ASCENT®
CENTER FOR TECHNICAL KNOWLEDGE

AutoCAD® 2027
Beyond the Basics

Learning Guide
Mixed Units - Edition 1.0

ASCENT - Center for Technical Knowledge®
AutoCAD® 2027
Beyond the Basics
Mixed Units - Edition 1.0

Prepared and produced by:

ASCENT Center for Technical Knowledge
11201 Dolfield Blvd, Suite 112
Owings Mills, MD 21117

866-527-2368
www.ASCENTed.com

Lead Contributor: Renu Muthoo

ASCENT - Center for Technical Knowledge (a division of Rand Worldwide Inc.) is a leading developer of professional learning materials and knowledge products for engineering software applications. ASCENT specializes in designing targeted content that facilitates application-based learning with hands-on software experience. For over 25 years, ASCENT has helped users become more productive through tailored custom learning solutions.

We welcome any comments you may have regarding this guide, or any of our products. To contact us please email: feedback@ASCENTed.com.

Contents

Preface

AutoCAD® 2027: Beyond the Basics is designed for users working with AutoCAD® 2027 on a Windows operating system. This content does not apply to AutoCAD for Mac software.

The objective of this course is to enable you to create, modify, and work with 2D drawings using the AutoCAD software.

AutoCAD 2027 Beyond the Basics continues on from the topics covered in *AutoCAD 2027: Essentials*. It covers more sophisticated techniques that extend your mastery of the software. For example, here you go beyond the basic skill of using a template to understand the process of setting up a template, creating annotation styles, and how to work with external references.

Topics Covered

- Using more advanced editing and construction techniques

- Adding parametric constraints to objects

- Creating local and global blocks

- Setting up layers, styles, and templates

- Attaching external references

Prerequisites

- Access to the 2027.0 version of the software, to ensure compatibility with this learning content. Future software updates that are released by Autodesk may include changes that are not reflected in this content. The practices and files included are not compatible with prior versions of the software (e.g., 2026).

- Knowledge of AutoCAD basics as taught in *AutoCAD: Essentials* or equivalent experience.

- A working knowledge of your operating system.

Note on Software Setup

This guide assumes a standard installation of the software using the default preferences during installation.

Note on Learning Guide Content

ASCENT's learning guides are intended to teach the technical aspects of using the software and do not focus on professional design principles and standards. The practices aim to demonstrate the capabilities and flexibility of the software rather than following specific design codes or standards.

Lead Contributor: Renu Muthoo

Renu is a learning content developer for Autodesk products at ASCENT. She has over 25 years of experience working with Autodesk products and specializes in AutoCAD and design visualization software.

Holding a bachelor's degree in Computer Engineering, Renu began her career as an Instructional Designer, co-authoring 3ds Max and AutoCAD books. At ASCENT, she continues her passion for instructional design by developing off the shelf and custom courseware for AutoCAD, AutoCAD Toolsets (Electrical, Mechanical, Raster Design, and Plant 3D), Autodesk 3ds Max, and other software products. An Autodesk Certified Professional in AutoCAD, Renu also enjoys educating users by sharing her knowledge through webcasts and blogs.

Renu Muthoo has been the Lead Contributor for *AutoCAD: Beyond the Basics* since 2015.

In This Guide

The following highlights the key features of this guide.

Feature	Description
Practice Files	The Practice Files page includes a link to the practice files and instructions on how to download and install them. The practice files are required to complete the practices in this guide.
Chapters	A chapter consists of the following: Learning Objectives, Instructional Content, Practices, Chapter Review Questions, and Command Summary. • **Learning Objectives** define the skills you can acquire by learning the content provided in the chapter. • **Instructional Content**, which begins right after Learning Objectives, refers to the descriptive and procedural information related to various topics. Each main topic introduces a product feature, discusses various aspects of that feature, and provides step-by-step procedures on how to use that feature. Where relevant, examples, figures, helpful hints, and notes are provided. • **Practice** for a topic follows the instructional content. Practices enable you to use the software to perform a hands-on review of a topic. It is required that you download the practice files (using the link found on the Practice Files page) prior to starting the first practice. • **Chapter Review Questions**, located close to the end of a chapter, enable you to test your knowledge of the key concepts discussed in the chapter. • **Command Summary** concludes a chapter. It contains a list of the software commands that are used throughout the chapter and provides information on where the command can be found in the software.
Appendices	Appendices provide additional information to the main course content. It could be in the form of instructional content, practices, tables, projects, or skills assessment.

Errata Sheets

If there are any updates or corrections to this guide, they will be published in an errata sheet.

Access it here: *https://resources.ascented.com/errata-sheets-autodesk*

or

visit **ASCENTed.com > RESOURCES > RESOURCE CENTER > Errata Sheets** and select **Autodesk** from the drop-down list.

Practice Files

To download the practice files for this guide, use the following steps:

1. Type the URL *exactly as shown below* into the address bar of your Internet browser to access the Course File Download page.

   Note: If you are using the ebook, you do not have to type the URL. Instead, you can access the page by clicking the URL below.

   ## https://www.ascented.com/getfile/id/pseudocranichisPF

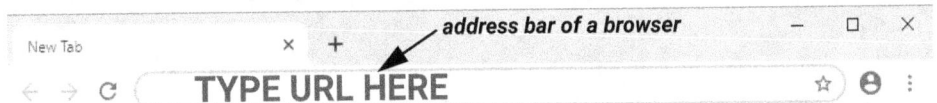

2. On the Course File Download page, click the **DOWNLOAD NOW** button, as shown below, to download the .ZIP file that contains the practice files.

3. Once the download is complete, unzip the file and extract its contents.

   The recommended practice files folder location is:
   C:\AutoCAD 2027 Essentials and Beyond the Basics Practice Files

   Note: It is recommended that you do not change the location of the practice files folder. Doing so may cause errors when completing the practices.

Stay Informed!
To receive information about upcoming events, promotional offers, and complimentary webcasts, visit:
www.ASCENTed.com/updates

Working Effectively with AutoCAD

You will explore how to work with the ribbon, navigate workspaces, and use keyboard shortcuts. Additionally, you will learn methods for copying and pasting to duplicate information between drawings, advanced grip techniques for editing objects, and the use of extra layer tools.

Learning Objectives

- Create and save a custom workspace.
- Set up the ribbon to dock and hide palettes.
- Input commands using Command line and dynamic input.
- Create new objects of the same type and properties as a selected object.
- Cycle through overlapping objects and select one.
- Control the transparency and visibility of objects in a drawing.
- Switch between multiple open drawings and copy and paste information between drawings.
- Modify objects using grips.

1.1 Creating a Custom Workspace

As you learn the various ways of working with the AutoCAD® software, you need to set up your personal workspace. You can specify how the ribbon tabs and panels display, which tool palettes you want open, and how you want them to be organized, as shown in the example in Figure 1–1. When you are finished, you can create a new workspace to save the arrangement.

Figure 1–1

- (Workspaces) controls the display of ribbon tabs and panels, tool palettes and other palettes, and even the Command Line. You can select from the default workspaces, as shown in Figure 1–2, or create a custom version.

  - To maximize the drawing window, you can temporarily toggle off the ribbon and all of the tool palettes in the *Status Bar* by clicking (Clean screen). The *Quick Access Toolbar*, Command Line, and *Status Bar* are still displayed.

Figure 1–2

- The **Drafting & Annotation** workspace is the default. When you set it to be current, the default ribbon tabs and panels display. Any palettes and toolbars that you have displayed are closed. Most of the tools you need can be found in the ribbon.

How To: Create a Custom Workspace

1. Set up the ribbon as you want it to be displayed.

2. Open the tool palettes that you want to include in the workspace, close any that you do not want to display, and arrange them in the drawing window.

3. In the *Status Bar,* expand the *Workspace* drop-down list, and select **Save Current As...**.

4. In the *Save Workspace* dialog box, type a name for the new workspace and click **Save**, as shown in Figure 1–3.

Figure 1–3

- The new workspace becomes the current workspace.

- Selecting **Workspace Settings** opens a dialog box in which you can control the display and order of the workspaces in the list and add separator lines between names in the list, as shown in Figure 1–4. You also have the option of saving or not saving any changes to the workspace.

Figure 1–4

Docking and Hiding Palettes

Many floating windows and palettes, such as *Properties*, *DesignCenter*, and *Tool Palettes*, can remain open at all times. You can dock and hide or anchor them to one side of the drawing window.

To dock a palette, select the title bar and drag it to one side of the drawing window until it docks. Alternatively, you can right-click on the title bar and select **Anchor Left <** or **Anchor Right >**. **Allow Docking** should be selected for **Anchor Left <** and **Anchor Right >** to be available.

- To hide the docked palette, click ◄ to minimize it, as shown in Figure 1–5.

Figure 1–5

- When palettes are hidden, you can display either **Text only** or **Icons only**, as shown in Figure 1–6.

Figure 1–6

- When the palette is hidden, hover the cursor over the title bar to display the full palette, as shown in Figure 1–7.

Figure 1–7

- To keep a palette open, click ➡ (Auto-hide).

- To close a palette, click ✖ (Close).

- The palettes provided in the AutoCAD software are grouped together in the *View* tab> *Palettes* panel, as shown in Figure 1−8.

- Open palette icons are highlighted with a blue background, as shown for the *Properties* palette in Figure 1−8.

Figure 1−8

Setting Up the Ribbon

The ribbon is the primary place for starting commands. The ribbon can be docked to the top or side of the drawing window, or be kept floating. You can control how much of the ribbon displays, and you can drag and drop the ribbon panels to the drawing window or in a ribbon tab.

- Some of the panels contain extra tools. Click ▼ to expand the panel and display them. Click 📌 (Pin) to keep the expanded panel displayed in the drawing window, as shown in Figure 1−9.

Figure 1−9

- Some of the ribbon panels display ⬃ in their bottom right corners, which enables you to open a related dialog box.

Displaying the Ribbon

When the ribbon is docked at the top of the interface, you can control how it displays by clicking to the right of the tabs. By default, it is set to **Cycle through All,** which cycles through the display settings of **Minimize to Tabs, Minimize to Panel Titles**, and **Minimize to Panel Buttons**, as shown in Figure 1–10.

Minimize to Tabs

Minimize to Panel Titles

Minimize to Panel Buttons

Figure 1–10

- When the ribbon is minimized to tabs, select the tab to display the panels.

- When the ribbon is minimized to panel titles, hover the cursor over the title to display the commands, as shown in Figure 1−11.

Figure 1−11

- Click to revert back to the default ribbon which displays the tabs, panels, and tools within the panels.

Relocating Individual Panels

Ribbon panels can be moved around. You can drag and drop panels to reorder them in a specific ribbon tab (but not between different tabs). You can also float an individual panel in the drawing window, as shown in Figure 1−12.

Figure 1−12

- To float an individual panel, drag and drop it on the drawing window. To re-dock the panel, drag it back to the ribbon.

- If you have a dual-monitor setup, individual panels can be moved to the second monitor and left open.

Docking/Floating the Ribbon

If you want to increase your drawing window space, you can float the ribbon or dock it to one side of the drawing window, as shown in Figure 1–13. The ribbon then becomes like other palettes that you can hide and display.

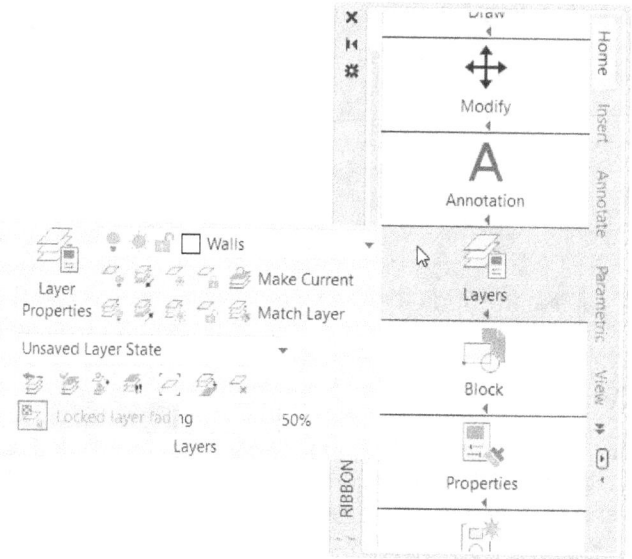

Figure 1–13

How To: Float and Dock the Entire Ribbon

1. Right-click in an empty space in the ribbon and select **Undock**, as shown in Figure 1–14.

Figure 1–14

2. The ribbon floats in the drawing window. If you want the ribbon to be docked to the side, click and hold on the ribbon title and drag it to the side of the drawing window.

- When the ribbon is docked, you can click ◄ (as shown in Figure 1–15) to hide the palette.

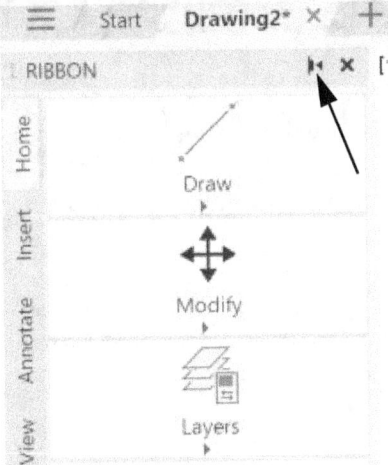

Figure 1–15

💡 Hint: Tool Palette Groups

You can associate a tool palette group with a tab, so that when you right-click on the tab and select **Show Related Tool Palette Group**, the tool palette group automatically opens. You can select from existing groups, as shown in Figure 1–16. This makes it easy to open the tool palettes you want to use.

Figure 1–16

- If a tab does not have a related tool palette group, the **Show Related Tool Palette Group** option is grayed out in the shortcut menu.
- When you select **Show Related Tool Palette Group**, it opens the *Tool Palette* window, if it was not already open.

Practice 1a
Set Up Workspaces

Practice Objective

- Create a custom workspace and switch between workspaces.

In this practice, you will create a custom workspace, as shown in Figure 1–17, and note the effects of switching workspaces.

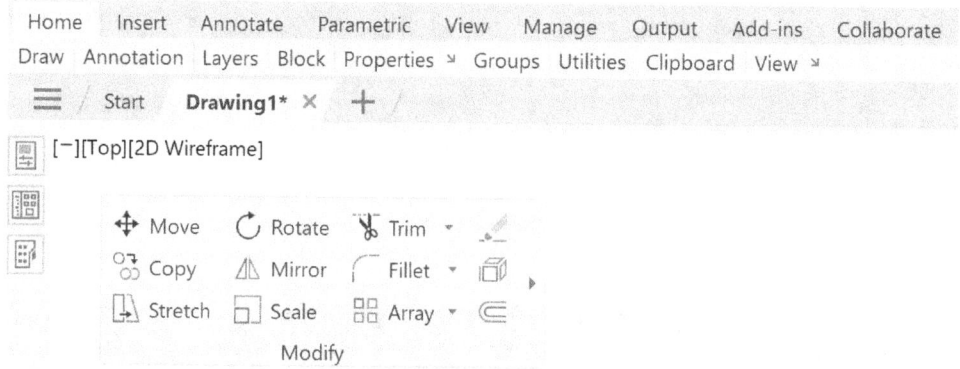

Figure 1–17

1. Start a new drawing based on the previous used/default AutoCAD template.

2. In the *Status Bar*, expand ⚙ ▼ (Workspaces) and select **3D Modeling**. Note all the tabs and panels.

3. Change back to the **Drafting & Annotation** workspace. What are the differences?

4. Open the *Properties* palette (*View* tab>*Palettes* panel or press <Ctrl>+<1>). Right-click on the title bar and select **Allow Docking** and **Anchor Left <** to dock it to the left side of the drawing window.

5. The palette displays as a bar along the left edge of the drawing window. If the palette displays in the maximize position, hover the cursor on the title bar of the docked palette and click ▶◀ to minimize the palette such that only the palette bar displays.

6. Right-click on the palette title bar and select **Icons only**. Note how the palette displays as an icon near the top left corner of the drawing window.

7. Open the *DesignCenter* (press <Ctrl>+<2>) and *Tool Palettes* (press <Ctrl>+<3>). Dock and minimize both of them (as icons) to the same side of the drawing window as the *Properties* palette, as shown in Figure 1–17.

8. In any ribbon tab, click and hold the panel bar (for example, the *Modify* panel in the *Home* tab) and drag it onto the drawing window.

9. Set the ribbon to **Minimize to Panel Titles** by using ⬛▾.

10. In the *Status Bar*, expand ⚙ ▾ (Workspaces) and select **Save Current As....**

11. In the *Save Workspace* dialog box, type **My 2D Workspace** and click **Save**. In the *Status Bar*, expand ⚙ ▾ (Workspaces) and note that the new workspace is listed there and is currently active.

12. Switch to the **Drafting & Annotation** workspace. What are the differences?

13. Stay in the **Drafting & Annotation** workspace and close the file. Do not save it. Your newly created workspace is still available to use in other drawing files.

End of practice

1.2 Using the Keyboard Effectively

The Command Line and Dynamic Input use information typed on the keyboard, as shown in Figure 1–18. For example, you can start the **Line** command by typing the command name (**line**) or shortcut (**L**). When you press <Enter> to start the command, its options display in the Command Line. To display the options in the Dynamic Input, select the down arrow. To use one of the options, you can type the capitalized letter(s) of the option or select it in the Command Line.

Figure 1–18

- All AutoCAD command can be typed in the Command line or Dynamic Input.

- ![icon] (Dynamic Input) should be toggled on (in the *Status Bar*) for the command prompts to display at the cursor location.

- You can start typing the first letters of a command name and then select the command in the **AutoComplete** list.

- You can quickly search for additional information about a command or system variable in the AutoComplete suggestion list. Hover the cursor over the required item in the list. A tooltip displays, providing a description of the command's functions, as shown in the left of Figure 1–19.

- The Autocomplete list in the Command line provides the **Search in Help** or **Search on Internet** icons, as shown in the right of Figure 1–19.

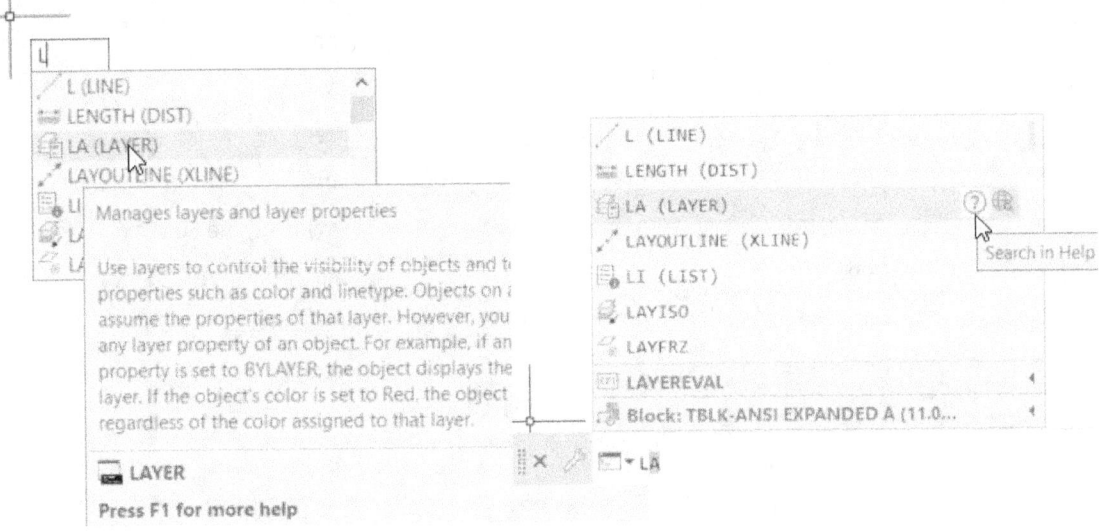

Figure 1–19

- You can easily reuse any command or number that you have typed. Press <Up Arrow> or <Down Arrow> to scroll through your typed input, and press <Enter> when you reach the command that you want to reuse.

- You can quickly select from a list of the most recent commands by expanding ⊡ ▾ in the Command Line.

- You can also copy and paste information from the Text Window to the Command Line. Highlight the text, right-click, and select **Paste to Cmdline**.

Command Aliases

Rather than typing the entire command name, you can use abbreviations called *command aliases*. The following aliases are some of the standard ones in the AutoCAD software.

> **Note:** Click ⊡ (Command Aliases) in the Express Tools tab>Tools panel to add or modify command aliases in the file **acad.pgp**.

To locate most commands, try typing the first character of the command, then try the first two, and then try the first three. Other commands use various letters. Some examples are listed below:

Alias	Command	Alias	Command
A	Arc	LT	Linetype
AA	Area	M	Move
AR	Array	MI	Mirror
B	Block	MS	Mspace
BR	Break	O	Offset
C	Circle	OS	Osnap
CHA	Chamfer	PE	Pedit (Polyline Edit)
CO, CP	Copy	PL	Pline (Polyline)
D	Dimstyle	PR	Properties
DAL	Dimaligned	PS	Pspace
DAN	Dimangular	PU	Purge
DBA	Dimbaseline	R	Redraw
DCO	Dimcontinue	RA	Redrawall
DDI	Dimdiameter	RE	Regen
DI	Distance	REC	Rectang (Rectangle)
DIV	Divide	REN	Rename
DLI	Dimlinear	RO	Rotate
DRA	Dimradius	S	Stretch
E	Erase	SC	Scale
ED	Textedit (ddedit)	SP	Spell
EX	Extend	T, MT	Mtext (Multiline Text)
F	Fillet	TR	Trim
H	Hatch	U	Undo
HE	Hatchedit	V	View
I	Insert	W	Wblock
L	Line	X	Explode
LA	Layer	Z	Zoom

Shortcut Keys

Another quick way to launch commands or change settings is to use the *shortcut keys* (also called *accelerator keys*). Many of these keystrokes follow the Microsoft Office standard.

To use the default shortcut keys, press <Ctrl> and a letter or number. You can also define customized key combinations in the *Customize* dialog box.

+<A>	Select All		+<N>	New drawing
+<B>	Snap on/off		+<O>	Open drawing
+<C>	Copy to the Clipboard		+<P>	Plot
+<D>	Dynamic UCS on/off		+<R>	Cycles layout viewports
+<E>	Toggle Isometric plane		+<S>	Save
+<F>	Object Snap on/off		+<T>	Tablet on/off
+<G>	Grid on/off		+<U>	Polar on/off
+<J>	Executes last command		+<V>	Paste from the clipboard
+<K>	Create Hyperlink		+<W>	Selection cycling on/off
+<L>	Ortho on/off		+<X>	Cut to clipboard

+<1>	Properties palette on/off		+<7>	Markup Set Manager on/off
+<2>	DesignCenter on/off		+<8>	QuickCalc on/off
+<3>	Tool Palettes on/off		+<9>	Command Line on/off
+<4>	Sheet Sets on/off		+<0>	(zero) Cleanscreen on/off

Function Keys

Function keys control most of the toggles for the drafting settings and several other features.

<F1>	Help		<F7>	Grid on/off
<F2>	Text Screen		<F8>	Ortho on/off
<F3>	Osnap on/off		<F9>	Snap on/off
<F4>	3DOsnap on/off		<F10>	Polar on/off
<F5>	Isoplane switch		<F11>	Osnap Tracking on/off
<F6>	Dynamic UCS on/off		<F12>	Dynamic Input on/off

Practice 1b
Use the Keyboard Effectively

Practice Objectives

- Draw objects using keyboard commands.
- Use various techniques for entering information.

In this practice, you will draw lines, circles, and trim objects (as shown in Figure 1–20) using keyboard commands. You will select commands in the *AutoComplete* list using partial keyboard commands. You will also be able to toggle Command Line on and off using keyboard commands.

Note: The size of the dimensions has been changed in the Figure for printing clarity.

Figure 1–20

1. Start a new drawing based on **Mech-Inches.dwt**, which is located in your practice files folder.

2. Draw the objects shown above in Figure 1–20. Use the command aliases **L (Line)**, **C (Circle)**, and **TR (Trim)** to start the required commands. Type the distances using Polar Tracking and Dynamic Input.

   Note: Verify that ⊞ *(Dynamic Input) is toggled on so that command prompts display at the crosshairs.*

3. Set the layer to **Dimensions**. To test the AutoComplete list of command names, type **D** and select **DIM** (the shortcut for **Dimension** command) in the list. This starts the command. Dimension the objects. If the *Select Annotation Scale* dialog box opens, set the *Scale* to **1:1** and click **OK**.

4. Save the drawing as **Jig.dwg** and close it.

End of practice

1.3 Object Creation, Selection, and Visibility

Object Creation

You can use **Add Selected** to create new objects of the same type and properties as the selected object. Select an object, right-click, and select **Add Selected** as shown in Figure 1–21. The AutoCAD software launches the command that was used to create the selected object and sets some of the properties (such as the layer or color) to be the same as the original object.

Figure 1–21

Selecting Similar Objects

You can use **Select Similar** (as shown in Figure 1–21) to select an object and automatically select other objects of the same type and properties at the same time. For example, if you select a red rectangle on the layer **Walls**, all of the other red rectangles on the layer **Walls** are also selected.

How To: Select Similar Objects

1. Select an object.
2. Right-click and select **Select Similar**. All of the other objects that match the settings are selected.

• If you select more than one object and then use **Select Similar**, all of the objects that match the properties of all of the selected objects are selected.

How To: Modify Select Similar Settings

1. Without any object selected, at the Command Line, type or dynamically input **selectsimilar**.
2. At the Select objects prompt, press <Down Arrow> and select **SEttings**.
3. In the *Select Similar Settings* dialog box (shown in Figure 1–22), select the property types by which you want to filter the selection set.

Figure 1-22

- The properties that are set in the dialog box are used to filter the selection process. The objects that are selected have the same properties.

- If you clear the **Name** option in the dialog box, the command looks for all of the objects that match the properties no matter what type they are.

Object Selection Cycling

If you need to select an object in a location in which many objects overlap, you can use **Object Selection Cycling**. When it is toggled on, and you hover the cursor over an area where some objects are overlapping, 🗗 displays, indicating that more than one object can be selected. Clicking on the object displays the *Selection* dialog box where you can select an object from the list, as shown in Figure 1-23.

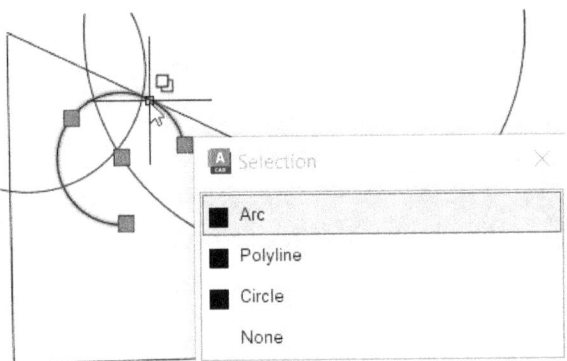

Figure 1-23

How To: Use Object Selection Cycling

1. In the *Status Bar*, toggle on 📑 (Selection Cycling).
2. Hover the cursor over some overlapping objects close to where the objects intersect. 🔲 displays, indicating that there are overlapping objects.
3. Click to open the *Selection* dialog box.
4. Select the object that you want to use.

Object Visibility

You can control whether objects are displayed or hidden in the drawing. The **Isolate Objects**, **Hide Objects**, and **End Object Isolation** commands control this display.

Isolate Objects	Select the objects that you want to isolate, right-click, and select **Isolate>Isolate Objects**. The selected objects display and all other objects are hidden.
Hide Objects	Select the objects that you want to hide, right-click, and select **Isolate>Hide Objects**. The selected objects are hidden.
End Object Isolation	Right-click anywhere in the drawing window and select **Isolate>End Object Isolation**. All hidden objects display.

- If a drawing contains hidden or isolated objects, 🔺 (Unisolate Objects) (highlighted) displays in the *Status Bar*.

- If a drawing does not contain hidden objects, 🔺 (Isolate Objects) displays in the *Status Bar*.

How To: Isolate or Hide Objects

1. Right-click and select **Isolate>Isolate Objects** or **Hide Objects**, as shown in Figure 1−24. You can also use ⌷ (Isolate/Hide/Unisolate) in the *Status Bar*.

Figure 1−24

2. If you selected objects before starting the command, the objects are hidden or isolated. If you did not select objects, you are prompted to select them.

3. To display the isolated or hidden objects, right-click and select **Isolate>End Object Isolation** or click ⌷ (Unisolate Objects) in the *Status Bar*, and select **End Object Isolation.**

*   If objects are already hidden or isolated, you can add additional objects to the isolated selection set by clicking ⌷ (Unisolate Objects) in the *Status Bar*, and selecting **Isolate Additional Objects**, as shown in Figure 1−25.

Figure 1−25

Setting Transparency

Transparency can be applied to objects similar to applying other properties (such as Layer, Color, or Linetype). It can be set individually, ByLayer, or ByBlock. It is very useful when displaying hatches, as shown in Figure 1–26.

Transparency = 0   Transparency = 50

Figure 1–26

- Transparency values vary from **0** (least transparent) to **90** (most transparent).

- When you are creating or editing objects, you can set the transparency in the *Home* tab> expanded *Properties* panel. You can also expand the *Transparency* drop-down list and select one of the options shown in Figure 1–27.

Figure 1–27

- Transparency is also available in the *Properties* palette when objects have been selected.

- You can toggle (Transparency) on and off in the *Status Bar*.

- Transparency can be set in *Layer Properties Manager*, as shown in Figure 1–28. It can also be modified by layer in a viewport.

Figure 1–28

- Transparency can be set for **Match Properties**, as shown in Figure 1–29, and for **Quick Select** and **Filter**.

Figure 1–29

- To plot transparent objects, select the **Plot transparency** option in the *Plot* dialog box, as shown in Figure 1–30. This is toggled off by default because the file must be converted into raster for the transparency to plot.

Plot options

☐ Plot in background
☐ Plot object lineweights
☑ Plot transparency
☐ Plot with plot styles
☐ Plot paperspace last
☐ Hide paperspace objects
☐ Plot stamp on
☐ Save changes to layout

Figure 1–30

Practice 1c
Object Creation, Selection, and Visibility

Practice Objective

- Modify the display of objects using various commands and options.

In this practice, you will modify the way objects display in a drawing using **Select Similar**, **Hide Objects**, and **Isolate Objects**. You will also modify the display of objects using the **Transparency** option.

Task 1: Use selection and visibility tools.

1. Open **Office-Plan1-A.dwg** from your practice files folder.

2. In the *Status Bar*, ensure that ⬚ (Isolate Objects) is displayed. If not, select it from the ☰ (Customization) list.

3. Select one of the double sided corner desks on the layer Cubicles (blue color).

4. Right-click and select **Select Similar**. All of the double sided corner desks are selected, as shown in Figure 1–31. Press <Esc> to exit the command.

Figure 1–31

5. Select one of the red desks and one of the red chairs and use **Select Similar**. All of the chairs are selected along with a few desks (there are different types of desks; only those desks which are similar to the selected one are selected).

6. In the *Status Bar*, click (Isolate Objects) and select **Hide Objects**. Note how the selected objects are hidden and (Unisolate Objects) is highlighted in the *Status Bar*.

7. Use **Select Similar** to select the rest of the red-colored furniture objects. Hide them as well ((Unisolate Objects)>**Hide Objects**). You might have to select some red objects individually and hide them.

8. In the *Status Bar*, click (Unisolate Objects) and select **End Object Isolation** to unhide the objects.

Task 2: Modify object transparency.

1. Toggle on the layer **Hatching**.

2. In the *Status Bar*, toggle on (Transparency).

3. Select one of the hatches.

4. In the *Hatch Editor* contextual tab>*Properties* panel, for the **Hatch Transparency**, use the slider bar to increase it and note that it lightens the selected hatch. Close the *Hatch Editor*.

5. Open *Layer Properties Manager*.

6. In the *Hatching* row, set the *Transparency* value to **50**, as shown in Figure 1–32.

S...	Name		▲	O..	F...	L...	P...	Color		Linetype	Lineweight		Transp...	N..	Description
	0			💡	☀	🔓	🖨	■	wh...	Continu...	—	Defa...	0		
	Border			💡	☀	🔓	🖨	■	blue	Continu...	—	Defa...	0		
	Cubicles			💡	☀	🔓	🖨	□	132	Continu...	—	Defa...	0		
	Defpoints			💡	☀	🔓		■	wh...	Continu...	—	Defa...	0		
	Dimensions			💡	☀	🔓	🖨	□	red	Continu...	—	Defa...	0		
	Doors			💡	☀	🔓	🖨	□	40	Continu...	—	Defa...	0		
	Electrical			💡	☀	🔓	🖨	□	132	Continu...	—	Defa...	0		
	Furniture			💡	☀	🔓	🖨	□	red	Continu...	—	Defa...	0		
	Hatching			💡	☀	🔓	🖨	□	red	Continu...	—	Defa...	50		
	Headers			💡	☀	🔓	🖨	■	wh...	Continu...	—	Defa...	0		
	HVAC							□	40	Continu...		Defa...	0		

Figure 1–32

7. All of the other hatches (except the one selected in Step 3) are lightened because they are all on the same layer, and each of their *Transparency* options is set to **ByLayer**.

8. Save and close the drawing.

End of practice

1.4 Working in Multiple Drawings

You can open multiple drawings in the same session of the AutoCAD software, as shown in Figure 1–33. This can make it easier to copy information across drawings.

Figure 1–33

By default, the *Files Tab* bar is displayed along the top of the drawing window and has the

≡ (Files tab menu), and the *Start* tab always displayed. The *Start* tab is the first active tab. If any other drawing is active, clicking the *Start* tab displays the initial *Start* window, which contains tools to create new drawings, open existing ones, open the recently used files, and many other file and help related options.

File Tabs

The *File Tabs* or the *Drawing Tabs* along the top of the drawing window are an easy way to switch between open drawing files and the initial Start window.

Switching Windows

The *File Tabs* along the top of the drawing window display the names of the open drawings.

- The names of all of the open drawings display as tabs in the *File Tabs* bar. The currently active drawing tab displays with a white background.

- They display in the order in which they are opened, but you can change their order by dragging and moving the tabs.

- You can cycle between the drawings by pressing <Ctrl>+<Tab> or by selecting the required file tab in the *File Tabs* bar. The selected drawing tab opens the drawing and makes it active.

- At the beginning of the *Files Tab* bar is the ≡ (Files tab menu), which displays a complete list of open files, as shown in Figure 1–34. Here you can select the required filename to switch to that open drawing file. You can hover your cursor on a drawing to display all the layouts for that drawing and open the drawing in the required layout tab, as shown in Figure 1–34. The *Files* tab menu also provides you with options to create or open a drawing along with saving and closing all drawings together.

Figure 1–34

- You can also open and make another drawing active by clicking (Switch Windows) in the *View* tab>*Interface* panel, and then selecting the drawing from the list, as shown in Figure 1–35.

C:\AutoCAD 2020 Fund Practice Files\Office-

Drawing5.dwg

✓ Drawing6.dwg

Figure 1–35

- If you want all of the open drawings to display together, click ⊟ (Tile Horizontally), ⊓⊓ (Tile Vertically), or ⧉ (Cascade).

Floating Windows

You can display multiple drawings at the same time as floating windows. The floating drawing tabs enable you to work on multiple drawings side by side without having to switch between tabs.

- You can pull (click and drag) the drawing tabs and display them as separate drawing windows, as shown in Figure 1–36.

Figure 1–36

- As with any other windows function, you can resize the windows, place them side by side or let them overlap one on top of the other. If you have a second monitor, you can easily drag the floating drawing onto that screen and have the two drawing files displayed on two separate screens side by side.

- If you want to keep the drawing in the overlapping mode, then the currently active drawing remains on top. If you want to keep the floating window always on top, click [icon] to pin it. It ignores the active drawing and allows the floating drawing to always stay on top of the main application window.

- The floating window has its own Command Line, Dynamic Input, and *Layout Tabs* bar.

- The ribbon, the *Quick Access Toolbar*, and the *Status Bar* are only available in the main application window, but you can use them in the floating drawing window as well. These tools are associated with the drawing that is currently active. To make the drawing current, click inside it and the cursor displays in the current drawing.

- If you do not want to have the floating drawing tabs as separate windows, you can simply drag and drop the floating drawing window back onto the *File Tabs* bar, as shown in Figure 1−37.

Figure 1−37

Appearance and Preview

The file tabs include some visual tools.

- A drawing file that is open as read-only is indicated by a lock on its tab.

- A drawing file that has been modified since its last save is indicated by an asterisk on its tab.

- To display a preview image of the model tab and layouts of any other open drawing, hover the cursor over its filename tab, then hover the cursor over one of the previews to highlight it, as shown in Figure 1−38. Select the preview to switch to that model or layout.

Figure 1−38

- When a preview image is highlighted, the icons at the top of the preview enable you to 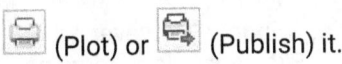 (Plot) or (Publish) it.

Shortcut Menu

You can right-click on any file tab to display a menu (shown in Figure 1–39) with various file commands, including options to create, open, save, and close files.

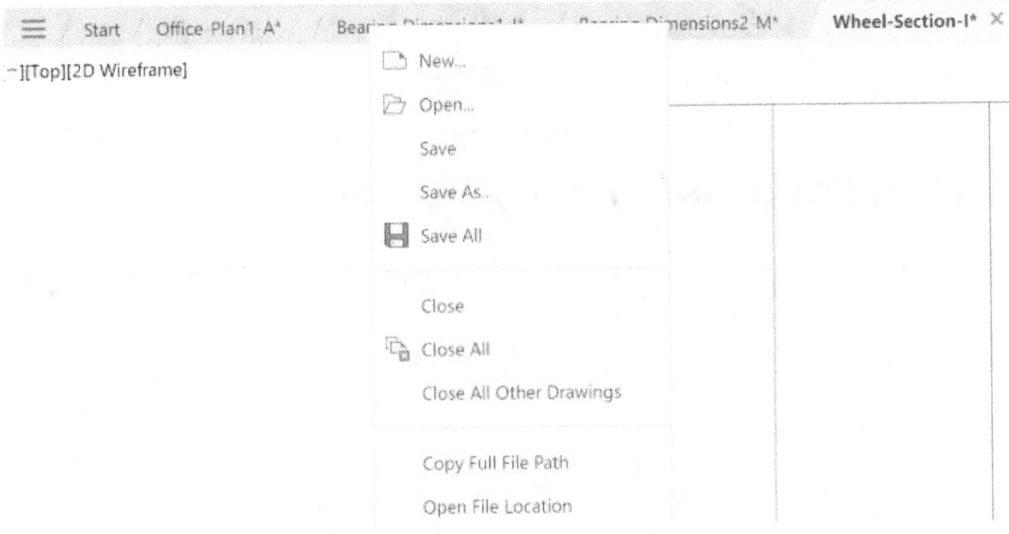

Figure 1–39

- You can use **Close All** to close all of the drawings except the ≡ (File tab menu) and the *Start* tab.

- Select **Close All Other Drawings** to close all of the drawings except the ≡ (File tab menu), *Start* tab, and the drawing where you opened the shortcut menu from.

- Selecting any of the closing options prompts you to save/discard the drawing files that have any changes that were not saved prior to closing them.

- Other options include copying the full file path to the clipboard and opening the file location in Windows Explorer.

Toggle File Tabs Bar On/Off

By default, the *File Tabs* bar displays along the top of the drawing window. However, when maximum screen real estate is more important, you can hide the *File Tabs* bar by toggling (File Tabs) off in the *View* tab>*Interface* panel, as shown in Figure 1–40.

Figure 1–40

Selecting Drawings in the Application Menu

The Application Menu provides access to all of the already saved open drawings and recently used drawings, as shown in Figure 1–41.

Figure 1–41

- When you hover the cursor over a drawing name, a thumbnail of the drawing displays. Hover the cursor a while longer to display more information about the file.

- Click (Recent Documents) to display a list of recently used drawing files or click (Open Documents) to display a list of open drawing files.

- You can customize the way the drawings are listed and displayed, as shown in Figure 1-42.

Figure 1-42

- Expand (Close) in the Application Menu to close either the current drawing or all open drawings, as shown in Figure 1-43.

Figure 1-43

1.5 Copying and Pasting Between Drawings

You can place information on the clipboard by copying or cutting it from a document. You can then paste the information from the clipboard into the same document or into a different one, even in a different application. To copy, move and paste information between drawings you must use the Windows **Copy** command. The AutoCAD **Copy** command does not work between drawings.

- The various **Cut**, **Copy**, and **Paste** commands are available in the *Home* tab>*Clipboard* panel and in the shortcut menu.

Cut to the Clipboard

When using the Windows **Cut** command, you have the following options:

	Cut Clip	Removes the selected objects from their file and places them on the clipboard.
	Cut with Base Point	Enables you to select the base point before selecting the objects to be cut. This option provides more control over the location of the objects when they are placed. The base point is only significant when the objects are pasted into the AutoCAD software.

Copy to the Clipboard

When using the Windows **Copy** command, you have the following options:

	Copy Clip	Copies the selected objects to the clipboard, using the lower left corner of the bounding box of all of the objects as the base point. <Ctrl>+<C> starts the command.
	Copy with Base Point	Enables you to select the base point before the objects are selected. This option provides more control over the location of the objects when they are placed. The base point is only significant when the objects are pasted into the AutoCAD software.
NA	**Copy Link**	Type **copylink** at the Command Line. It copies the contents of the current view to the clipboard.

Paste from the Clipboard

When using the Windows **Paste** command, you have the following options:

	Paste	Prompts you to select a location for the base point at which it then places the objects. <Ctrl>+<V> starts the command.
	Paste as Block	The copied objects are placed as a block. The AutoCAD software gives the block an arbitrary name. This option is only available if the objects on the clipboard are AutoCAD objects.
	Paste to Original Coordinates	Places the objects at the same coordinates as in the drawing from which they were taken. This option is only available if the objects on the clipboard are AutoCAD objects.
	Paste as Hyperlink	Creates a hyperlink of an object, text or file already copied to clipboard, and then associates it with another object.
	Paste Special	Enables you to control the format of an already copied data while pasting it into the active drawing.

Drag-and-Drop Copying

When two drawing windows are open, you can also *drag and drop* objects to copy them from one drawing into another.

How To: Copy Using Drag and Drop

1. Without a command running, select the objects that you want to copy.

2. Hold the mouse button with the cursor on the objects (do not select a grip).

3. Drag the objects into the other drawing window and release the mouse button.

Match Properties Across Drawings

(Match Properties) works across drawings. You can select an object in one drawing and apply its properties to objects in another drawing.

Match Properties works for general object properties, such as color, linetype, and lineweight, and for the formatting of some specific object types, including text, dimensions, hatching, and tables.

(Match Properties) is located in the *Home* tab>*Properties* panel.

Practice 1d
Work in Multiple Drawings

Practice Objectives

- Switch between drawings and display them as floating windows.
- Copy and paste objects between drawings.

In this practice, you will switch between multiple drawings using file tabs and Open Documents. You will display drawings side by side in separate drawing windows. You will then copy and paste objects between the drawings, as shown in Figure 1–44.

Figure 1–44

1. Open **Bighouse1-A.dwg** and **Floor Plan-A.dwg** from your practice files folder. Close any other open drawings.

   - You can use <Ctrl> to select both files in the *Select File* dialog box and click **Open** to open them together.

2. If not already active, in the *File Tabs* bar, select the **Bighouse1-A.dwg** tab to activate it. Hover your cursor over the **Floor Plan-A.dwg** tab to display the preview images of the drawing and its layouts, as shown in Figure 1–45. Select the **Model** preview to switch to **Floor Plan-A.dwg** with its *Model* tab active.

   • Depending on the selection of the filenames while opening them, your drawing tabs might be reversed. You can click and drag them to display as shown in Figure 1–45.

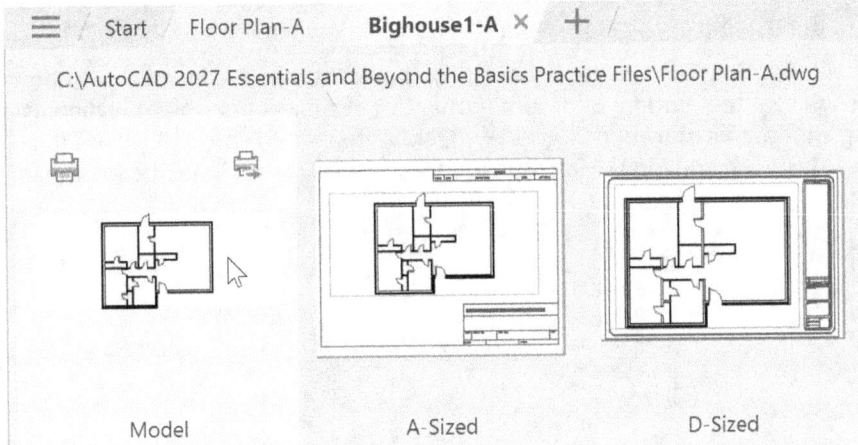

Figure 1–45

3. Thaw the layer **Text** (in **Floor Plan-A**).

4. In the Application Menu, click (Open Documents) and display the thumbnails of the two drawings by hovering the cursor over them, as shown in Figure 1–46. Select **Bighouse1-A.dwg** to make that drawing current. Press <Esc>.

Figure 1–46

5. Click, hold, and drag **Floor Plan-A.dwg** out of the *File Tabs* bar and place it on top of the **Bighouse1-A.dwg** as shown in Figure 1–47.

   *Note: If you have a second monitor, you can move **Floor Plan-A.dwg** to that screen.*

6. Resize the **Floor Plan-A** drawing window so that it is completely inside the main drawing window and click to pin on top, as shown in Figure 1–47.

7. Zoom to the extents of the **Floor Plan-A.dwg**, as shown in Figure 1–47.

8. Click inside **Bighouse1-A.dwg** so that the cursor is now active inside its window. Pan and zoom such that the Primary Bedroom (upper left corner of floor plan) is displayed in the drawing window, as shown in Figure 1–47. Note that when you click inside the **Bighouse1-A.dwg**, the **Floor Plan-A.dwg** still stays on top as it has been pinned there.

Figure 1–47

9. Ensure that your cursor is active in the **Bighouse1-A.dwg**. Start the (Match Properties) command (*Home* tab>*Properties* panel). Select the text **PRIMARY BEDROOM** as the source object. Note that the cursor changes into a brush with a little square.

10. Click inside **Floor Plan-A.dwg** once to activate it (the brush cursor is now available in **Floor Plan-A.dwg**). Select each of the text labels in **Floor Plan-A.dwg** as the destination object, as shown in Figure 1–48. Press <Enter> to exit the command. The text properties are matched in both drawings.

Figure 1–48

11. Make **Bighouse1-A.dwg** the active window by clicking in it. In the *Home* tab>*Clipboard* panel, click (Copy with Base Point). For the basepoint, select the corner of the walls behind the fireplace (in the primary bedroom). Select the fireplace (they might be separate objects) and the short diagonal walls that frame it, as shown in Figure 1–49. Press <Enter>.

Figure 1–49

12. Click inside **Floor Plan-A.dwg** once to activate it. In the *Home* tab>*Clipboard* panel, click (Paste). For the insertion point, select the top left corner of the larger bedroom to paste the fireplace there.

13. Click, hold, and drag the **Floor Plan-A.dwg** drawing window back on the *File Tabs* bar, as shown in Figure 1–50.

Figure 1–50

14. Close both drawings without saving the changes.

End of practice

1.6 Using Grips Effectively

Grips are a very powerful tool and using them helps you to quickly and easily modify drawings. You can increase the effectiveness of using grips by changing the base point, copying with grips, using the reference option, stretching multiple objects (as shown in Figure 1–51), and modifying grip settings.

Figure 1–51

- If (Dynamic Input) is on, dynamic dimensions (and if it is a multifunctional grip, a dynamic list of options) display when you hover the cursor over a grip. Select one of the optional commands, such as **Stretch**, **Lengthen**, or **Add Vertex**.

- When you select a grip you can edit the dimensions to stretch the object. Use <Tab> to highlight the dimension that you want to change.

- Depending on which grip is selected, the Stretch mode either stretches or moves the object. Centers of circles and midpoints of lines move the objects. Standard blocks move because they cannot be stretched. Dynamic blocks have special grips.

- Pressing <Enter> while a grip is hot, sequentially toggles through **Move, Rotate, Scale, Mirror**, and then back to **Stretch**.

- To clear grips from objects, press <Esc> or right-click and select **Exit**.

Changing the Base Point

The hot grip becomes the default base point for moving, rotating, etc. To use a different base point, right-click and select **Base Point** as shown in Figure 1–52 (or type **B** in the Command Line). Select the new base point and continue with the command.

Figure 1–52

Copying with Grips

Use the **Copy** option with any of the grip editing modes to create multiple copies while you move, rotate, etc.

How To: Copy with Grips

1. Select the objects and make one grip hot.
2. Right-click and select the editing mode (**Stretch, Move, Rotate**, etc.).
3. Select the **Copy** option in the shortcut menu or Command Line.

4. Select (or type) the second point, rotation angle, mirror line, or scale factor.

- If you hold <Ctrl> while selecting the location for additional copies, the new objects snap to the same spacing as the first copy, as shown in Figure 1–53.

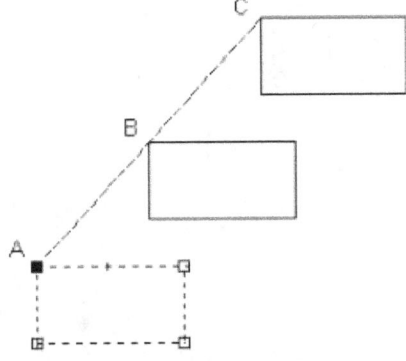

Figure 1–53

Rotate and Scale with the Reference Option

The **Reference** option enables you to select reference points in your drawing to describe the rotation angle or scale factor.

How To: Rotate and Scale with Grips and Reference

1. Select the objects that you want to rotate or scale.

2. Select the grip to be the base point for rotating or scaling.

3. Right-click and select **Rotate** or **Scale**.

4. Right-click and select **Reference**.

- **For Rotate:** Specify the reference angle by typing the angle or selecting two points. Specify the new angle by typing the angle or selecting a second point. The first point of the new angle is the base point.

- **For Scale:** Specify the reference length by typing the length or selecting two points. Specify the new length by typing the length or selecting a second point. The first point of the new length is the base point.

For example, you might want to straighten a rectangle that is rotated at an unknown angle, as shown in Figure 1-54. Select the rectangle and then select the grip at point 1 as the base point for rotation. Right-click and select **Rotate** and **Reference**. For the *Reference angle*, select the end points at **1** and **2** (this is the current angle of the object). For the *New angle*, type **0**.

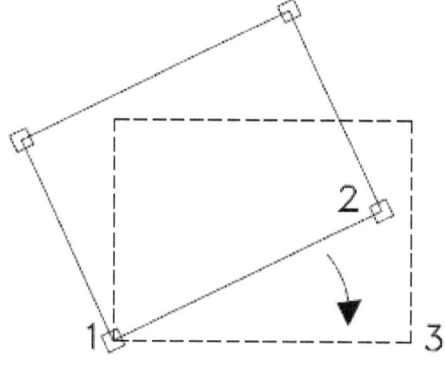

Figure 1-54

• The **Reference** option is also available with the regular **Rotate** and **Scale** commands.

Stretching Multiple Objects

In the Stretch mode, only hot grips or objects that contain hot grips are stretched. You can make multiple grips hot by holding <Shift> when selecting each grip, as shown in Figure 1-55.

Figure 1-55

How To: Stretch with Grips

1. Select the objects that you want to stretch.
2. Hold <Shift> and select all of the grips that you want to move using **Stretch**.
3. Release <Shift>.
4. Select the grip that you want to use as a base point.
5. Select the point that you want to use as the second point of displacement.

Converting to Arcs or Lines

The multi-functional grips of certain objects (such as polylines) enable you to convert an object segment into an arc or an arc segment into a line.

How To: Convert an Object Segment into an Arc or Line Segment

1. Select the object to display its multi-functional grips, as shown for a rectangular object in Figure 1–56.

Figure 1–56

2. Hover your cursor over the top middle bar grip, as shown in Figure 1–57. You can stretch, add a vertex, and convert to an arc using the grip options.

Figure 1–57

3. Click **Add Vertex** and move that point to add a vertex and manipulate the shape of the object, as shown in Figure 1–58.

Figure 1–58

4. Hover your cursor over one of the bar grips and select **Convert to Arc**. Move the cursor to define the position and radius of the arc, as shown in Figure 1–59.

Figure 1–59

Grip Settings

In the *Options* dialog box (expand the Application Menu and click **Options**), in the *Selection* tab, there are several settings related to grips, as shown in Figure 1–60.

Figure 1–60

- *Grip size* enables you to control the size of the grip as it displays in the drawing window.

- You can also change the grip colors by clicking **Grip Colors...** and adjusting the values in the *Grip Colors* dialog box, as shown in Figure 1–61.

Figure 1–61

In addition to grip size and color, you can set the following:

Show grips	Turns grips on or off globally.
Show grips in blocks	Controls whether grips only display on a block's insertion point (off) or on all nested objects in the block (on). Normally it is easier to work with this option off. This only applies to standard blocks. Dynamic blocks still display grips.
Show grip tips	Grip tips are not available in the basic AutoCAD software, but can display for objects from software such as the AutoCAD® Architecture software.
Show dynamic grip menu	Controls whether a menu displays next to a dynamic grip.
Allow Ctrl+cycling behavior	Controls whether you can use <Ctrl> to cycle through the grip's options.
Show single grip on groups	Displays a single grip for an object group.
Show bounding box on groups	Displays a bounding box around the extents of grouped objects.
Object selection limit for display of grips	If you select more objects than the number set here, grips do not display on them.

Practice 1e
Use Grips Effectively

Practice Objective

*   Modify a drawing using grips.

In this practice, you will use grips to edit the schematic drawing, as shown in Figure 1–62.

Figure 1–62

1. Open **Computer-I.dwg** from your practice files folder.

2. Use grips to add three, evenly spaced computers to **PRODUCTION**. Use <Ctrl> when selecting the locations for the copies, to place them at even intervals.

3. Use grips to stretch the red rectangle to include the new computers. Use <Shift> to select more than one hot grip.

4. Select the three, yellow polylines connecting the **ACCOUNTING** computers to the hubs. **Mirror** and **Copy** the three polylines to the **PRODUCTION** computers using grips and a base point at the midpoint of the middle hub.

- Hint: After selecting the three middle grips using <Shift>, use the shortcut menu to select **Mirror** and hold <Ctrl> to make mirrored copies. Select the three middle grips of the mirrored copies, right-click and select **Move** to move those to the **PRODUCTION** computers.

5. Use grips to manipulate the new lines so they match up with the new computers.

6. Save and close the drawing.

End of practice

1.7 Additional Layer Tools

The additional layer commands in the *Home* tab>*Layers* panel, can help you to work quickly with layers. They include commands that enable you to select layers rather than their names, and to change their layer state or current status.

Changing Object Layer States

The commands to freeze, toggle off, lock, and unlock layers are the most basic of the additional layer commands. They can be accessed in the *Home* tab>*Layers* panel, as shown in Figure 1–63.

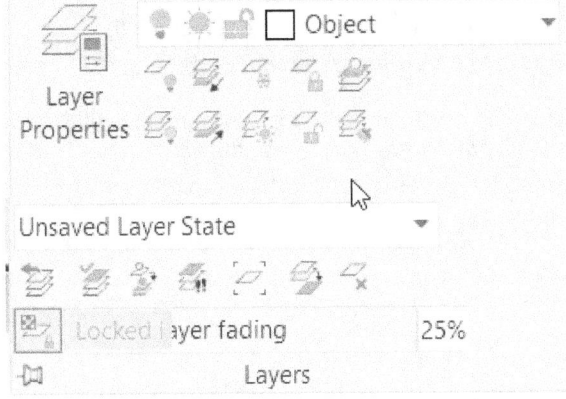

Figure 1–63

How To: Freeze or Turn Layers Off

1. Start (Layer Freeze) or (Layer Off).
2. Select an object on the layer that you want to change. It changes automatically.
3. You can continue selecting objects on other layers as required.
4. Press <Enter> to finish the command.

   Two other commands are helpful with layer states:

   - (Turn All Layers On)

   - (Thaw All Layers)

Settings

Layer Freeze and **Layer Off** have settings for how blocks, Xrefs, and Viewports respond to the commands. These settings remain in effect until you change them.

Block selection	Sets the nesting level of a block or Xref:
	• **Block (default):** Freezes or turns off the layer on which the block was inserted. If it is part of an Xref, it freezes the layer of the object.
	• **Entity:** Only freezes or turns off the layer in the block or Xref that you actually select.
	• **None:** Freezes or turns off the layer on which the block or Xref was inserted.
Viewports	Sets the way the command responds when you are working in a Paper Space viewport.
	• **VPFreeze (default):** Only freezes or turns off the layer in the current viewport.
	• **VP Freeze in All Viewports except Current:** In the *Home* tab>extended *Layers* panel, use ⬚ (VP Freeze in All Viewports except Current) to freeze a selected layer in all other viewports except the active one.
	• **Freeze/Off:** Freezes or turns off the layer across the entire drawing.

How To: Lock or Unlock Layers

1. Click ⬚ (Layer Lock) or ⬚ (Layer Unlock).

2. Select an object on the layer that you want to change. It changes automatically.

• A small padlock icon displays when you hover the cursor over a locked layer, as shown in Figure 1−64.

Figure 1−64

- Locked layers fade but are still displayed in the drawing. Use the **Locked layer fading** slider in the extended *Layers* panel to control how much the layers fade, as shown in Figure 1–65.

Figure 1–65

Isolating Layers

(Layer Isolate) is similar to changing the layer state, but it locks and fades (or turns off) all of the objects in a drawing EXCEPT those that are on the layers that you selected to isolate, as shown in Figure 1–66. When you have finished working with the isolated layers, you can return them to their original layer state.

Figure 1–66

How To: Isolate Layers

1. Click (Layer Isolate).
2. Select objects on the layer(s) in which you want to work.
3. Press <Enter>. All of the other layers are locked and faded.
- If you only select one layer to isolate and it is not the current layer, it becomes current.

- The layers that are not selected to be isolated are either locked and faded or toggled off. To change this, start the **Layer Isolate** command, select **Settings**, and select the required option, as shown in Figure 1–67.

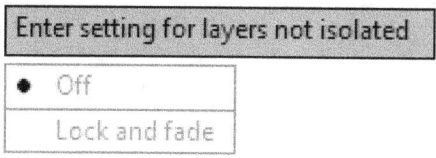

Figure 1–67

- When you select **Off** you are prompted to set the way it works in Paper Space viewports. The **Vpfreeze** option freezes the unisolated layers in the active viewport, and the **Off** option turns the unisolated layers off in all of the viewports.

How To: Unisolate Layers

1. Click ⬒ (Layer Unisolate).
2. All of the isolated layers are restored.

- ⬒ (Layer Previous) also restores layers that have been isolated and changes the current layer back to the original if **Layer Isolate** was last used to change it.

Changing an Object's Layer

There are other ways of changing the layers of objects in a drawing, including ⬒ (Change to Current Layer) and ⬒ (Copy Objects to New Layer). These commands change an object's layer by selecting other objects.

How To: Change to the Current Layer

1. Click ⬒ (Change to Current Layer).
2. Select the objects that you want to place on the current layer.
3. Press <Enter> to complete the command and note that the objects are moved to the current layer.

How To: Copy an Object to a New Layer

This command creates new copies of selected objects and places them on a new layer. You can then move the copies to a new location while you are still in the command or leave them on top of existing objects.

1. Click 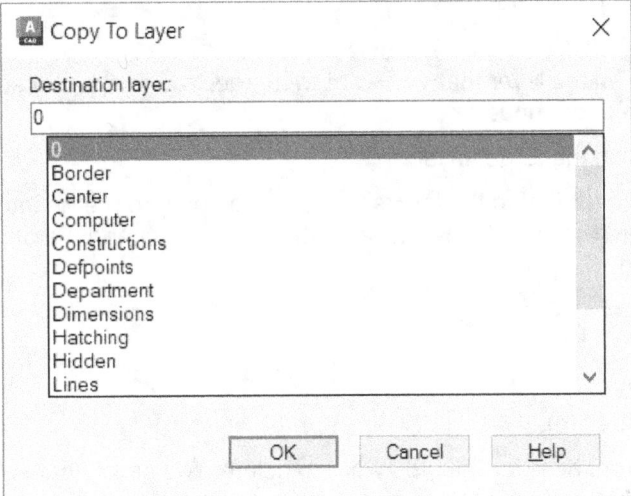 (Copy Objects to New Layer).

2. Select the objects that you want to copy and press <Enter> to complete the selection set.

3. Select an object on the destination layer or use the **Name** option to open the *Copy To Layer* dialog box, in which you can select a layer name, as shown in Figure 1–68.

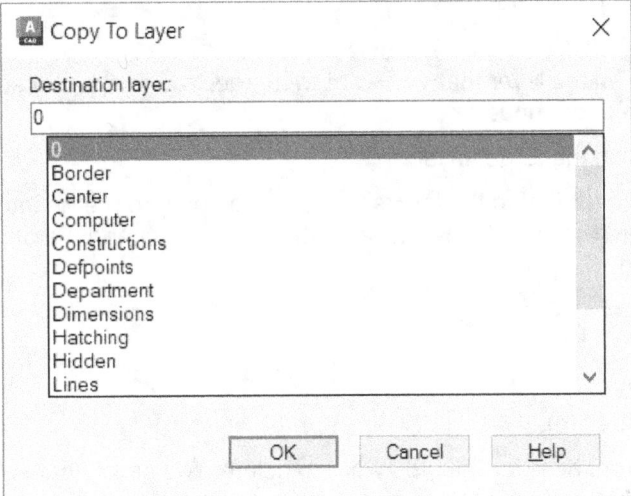

Figure 1–68

4. Select a base point from which to copy. If you want the new copies to be on top of the originals, you can press <Enter> to exit without moving the objects.

5. Select a second point to place the new objects on the selected layer.

*   The new layer to which objects are going to be copied must exist for this command to be used.

Modifying Layers

In the *Home* tab>extended *Layers* panel, use (Layer Merge) to move all of the objects on selected layers to a target layer. It automatically then purges the empty layer.

(Layer Delete) removes a layer and any objects associated with that layer.

- The default response to the final prompt of *Do you wish to continue?* for each of these commands is **No**. You must specify **Yes** to complete the process.

How To: Merge Layers

1. Click (Layer Merge).
2. Select an object on the layer that you want to merge. You can select several layers before pressing <Enter> to continue.
3. Select an object on the target layer.
4. A warning box opens, listing the layers that you are going to merge into the target layer. If you type **Y** for **Yes**, the objects are moved to the target layer and the other layers are deleted from the drawing.

How To: Delete Layers

1. Click (Layer Delete).
2. Select an object on the layer that you want to delete. You can select several layers before pressing <Enter> to continue. If you select multiple layers, the objects disappear from the drawing as you click them.
3. A warning box opens, listing the layers that you are going to delete. If you type **Y** for **Yes**, the objects and layers are deleted from the drawing.
   - If blocks are associated with the layer, they are redefined with objects from the deleted layer.

💡 **Hint: Layer Translator (LAYTRANS command)**

The ▤ (Layer Translator) enables you to move all the elements on a selected layer to another new layer that you have to create first. In the *Layer Translator* dialog box (as shown in Figure 1–69), create a new layer where you want the objects of the old layer to be moved

into. It automatically then purges the empty layer. The ▤ (Layer Translator) tool is available in the *Manage* tab>*CAD Standards* panel.

Figure 1–69

Layer Walk

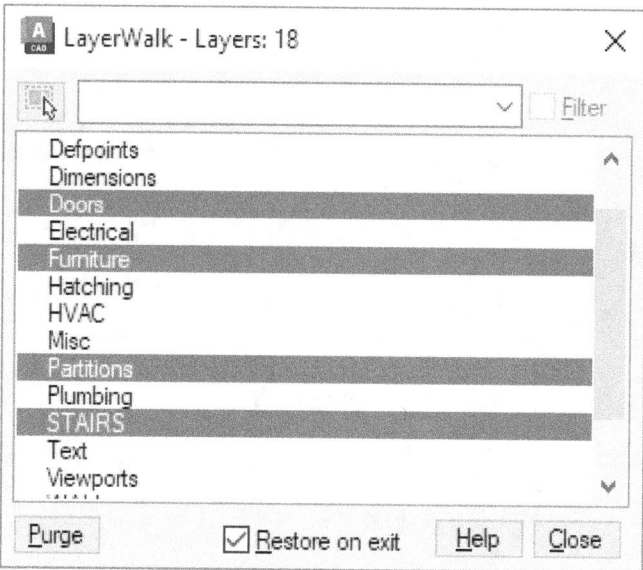 (Layer Walk) provides an interface in which you can quickly display objects on specified layers and then modify them in a dialog box, as shown in Figure 1–70. Use this command to find out which layers the objects display on and then use other commands to move them to the correct layer.

Figure 1–70

- You can either select from the list of layer names in the *LayerWalk* dialog box or use

  (Select Objects) to select objects in the drawing window.

- Use <Ctrl> and <Shift> or drag to select multiple layers.

- Double-click on the name if you always want a layer to be displayed. An asterisk displays next to the name. You can also right-click and select **Hold Selection**. You can release the hold layers individually or as a group by right-clicking and selecting **Release Selection** and **Release All**.

- If a layer does not contain any objects, you can click **Purge** to remove it from the drawing.

- When you have finished working in the dialog box, you can display the layer setup in your drawing if you clear the **Restore on exit** option. If it is selected, the modifications you made in the dialog box are not displayed in the drawing window.

Filtering Layers

You can use filters to select layers more quickly. Type information including a wildcard character (such as *) and press <Enter> to only display the layer names that match the filter, as shown in Figure 1–71.

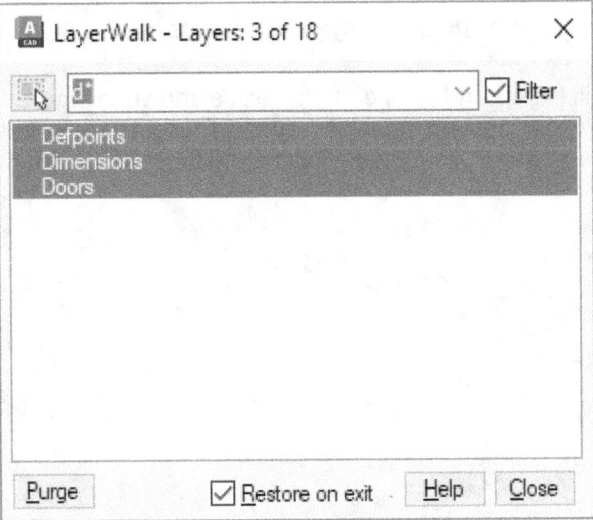

Figure 1–71

- To save a filter, right-click in the *Layer* list and select **Save Current Filter**. The filter is added to the drop-down list.

- All of the layers display if you clear the **Filter** option.

- In the *LayerWalk* dialog box, right-click and select **Save Layer State** to save the current selection of layers to be used later in *Layer State Manager*.

- In the *LayerWalk* dialog box, right-click and select **Inspect...** to display the number of layers in the drawing, number of layers selected, and number of objects on the selected layers, as shown in Figure 1–72.

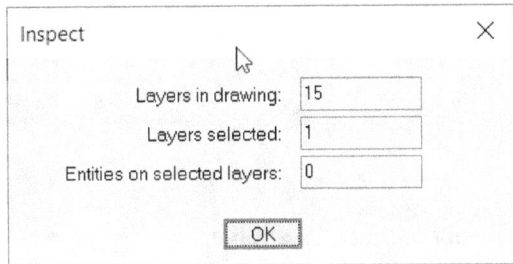

Figure 1–72

Practice 1f
Use Layer Tools

Practice Objective

*   Modify the layers using the additional layer commands.

In this practice, you will freeze and toggle off layers, as shown in Figure 1–73, and then restore the layer states. You will isolate and unisolate layers. You will use the **Layer Walk** and **Layer Merge** commands to determine whether any layers are incorrect in the drawing and then fix them as required.

Figure 1–73

1.   Open **Bank-A.dwg** from your practice files folder.

2.   In the *Home* tab, expand and pin the *Layers* panel.

3.   Practice freezing and toggling off layers using (Layer Freeze) and (Layer Off).

4. Restore the layer states using ⬚ (Turn all Layers On) and ⬚ (Thaw All Layers).

5. You can also try isolating layers using ⬚ (Layer Isolate) and ⬚ (Layer Unisolate).

6. Set the current layer to **Electrical**.

7. Click ⬚ (Layer Freeze). At the *Select an object* prompt, press <Down Arrow> and select **Settings>Block selection>Block**. Select a door to freeze and note what happens. All the doors disappear from the drawing.

8. Click ⬚ (Thaw All Layers).

9. Hover your cursor on one of the text in the drawing. Note that the text is on layer **Walls**.

10. Set the current layer to **Text**.

11. Click ⬚ (Change to Current Layer). Select the text and note how the color changes to blue, which is the color of the layer **Text**.

12. Click ⬚ (Layer Walk). In the *Layer Walk* dialog box, select **Doors**. Only the objects that are on layer Doors are displayed with everything else disappearing. Similarly, select **Furniture** and **STAIRS** to display the objects on each layer. Select the layer **Walls** first and then select the layer **WALL**. Note that the walls in the drawing are on two different layers with most of them being on layer **Walls** and few of them being on layer **WALL**. Close the *Layer Walk* dialog box.

13. Set layer **0** to be the current layer. Click ⬚ (Layer Merge) and select an object on the layer **Walls** (top most horizontal wall of the layout). Note that all the walls on the layer **Walls** are highlighted. Press <Enter>.

14. Select an object on the layer **WALL** (a wall between the rooms **VICE PRES** and **PRES**). Click **Yes**.

15. Expand the Layer Control in the *Layers* panel to verify that one of the wall layers is deleted and all the walls are on a single layer.

16. Save and close the drawing.

End of practice

Chapter Review Questions

1. What do Workspaces control?

    a. The available tabs in the ribbon and the display of Tool Palettes.

    b. The settings in the *Options* dialog box.

    c. The default template location.

    d. The drawings that are open in the AutoCAD software.

2. If some objects are already hidden or isolated, you cannot add additional objects to the isolated selection set.

    a. True

    b. False

3. How can you paste AutoCAD objects into a drawing at the same location as in the drawing from which they were copied?

    a. Select **Edit>Paste Special** in the Application Menu.

    b. Right-click and select **Paste to Original Coordinates**.

    c. Right-click and select **Paste as Block**.

    d. Select **Edit>Paste Special** in the Menu Browser.

4. If you have multiple drawings open, how can you switch between them? (Select all that apply.)

    a. Use **Open** to open the drawing again.

    b. Press <Shift>+<Tab>.

    c. Use **Application Menu>Open Documents**.

    d. Use *View* tab>*Interface* panel, expanded *Switch Windows* drop-down list.

5. What is a function of the **Layer Walk** command?

    a. Toggle the visibility of layers on and off by selecting them in the *LayerWalk* dialog box.

    b. Change the properties of a layer.

    c. Change the layer on which an object is located.

    d. Create new layers in the *LayerWalk* dialog box.

6. When selecting an object and then a grip, which of the following commands is started by default?

    a. Stretch

    b. Copy

    c. Scale

    d. Move

Command Summary

Button	Command	Location
	Clean Screen	• **Status Bar** • **Command Prompt:** <Ctrl>+<0> (zero), cleanscreenON or cleanscreenOFF
	Command Aliases	• **Ribbon:** *Express Tools* tab>*Tools* panel
	File Tabs bar	• **Ribbon:** *View* tab>*Interface* panel
	Workspace Switching	• **Status Bar** • **Command Prompt:** wscurrent
Clipboard		
	Copy	• **Ribbon:** *Home* tab>*Clipboard* panel • **Shortcut Menu:** Copy • **Command Prompt:** copyclip or <Ctrl>+<0>
	Copy with Base Point	• **Shortcut Menu:** Copy with Basepoint • **Command Prompt:** <Ctrl>+<Shift>+<C> or copybase
	Cut	• **Ribbon:** *Home* tab>*Clipboard* panel • **Shortcut Menu:** Cut • **Command Prompt:** <Ctrl>+<X> or cutclip
	Paste	• **Ribbon:** *Home* tab>*Clipboard* panel • **Shortcut Menu:** Paste • **Command Prompt:** <Ctrl>+<V> or pasteclip
	Paste as Block	• **Ribbon:** *Home* tab>*Clipboard* panel • **Shortcut Menu:** Paste as Block • **Command Prompt:** pasteblock
	Paste to Original Coordinates	• **Ribbon:** *Home* tab>*Clipboard* panel • **Shortcut Menu:** Paste to Original Coordinates • **Command Prompt:** pasteorig
Layer		
	Change to Current Layer	• **Ribbon:** *Home* tab>expanded *Layers* panel • **Command Prompt:** laycur
	Copy Objects to New Layer	• **Ribbon:** *Home* tab>expanded *Layers* panel • **Command Prompt:** copytolayer

Button	Command	Location
	Layer Delete	• **Ribbon:** *Home* tab>expanded *Layers* panel • **Command Prompt:** laydel
	Layer Freeze	• **Ribbon:** *Home* tab>*Layers* panel • **Command Prompt:** layfrz
	Layer Isolate/Layer Unisolate	• **Ribbon:** *Home* tab>*Layers* panel • **Command Prompt:** layiso or layuniso
	VP Freeze in All Viewports except Current	• **Ribbon:** *Home* tab>expanded *Layers* panel • **Command Prompt:** layvpi
	Layer Lock/Layer Unlock	• **Ribbon:** *Home* tab>*Layers* panel • **Command Prompt:** laylck or layulk
	Layer Merge	• **Ribbon:** *Home* tab>expanded *Layers* panel • **Command Prompt:** laymrg
	Layer Previous	• **Ribbon:** *Home* tab>expanded *Layers* panel • **Command Prompt:** layerp
	Layer Off	• **Ribbon:** *Home* tab>*Layers* panel • **Command Prompt:** layoff
	Layer Walk	• **Ribbon:** *Home* tab>expanded *Layers* panel • **Command Prompt:** laywalk
	Thaw All Layers	• **Ribbon:** *Home* tab>*Layers* panel • **Command Prompt:** laythw
	Turn all Layers On	• **Ribbon:** *Home* tab>*Layers* panel • **Command Prompt:** layon

Window

Button	Command	Location
	Cascade	• **Ribbon:** *View* tab>*Interface* panel
	Switch Windows	• **Ribbon:** *View* tab>*Interface* panel
	Tile Horizontally	• **Ribbon:** *View* tab>*Interface* panel
	Tile Vertically	• **Ribbon:** *View* tab>*Interface* panel

Accurate Positioning

You will explore absolute, relative, and relative polar coordinates to specify a point and use tracking to determine a point based on existing references. You will also use construction lines and place reference points.

Learning Objectives

- Locate positions in a drawing and new points based on existing object snap points.
- Create guidelines that are infinite in one or both directions.
- Add individual points and multiple individual points.

2.1 Coordinate Entry

The AutoCAD® software has several ways of locating positions in a drawing by typing coordinates or by coordinate entry, as shown in Figure 2−1:

- Absolute Cartesian Coordinates (X,Y)

- Relative Cartesian Coordinates (@X,Y)

- Relative Polar Coordinates (@Distance<Angle)

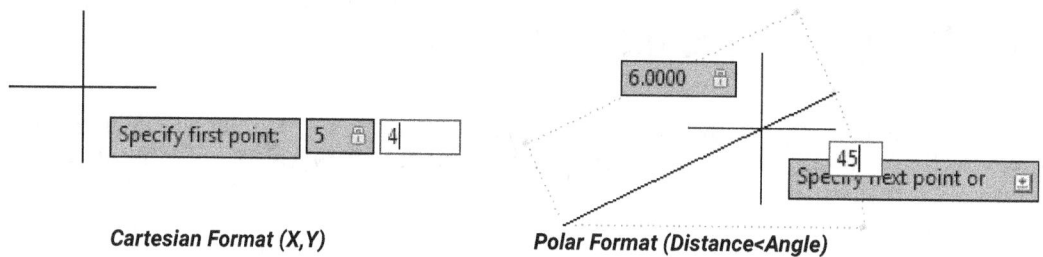

Cartesian Format (X,Y)   *Polar Format (Distance<Angle)*

Figure 2−1

Absolute Cartesian Coordinates (X,Y)

Absolute Cartesian coordinates (X,Y) specify a point's absolute location based on the origin (0,0). You can use absolute coordinates to specify the first point of a line or the center point of a circle. For example, typing **8,2** locates a point eight units in the X-direction and two units in the Y-direction from the origin, as shown in Figure 2−2.

Figure 2−2

- Absolute Cartesian Coordinates are useful when you are given the coordinates to use, such as in some mapping applications or drawings for numeric control machinery.

Relative Cartesian Coordinates (@X,Y)

Relative Cartesian coordinates specify a point's distance away from the last point entered using X- and Y-values.

- Relative Cartesian coordinates are useful when you are given an X- and Y-distance rather than a distance and angle.

- When using 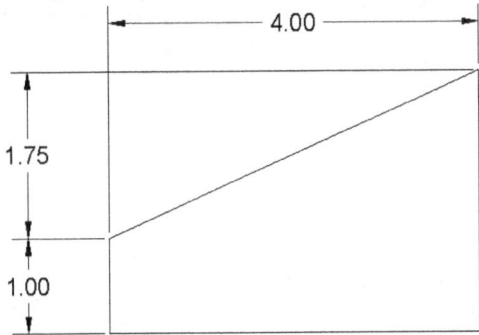 (Dynamic Input), the coordinates you type for the *next point* or *second point* in a command are automatically relative by default.

- If ⁺▬ (Dynamic Input) is toggled off, you have to force coordinates to be relative by putting @ in front of them (@X,Y). @ is a shorthand way of identifying the last point entered.

- When you type coordinates in the X,Y format, it overrides the default distance and angle format.

How To: Draw Using Relative Coordinates

In the example shown in Figure 2–3 the angled line is drawn using the specified dimensions and relative coordinates. The drawing requires X- and Y-values, rather than distance and angle values.

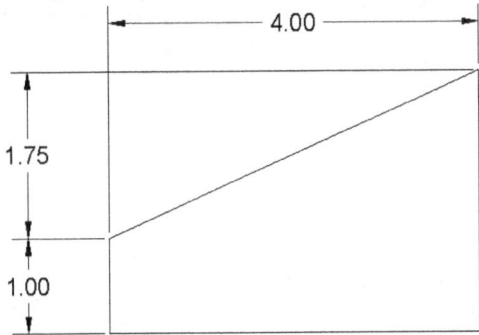

Figure 2–3

1. Verify that 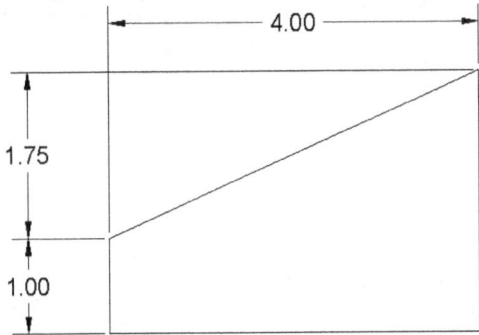 (Dynamic Input) is toggled on (highlighted).

2. Start the **Line** command.

3. Draw the short vertical segment **1 unit** straight up.

4. At the *Specify next point:* prompt, type **4,1.75** and press <Enter>. This places the endpoint of the segment **4 units** to the right (X-value) and **1.75 units** up (Y-value) from the last point.

    - When 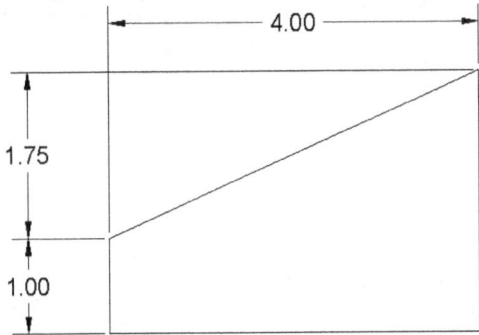 (Dynamic Input) is toggled on, the coordinates you type for the *next point* or *second point* in a command are automatically relative by default. Therefore, @ is not required.

5. At the *Specify next point:* prompt, type **0,-2.75** and press <Enter>. This places the endpoint of the segment **0 units** to the right (X-value) and **2.75 units** down (Y-value) from the last point.

6. Type **C** to close the object and complete the drawing.

- The X- or Y-values can be either positive or negative. For example, @6,0 is a point 6 units straight to the right of the last point, but @-6,0 is a point 6 units to the left (back along the X-axis).

Relative Polar Coordinates (@Distance<Angle)

When you are selecting the *next point* for a line, dynamic dimensions display the distance from the last point and angle, as shown in Figure 2–4. Specifying the distance and angle is another form of coordinates, known as polar coordinates.

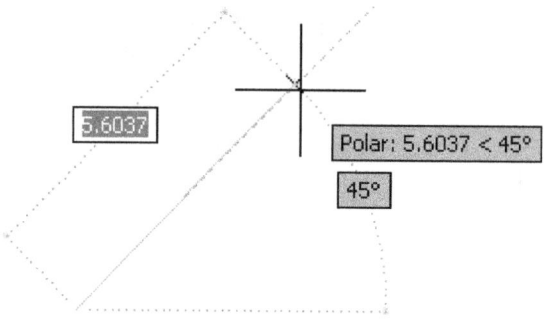

Figure 2–4

- Relative polar coordinates identify a point at a specific distance and angle from the last point selected.

- When drawing with ⊞ (Dynamic Input) toggled on, you can enter the distance, press <Tab>, and enter the angle.

- You can also type polar coordinates in the form of **distance <angle**. For example, **@10<45** identifies a point ten units away, up, and to the right at a 45-degree angle from the last point entered (with ⊞ (Dynamic Input) toggled off).

- You can use the AutoCAD angle scheme (shown in Figure 2–5) to help type the polar coordinates as **distance<angle** without needing to move the cursor to display the angle on the screen.

Figure 2–5

Notes on Coordinate Entry

- You can use coordinate entry with or without using 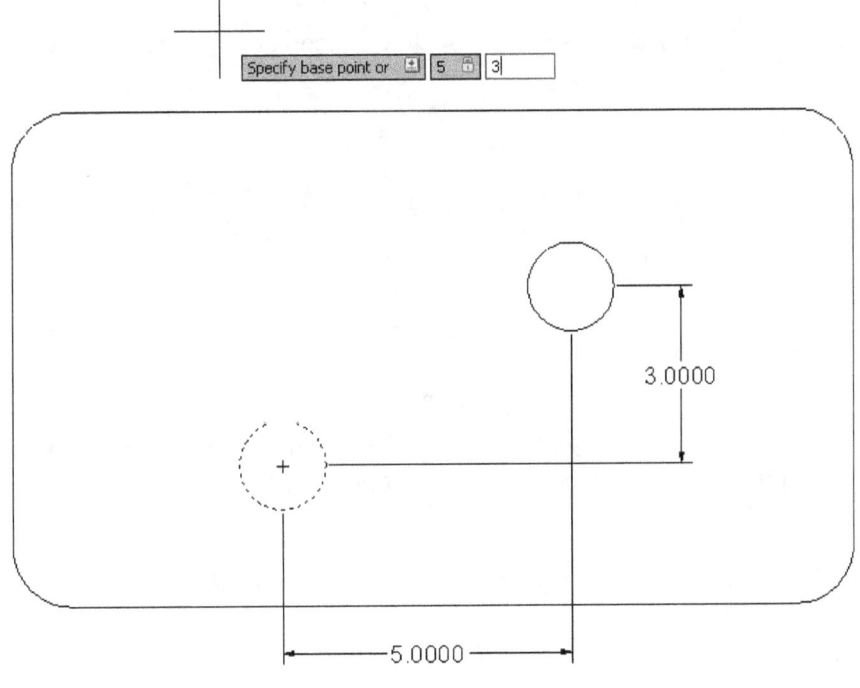 (Dynamic Input). If (Dynamic Input) is toggled off, you must use @ to make points relative to the last point.

- You can use @ alone to indicate the last point.

- You can force coordinates to be absolute, rather than relative, by typing # in front of the X,Y value. For example, #1,1 always goes to the absolute point 1,1.

- The Dynamic Input settings can be changed so that the default for the second or next point is absolute instead of relative. In the *Status Bar*, right-click on (Dynamic Input) and select **Dynamic Input Settings**. In the *Drafting Settings* dialog box, in the *Dynamic Input* tab> *Pointer Input* area, click **Settings...** and modify the settings in the *Pointer Input Settings* dialog box.

- Relative coordinates can be useful in commands (such as **Move** and **Copy**), and in drawing commands. For example, you can use relative coordinates to copy an object at precise X- and Y- distances from the original. To copy the circle on the lower left (as shown in Figure 2−6), use the coordinates **5,3** as the second point.

Figure 2−6

💡 Hint: The User Coordinate System

The *User Coordinate System* (UCS) refers to the system of X-, Y-, and Z-coordinates, which define the AutoCAD Cartesian workspace. In the lower left corner of the window, a horizontal line labeled **X** and a vertical line labeled **Y** display. This is called the *UCS icon*, as shown in Figure 2–7.

Figure 2–7

To hide the UCS icon, click 🔼 (Hide UCS Icon) in the *View* tab>*Coordinates* panel, as shown in Figure 2–8. You might need to toggle on the *Coordinates* panel, as it is off by default (right-click in any panel of the *View* tab and select **Show Panels>Coordinates**). To have the UCS icon remain in the lower left corner of the screen (rather than moving with the 0,0 point),

click 🔼 (Show UCS Icon). By default, 🔼 (Show UCS Icon at Origin) is selected.

Figure 2–8

Typically, you work with a fixed coordinate system called the *World Coordinate System* or WCS. The UCS can also be changed to adjust the orientation of the drawing plane, which is primarily used in for 3D models.

To return to the standard World Coordinate System at any time, click 🔼 (World) in the *View* tab>*Coordinates* panel.

Practice 2a
Draw Using Coordinate Entry

Practice Objective

- Draw an object using typed coordinates.

In this practice, you will draw the object (as shown in Figure 2–9) using typed coordinates. You are not required to dimension the object.

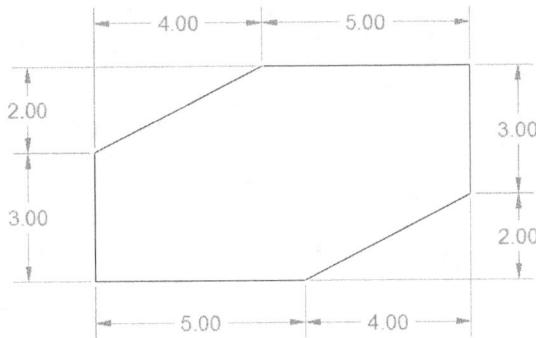

Figure 2–9

1. Start a new drawing based on **Mech-Inches.dwt**, which is located in your practice files folder. Save it as **New Plate.dwg**.

2. Toggle on ⊞ (Dynamic Input) if it is not already on.

3. Start the **Line** command.

4. For the first point, type the absolute coordinates **5,5** and press <Enter>.

5. For the next point, type **5<0** and press <Enter>. This draws the first segment 5 units straight to the right (angle 0) from the last point.

6. For the next point, type **4,2** and press <Enter>. This places the endpoint 4 units to the right (X-value) and 2 units up (Y-value) from the last point.

7. For the next point, type **3<90** and press <Enter>.

8. For the next point, type **5<180** and press <Enter>.

9. For the next point, type **−4,−2** and press <Enter> to draw the angled segment down and to the left.

10. Type **C** and press <Enter> to close the figure.

11. Save and close the drawing.

End of practice

2.2 Locating Points with Tracking

Object Snap Tracking Review

You can use the technique of Object Snap Tracking to locate a new point based on existing object snap points. In other words, you can track from two points to find the intersection point of their tracking lines. For example, you can find the precise center of an object in your drawing by tracking from the midpoints of two sides, as shown in Figure 2–10.

Midpoint: < 0°, Endpoint: < 90°

Figure 2–10

- (Object Snap) and (Object Snap Tracking) must both be toggled on to use Object Snap Tracking.

- Hover the cursor over the object snap point and then move it away vertically or horizontally to display the tracking line.

- You can select one point and type a distance to move in one direction along a tracking line from that point.

Temporary Track Point

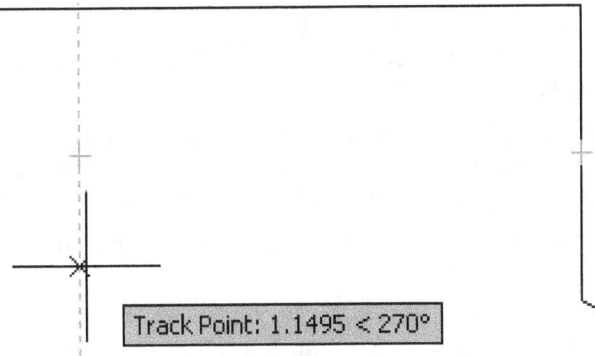 (Temporary Track Point) can create additional tracking points, which can be useful when you are using Object Snap Tracking and need to have more than two tracking points. It enables you to find a location based on two distances from another point. For example, if you need to position a circle with its center five units to the left and three units up from an endpoint, you need to use Temporary Track Point to add the additional point.

- (Object Snap) and (Object Snap Tracking) must both be toggled on to use Temporary Track Point.

- You can start a Temporary Track Point by right-clicking and selecting **Osnap Overrides> Temporary track point** in the shortcut menu or by typing **TT** in the Command Line, after starting a draw command.

How To: Use a Temporary Track Point

1. In the *Status Bar*, toggle on (Object Snap) and (Object Snap Tracking).
2. Start a command, such as **Line** or **Circle**.
3. When prompted for a point, start (Temporary Track Point) by typing **tt**.
4. Hover the cursor over an existing point, which is then marked with a small plus mark.
5. Move the cursor to lock the required tracking angle from the temporary point, and then type a distance to move in relation to the temporary point, as shown in Figure 2−11.

Track Point: 1.1495 < 270°

Figure 2−11

- Tracking lines display when you have locked a tracking angle from the temporary point.

- **IMPORTANT:** Do not move the cursor directly over the cross that marks the temporary point. Doing so clears the point.

Practice 2b
Locate Points with Tracking (Mechanical)

Practice Objective

- Place holes at certain locations.

In this practice, you will use Object Snap Tracking and Temporary Track Point to place holes on a machine part, as shown in Figure 2–12. You are not required to dimension the part.

Figure 2–12

1. Open **Track-I.dwg** from your practice files folder.

2. Set the **Midpoint** *Object Snap* and verify that ▢ (Object Snap) and ◿ (Object Snap Tracking) are toggled on.

3. To draw a circle using the **Circle** command, hover the cursor over the midpoint of the left vertical line as a tracking point, and then pull the cursor to the right. Note that a tracking line is displayed. Type **3**, press <Enter>, and set the *diameter* (using the <Down Arrow>) to **1**.

4. Repeat this process to place the **0.25 diameter** circle, **1 unit** from the midpoint of the left vertical line, as shown above in Figure 2–12.

5. Start the **Circle** command again and start the **Temporary Track Point** override by right-clicking anywhere and selecting **Osnap Overrides>Temporary track point**.

6. Hover the cursor over the midpoint of the left vertical line, and pull the cursor to the right. Type **1.5** (as shown on the left in Figure 2–13) and press <Enter>. A small plus mark displays at the temporary track point. Move the cursor directly below the plus mark. A vertical tracking line displays. Type **0.75** (as shown on the right in Figure 2–13) and press <Enter>. This selects another point **0.75** units down from the first temporary point.

Figure 2–13

7. The cursor snaps to the point. Place a **0.25 diameter** circle at this temporary track point location.

8. Repeat this process to place the last circle (**0.25 diameter**) as shown in Figure 2–12, but move the cursor directly above the cross.

9. Save and close the drawing.

End of practice

Practice 2c
Locate Points with Tracking (Architectural)

Practice Objectives

- Draw the walls of a building.
- Position additional wall lines using tracking methods.

In this practice, you will create walls for a simple building outline using the **Polyline** command and then use the Object Snap Tracking and Temporary Track Point methods to help position interior partitions, as shown in Figure 2–14. You are not required to dimension the drawing.

Figure 2–14

1. Start a new drawing based on **AEC-Imperial.dwt,** which is found in your practice files folder.

2. Make the layer **Walls** current, if required (add for Metric only). Using the **Polyline** command, verify that the **Width** option is set to **0**, and then draw the outside of the building as shown in Figure 2–14. Start from the lower left corner and draw counter-clockwise.

   - (Object Snap Tracking) can help to position the point for the top left corner.

3. Offset the exterior walls **6"** to the inside.

4. Make the layer **Partitions** current and draw the interior partitions except the undimensioned partition wall.

5. Use ⬚ (Object Snap) and ◩ (Object Snap Tracking) to help position the bottom partition line and then make it **3"** wide.

6. From this wall, use the ⬚ (Object Snap) and ◩ (Object Snap Tracking) to draw the middle partition wall.

7. For the top-most floating wall, start the **Pline** command. Hover the cursor over the top left inner corner (Endpoint) of the wall. Enter **tt** (for **Temporary Track Point**) and press <Enter>.

8. Drag the cursor down, enter **5'** and press <Enter>. A plus mark is established. Drag the cursor right, enter **10'** and press <Enter>. The first point of the polyline is established. Draw the floating wall starting from this point.

9. Save the drawing as **Open Office.dwg** and close the drawing.

End of practice

2.3 Construction Lines

Use temporary construction lines as guidelines for creating the more permanent parts of your design, as shown in Figure 2–15. Regular lines can serve as construction lines, but do not always provide the required length. Construction lines and rays are infinite lines that can be used to help construct your drawing.

- **Construction Line** and **Ray** are located in the *Home* tab>expanded *Draw* panel.

Figure 2–15

Construction Lines

The **XLine** command creates a construction line that is infinite in both directions.

How To: Draw a Construction Line

1. In the *Home* tab>expanded *Draw* panel, click ✎ (Construction Line).
2. Select two points on the screen for the line to go through or select an option in the menu. If you select two points, you can create additional construction lines by continuing to select points at different angles around the first point.
3. Using the <Down Arrow> menu, select the **Hor**, **Ver**, or **Ang** options before selecting the first point if you want to make a series of horizontal, vertical, or angled construction lines.
4. If you want to create construction lines offset by a specific distance, select the **Offset** option in the <Down Arrow> menu.
5. The **Bisect** option creates a construction line that bisects a selected angle. It is determined by three points: angle vertex point, angle start point, and angle endpoint.

    - Construction lines are not affected by zooming.
    - Construction lines should be placed on a separate layer that can be toggled off or made non-plotable.

Rays

A ray extends infinitely in one direction from a specified point and you can input more than one ray from the same point.

How To: Draw a Ray

1. In the *Home* tab>expanded *Draw* panel, click ✏ (Ray).
2. Select the start point for the ray. This becomes the end point of the ray.
3. Select a through point for the ray.
4. Continue to select other through points to create additional rays at different angles, but with the same end point.
5. Press <Enter> to end the command.

   - Use object snaps to place construction lines and rays precisely on existing objects.
   - **Ray** does not have the same options as **Construction Line**.

Practice 2d
Use Construction Lines

Practice Objective

- Create guidelines that are used to add geometry.

In this practice, you will draw circles and then add more circles to the plate using construction lines for precise placement, as shown in Figure 2–16.

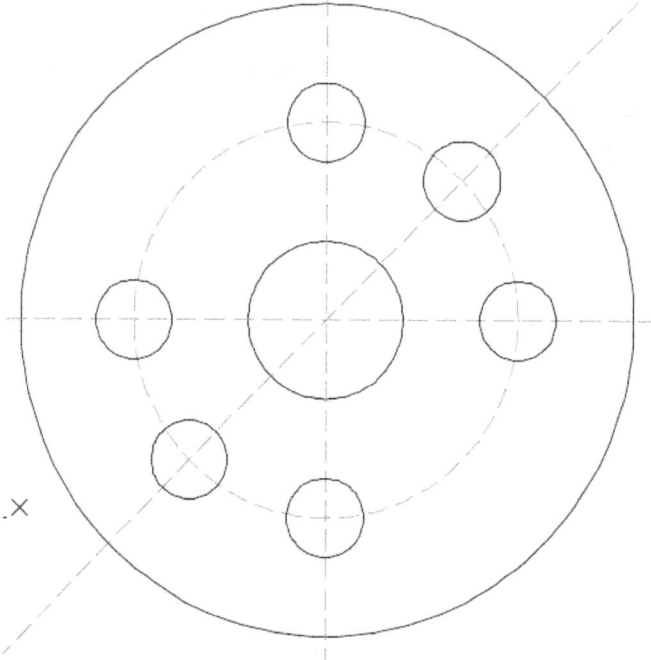

Figure 2–16

1. Create a new drawing based on **Mech-Inches.dwt**, which is located in your practice files folder. Save it as **Round Plate.dwg**.

2. Draw two circles (**R=2** and **R=8**) around the *center point* **10,5**. Use the **Zoom Extents** command to display the entire drawing.

3. Toggle on the **Center** object snap.

4. Set the current layer to **Constructions**.

5. Draw a third circle (**R=5**) around the same center point.

6. In the *Home* tab>expanded *Draw* panel, click (Construction Line). Use the <Down Arrow> menu to place the following three construction lines through the center point of the circles:

- Horizontal
- Vertical
- Angular at 45 degrees

Select the **Hor**, **Ver**, or **Ang** options in the <Down Arrow> menu before selecting the through point, which is the center of the circles, as shown in Figure 2–17.

Figure 2–17

7. Set the current layer to **Object**.

8. Draw six circles with **R=1.0** at the intersection (**Intersection** object snap) of the construction lines and the middle circle.

9. Toggle off the layer **Constructions**.

10. Save and close the drawing.

End of practice

2.4 Placing Reference Points

The **Point** command places permanent reference markers into a drawing. For example, a point could be used to mark the center point of an arc for future reference, or to mark the precise location of survey points on a map, as shown in Figure 2–18. The visibility of this reference marker can be toggled on and off as required.

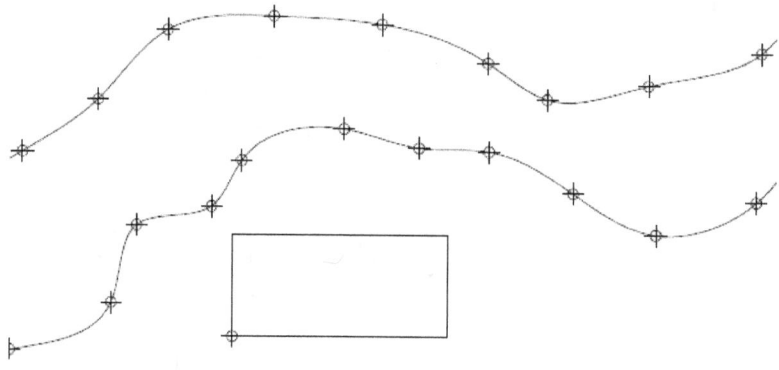

Figure 2–18

- You can add multiple individual points using ∴ (Multiple Points). Two other commands,

  (Divide) and (Measure), create groups of points in a pattern. You can access these point commands in the expanded *Home* tab>*Draw* panel, as shown in Figure 2–19.

Figure 2–19

- Once placed in a drawing, points can be moved or erased like other objects.

- Use the **Node** object snap to snap to a point.

Setting the Point Style

To change the appearance of points in your drawing, click ✨ (Point Style...) in the *Home* tab> expanded *Utilities* panel. The *Point Style* dialog box opens (as shown in Figure 2–20), enabling you to select from the available point styles.

- Changing the point style changes the display of all of the points in the drawing.

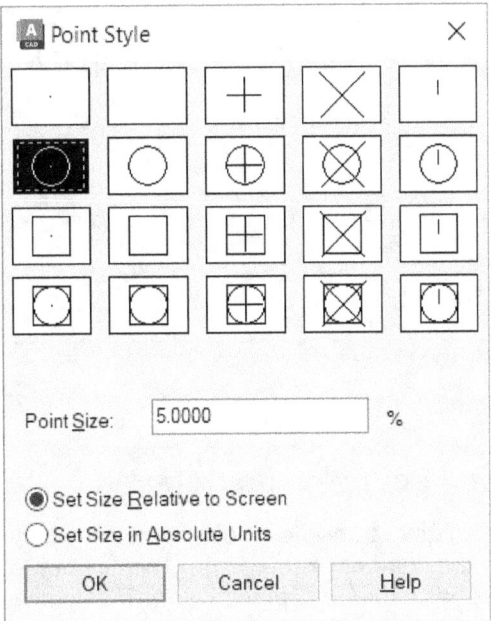

Figure 2–20

Creating Groups of Points

Creating groups of points can be very useful. For example, you might need to space electrical outlets evenly around a large room in a floor plan (as shown in Figure 2-21), or to place markers every 900 meters along a runway on a map.

Figure 2-21

Placing Evenly Spaced Points on an Object

The **Divide** command places points to divide an object into a specified number of equal segments. You can specify the number of segments. This is not the number of points: a line divided into three segments has two points placed along it as shown in Figure 2-22.

Figure 2-22

How To: Divide an Object

1. In the *Home* tab>expanded *Draw* panel, click ⸜⫯ (Divide).
2. Select the object that you want to divide.
3. Enter the number of segments. The points are evenly spaced, dividing the object into equal length segments between the points.

*   You can use the **Block** option to insert a block instead of a point style.

Placing Points at Specified Intervals on an Object

The **Measure** command places points at a specified distance along an object. You specify the *length of segments* (the distance between points). The software begins to measure from the end point closest to the location used to select the object.

How To: Measure an Object

1. In the *Home* tab>expanded *Draw* panel, click ⁂ (Measure).

2. Select the object that you want to measure.

3. Specify the length of the segment. The points are spaced at the specified distance along the object.

• If the object cannot be divided evenly, the remainder is left at the end of the object, opposite to where it was selected.

• You can use the **Block** option to insert a block instead of a point style.

Practice 2e
Place Points

Practice Objective

- Place points to mark the locations on objects.

In this practice, you will place points to mark the locations of the centers of holes in a plate. You will use **Point**, **Divide**, and **Measure** commands to position the points, as shown in Figure 2–23.

Figure 2–23

1. Open **Points-I.dwg** from your practice files folder.

2. Change the current layer to **Constructions**.

3. Draw a line from the midpoint of the left side (vertical line) of the plate, **10 units** straight to the right side.

4. Offset the line **2 units** on either side.

5. In the *Home* tab>expanded *Utilities* panel, click (Point Style) to open the *Point Style* dialog box. Select the cross with a circle or other visible point style and click **OK**.

6. In the *Home* tab>expanded *Draw* panel, click (Multiple Points). Place points at the midpoint and right endpoint of the middle construction line. Press <Esc> to end the command.

7. In the *Home* tab>expanded *Draw* panel, click (Divide) and select the top construction line. Type **8** as the number of segments. Note that seven points are added, evenly dividing the line.

8. In the *Home* tab>expanded *Draw* panel, click ⚹ (Measure) and select the bottom construction line closer to the left endpoint. Type **2.75** as the length of segments and press <Enter>. Three points are added, spaced at that distance apart.

9. Add **Node** as an additional Object snap.

10. Set the current layer to **Object**.

11. Start the **Circle** command and place a circle on one of the nodes (points). Select an appropriate radius for the circle such that it encloses the cross of the point.

12. Use the **Copy** command to copy the circle to the other points.

13. Toggle off the layer **Constructions**.

14. Save and close the drawing.

End of practice

Chapter Review Questions

1. With Dynamic Input toggled off, after you pick the first corner for a rectangle, what are the typed coordinates that can be used to make it 20 units long and 8 units high?

    a. 20,8

    b. @8,20

    c. 8,20

    d. @20,8

2. What does @ represent in the AutoCAD software?

    a. Indicates that Object Snap is going to be used.

    b. Indicates that a temporary tracking point is going to be used.

    c. Indicates a point relative to the last point.

    d. Used in place of 0.

3. What does the Temporary Tracking Point enable you to do that Object Snap Tracking alone does not?

    a. Find a location based on two distances from another point.

    b. Draw circles, lines, and rectangles.

    c. Find a location based on only the midpoints of two objects.

    d. Precisely pick a point without using an object snap.

4. The difference between construction lines and regular lines is that construction lines extend infinitely.

    a. True

    b. False

5. Which command would enable you to position points every 5 units along a line?

    a. Temporary Tracking Point

    b. Divide

    c. Point

    d. Measure

6. Relative coordinates are relative to the _____.

  a. Origin (0,0)

  b. Last point picked

  c. Nearest object snap

  d. Current screen display

Command Summary

Button	Command	Location
	Construction Line	• **Ribbon:** *Home* tab>expanded *Draw* panel • **Command Prompt:** xline or xl
	Divide	• **Ribbon:** *Home* tab>expanded *Draw* panel • **Command Prompt:** divide or div
	Hide UCS Icon	• **Ribbon:** *View* tab>*Coordinates* panel
	Measure	• **Ribbon:** *Home* tab>expanded *Draw* panel • **Command Prompt:** measure or me
	Point (Multiple Points)	• **Ribbon:** *Home* tab>expanded *Draw* panel • **Command Prompt:** point or po
	Point Styles	• **Ribbon:** *Home* tab>expanded *Utilities* panel • **Command Prompt:** ddptype
	Ray	• **Ribbon:** *Home* tab>expanded *Draw* panel • **Command Prompt:** ray
	Show UCS Icon	• **Ribbon:** *View* tab>*Coordinates* panel
	Show UCS Icon at Origin	• **Ribbon:** *View* tab>*Coordinates* panel
	Temporary Track Point	• **Shortcut Menu:** Snap Overrides>Temporary Track Point • **Command Prompt:** tt
	World	• **Ribbon:** *View* tab>*Coordinates* panel

Projects: Productivity Tools

Practice projects are provided for you to gain additional hands-on experience in the topics and commands previously covered. These projects are intended to be self-guided and do not include step-by-step information.

Learning Objectives

- *Schematic:* Modify a piping diagram using editing techniques such as trim and stretch.
- *Mechanical:* Create several parts using drawing tools in conjunction with Construction lines and object snap tracking.
- *Architectural:* Create several plans using various tracking, drafting tools, and Construction lines to establish the placement of the areas.

3.1 Schematic Project: Purifier Unit

In this project, you will use editing techniques to modify the piping diagram shown in Figure 3−1.

Figure 3−1

1. Open **Piping-I.dwg** from your practice files folder.

2. Use the **Stretch** command to stretch the Heater elements farther to the right, as shown in Figure 3−2.

Figure 3−2

3. Use grips to copy and rotate the gate valve (the blue hourglass shape) to the locations shown in Figure 3−3. Use the **Nearest** object snap to place the valves precisely on the lines.

4. Use **Trim** to remove the section of the line inside the valves, as shown in Figure 3−3.

Figure 3−3

5. Use grips to stretch the endpoint of the lines on the left side to connect with the **T** fittings, as shown in Figure 3−4.

Figure 3−4

3.2 Mechanical Project: 2 Views

In this project, you will create the front and top views of a part, as shown in Figure 3–5.

Figure 3–5

1. Start a new drawing based on **Mech-Inches.dwt**, which is located in your practice files folder and save it as **2Views.dwg**.

2. Use the drawing tools you have learned to create the two views, as shown in Figure 3–5.

   Use construction lines or ![icon] (Object Snap Tracking) to help align and draw the views. Place the hidden lines on the layer **Hidden**.

3. Switch to the *B-Sized* layout tab and display the views in a viewport scaled at **1:1**. If time permits, add annotative dimensions in the layout viewport, as shown in Figure 3–5.

3.3 Architectural/Civil Project: Formal Garden

In this project, you will create a formal garden plan. Use a construction line to establish the center line, and then use tracking and other methods to help place the various components as shown in Figure 3–6. The dimensions are for reference only. You are not required to draw them.

Figure 3–6

1. Start a new drawing based on **Civil-Feet.dwt**, which is located in your practice files folder and save it as **Formal Garden.dwg.**

2. In layer **0**, draw the **30' x 50' building** (extreme left rectangular object in Figure 3–6) with the **5' x 10' porch** along the backside center, as shown in Figure 3–6. (This template uses decimal feet - do not use the ' sign for feet).

3. Use the **XLine** command to establish the center line.

4. Draw the rectangular garden wall (**1'-0" thick**) and paths (**4'-0"**) with gates (**3'-0" on center of wall**), as shown in Figure 3–6. Use tracking or other construction lines to help you. Place the objects on the layer **Pavement Edge New**.

5. Add three semi-circular steps offset at **1'-0"** with the smallest step of **3'-0"** radius.

6. (Optional) If time permits, add the elliptical pool with a **10'** pool pavement. Add the path leading up to it. The path distance from the inner edge of the garden wall to the left endpoint of the ellipse axis is **35'**.

3.4 Mechanical Project: Cover Plate

In this project, you will draw one view of a mechanical part, as shown in Figure 3−7.

Figure 3−7

1. Start a new drawing based on **Mech-Inches.dwt**, which is located in your practice files folder.

2. Draw the objects shown in Figure 3−7 with the help of tools such as Dynamic Input, Direct Distance Entry, Polar Array, and Object Snap Tracking. Draw only the objects, not the dimensions. Note that all of the dimensions are mirror images unless otherwise indicated.

3. Save the drawing as **Cover Plate.dwg**.

3.5 Architectural Project: Addition

In this project, you will draw an addition to an existing house plan, as shown in Figure 3–8. The dimensions are for reference only.

Figure 3–8

1. Open **Addition-A.dwg** from your practice files folder.

2. Along the top right side, draw the addition shown in Figure 3–8. The walls are **5"** thick. Remember to use the appropriate layers. Use Dynamic Input, Direct Distance Entry, Object Snaps, Object Snap Tracking, and other drafting tools to help create the drawing.

    *   Use the dynamic **Door-Imperial** and **Window-Imperial** blocks from the *Architectural* tab in *Tool Palettes*.

    *   Use grips to adjust the length and depth of the window and door blocks to match the depth of the wall.

3. Save and close the drawing.

3.6 Mechanical Project: Block

In this project, you will use the Drafting Settings tools to help draw a mechanical object, as shown in Figure 3–9.

Figure 3–9

1. Start a new drawing based on **Mech-Inches.dwt**, which is located in your practice files folder. Save it as **Block.dwg**.

2. Draw the objects shown in Figure 3–9. Draw only the objects, not the dimensions.

Construction Hints:

*   Toggle on Dynamic Input and use Polar Tracking to draw the outline. Set the *Polar Angle* to **30 degrees** to draw the angled segments. Depending on how you construct the lines, Object Snap Tracking can help you to draw the top undimensioned segments.

*   Use Object Snap Tracking to place the three circles in relation to the outline.

3. Save and close the drawing.

3.7 Mechanical Project: Plate

In this project, you will use the Drafting Settings tools to help draw the object shown in Figure 3–10.

Figure 3–10

1. Start a new drawing based on **Mech-Inches.dwt**, which is located in your practice files folder. Save it as **Angled Plate.dwg**.

2. Draw the objects shown in Figure 3–10. Draw only the objects, not the dimensions.

Construction Hints:

- Start with the circle with a *diameter* of **1.8**.

- Use Object Snap Tracking to place the three **R.50** fillets (drawn as full circles) in relation to the larger circle. Draw the two angled segments on the right **Tangent** to the **R.50** circles. You will trim the circles later (after you complete the drawing) to convert them into fillets.

- Start at the bottom quadrant of the bottom circle and begin drawing the outline clockwise. Use Polar Tracking. Set the *Polar Angle* to **45 degrees** to draw the angled segments at the upper left side. Use Object Snap Tracking to draw the remaining segments of the outline.

- Use Object Snap Tracking to position the two circles with a *diameter* of **0.5**.

- Trim the three circles with a *radius* of **0.50** to convert them into fillets.

Parametric Drawing

You will learn how to add geometric and dimensional constraints to objects, modify parameters, and create user parameters.

Learning Objectives

- Control how geometry reacts using the *Geometric* constraints.
- Specify distances, radii, or angles that must be fulfilled by the geometry.
- Specify, modify, and delete an object's geometric constraints, and customize the constraint settings.
- Add dimensional constraints and convert the existing dimensions into constraints.
- Modify and add formulas to dimensional constraints.

4.1 Working with Constraints

Constraints and parametric tools provide ways of testing design options while maintaining specific relationships in a drawing. They are used extensively in software, such as the Autodesk® Inventor® software and the Autodesk® Revit® Architecture software. The AutoCAD® software uses them to enhance 2D sketching. There are two types of constraints: Geometric and Dimensional, as shown in Figure 4−1.

Figure 4−1

- Geometric constraints control how geometry reacts. For example, you can specify that a line remain horizontal or that two circles are concentric.

- Dimensional constraints specify distances, radii, or angles that must be fulfilled by the geometry. Dimensional constraints can include formulas referencing other constraints or using basic mathematical functions.

- When you hover the cursor over an object that has constraints, ⚏ displays, as shown in Figure 4−2.

Figure 4−2

4.2 Geometric Constraints

Once objects have been sketched, you can automatically and manually add constraints to the geometry by selecting them in the *Parametric* tab>*Geometric* panel, as shown in Figure 4–3. Click the required constraint icon and select the objects that you want to constrain.

Figure 4–3

Auto Constraining Objects

The **Auto Constrain** command enables you to automate the process of applying various constraints to multiple objects together. If you are working with rectangles or multiple lines or polylines, you can use the **Auto Constrain** command first to set up the parallel, perpendicular, horizontal, or vertical relationships. This command is best used to constrain rectangles as applying other constraints could force the rectangle away from the correct shape.

How To: Auto Constrain Objects

1. Draw the objects in the design.
2. In the *Parametric* tab>*Geometric* panel, click (Auto Constrain).
3. Select the objects that you want to constrain. The constraints are applied as shown on the rectangle in Figure 4–4.

   - One perpendicular, one horizontal, and four parallel constraints help a rectangle to keep its shape.

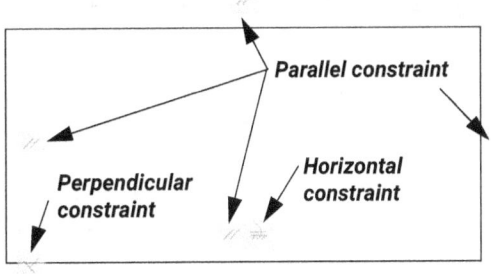

Figure 4–4

- Commands that duplicate objects, such as **Copy**, **Mirror**, and **Array**, also duplicate any related constraints.

Specifying Geometric Constraints

Before you start adding constraints, draw the objects, including any fillets or chamfers. The exact sizes and angles of the objects are not important.

- Linear objects include lines and polyline segments. For the purpose of constraints, a polyline segment can be selected separately from the rest of the polyline.

- Radial objects include circles, arcs, and ellipses.

Horizontal and Vertical

(Horizontal) and (Vertical) constraints force linear objects to remain horizontal or vertical. Select the linear object that you want to be horizontal or vertical, as shown in Figure 4-5.

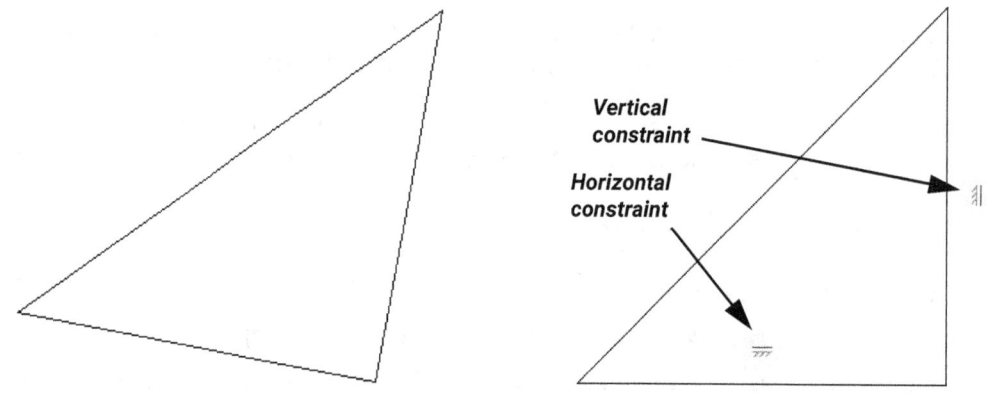

Figure 4-5

- You can also use these tools to align two points horizontally or vertically, such as center points for circles. When prompted to select an object, press <Enter> to select two points.

- Horizontal and Vertical constraints can also be used with ellipses and text.

Parallel and Perpendicular

(Parallel) constrains two linear objects, forcing them to take on the angle of the first object.

(Perpendicular) constrains the second linear element to rotate 90 degrees from the angle of the first linear object. Select a linear object and then a second linear object. The objects take on the angle or right angle of the first object, depending on the selected constraint. Examples of these constraints are shown in Figure 4–6.

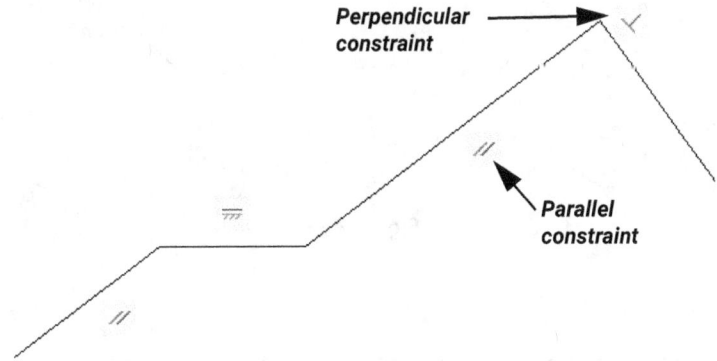

Perpendicular constraint

Parallel constraint

Figure 4–6

* Parallel and Perpendicular constraints can also be used with ellipses and text.

Tangent

(Tangent) constrains an object to the tangent of a radial object. At least one object needs to be a circle, arc, or ellipse, but the objects do not have to touch. Select one object and then select a second object. The elements are then forced to be tangent, as shown in Figure 4–7.

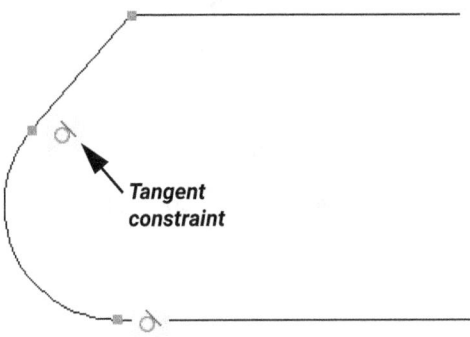

Tangent constraint

Figure 4–7

Smooth

(Smooth) ensures that the selected objects continue the same curvature values between a spline and other linear objects. Select the spline at the endpoint at which you want the curve to continue. Select the second linear element, which can be a line, polyline, or another spline. In Figure 4–8, the endpoint of the spline and the endpoint of the line (indicated by their grips) are selected.

Figure 4–8

Coincident

(Coincident) constrains two points to remain together or a point to remain touching another point on an object. Select a point on one object and then a point on a second object. The point on the second object is moved coincident to the point on the first object. In the example shown in Figure 4–9, the center of the circle has been constrained to the midpoint of the line. A constraint bar does not display with coincident constraints, but a small blue square displays.

Figure 4–9

- Coincident constraints can also move along an object, such as the end of the arc constrained to the line.

Concentric

(Concentric) constrains two radial objects, such as arcs, circles, or ellipses, to maintain the same center point. Select the first center point of a radial object, and then the second center point of another radial object. The two objects take on the center point of the first object, as shown on the right in Figure 4–10.

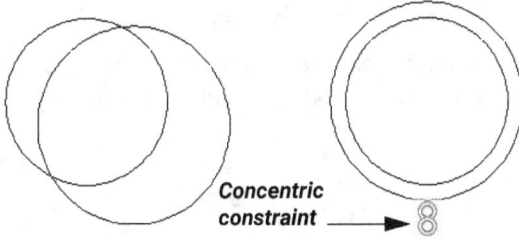

Figure 4–10

Colinear

(Colinear) constrains two lines to lie along the same infinite line. They do not need to be touching. Select the first line and then select the second line. The second line moves to line up with the first line, as shown in Figure 4–11.

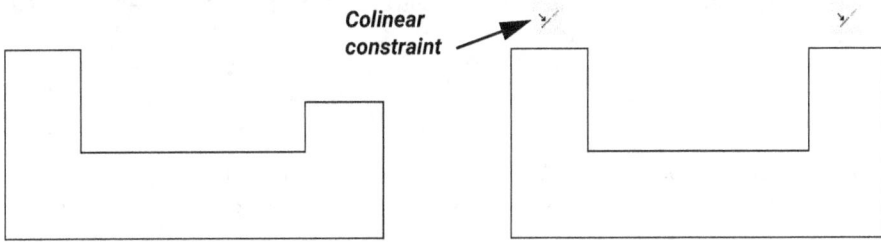

Figure 4–11

- Colinear constraints can also be used to make ellipses and text colinear with other objects, such as lines or ellipses.

Equal

≡ (Equal) constrains two linear elements to maintain the same length or two radial elements to maintain the same radius.

How To: Apply an Equal Constraint

1. Select the first object and then the second object.

2. The second object takes on the measurements of the first object. In Figure 4–12, the object on the right was not constrained and only the selected segment of the polyline changed in distance.

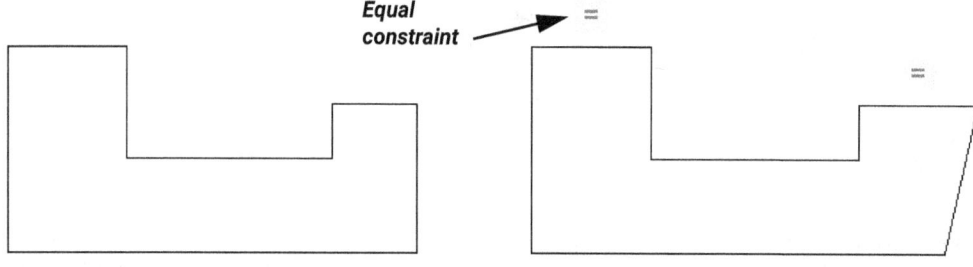

Figure 4–12

- When using Auto Constrain and the Equal constraint, it is applied to lines or polylines of the same length and circles of the same diameter.

Fix

🔒 (Fix) constrains a point on an object to remain fixed to a specific location on the World Coordinate System. You can also fix an entire object, rather than just a single point.

Symmetrical

[⁝] (Symmetrical) constrains two points on objects or forces objects to be symmetrical about a symmetry line.

- Add other constraints first before applying the symmetrical constraint.

How To: Add a Symmetrical Constraint

1. Select the first object or press <Enter> to select a point on an object.

2. Select the second object or point.

3. Select the symmetry line. The objects move into symmetry about the symmetry line, as shown in Figure 4–13.

Figure 4–13

Constraint Bars

Constraint bars are icons that display when geometric constraints are applied to objects. If more than one constraint is applied to an object, the icons touch, forming a bar. When you hover the cursor over a constraint in the constraint bar, the related objects highlight in the drawing.

- To toggle off individual constraint bars, click ✖, which displays when you hover the cursor over the bar, as shown in Figure 4–14.

Figure 4–14

- Toggling off the display of a constraint bar or an icon does not delete or remove the constraint. It only hides the icon.

- To display the constraints of selected objects, click [⌄] (Show/Hide Geometric Constraints) in the *Geometric* panel.

- To display all of the constraints in a drawing, click [⌄] (Show All Geometric Constraints).

- To hide all of the constraints in a drawing, click [⌄] (Hide All Geometric Constraints).

Modifying Geometrical Constraints

Objects that are constrained can still be modified using grips. When you select the grip, you can still stretch, move, rotate, and scale the objects as long as the constraints are satisfied, as shown on the left in Figure 4–15. Press <Shift> to cycle between maintaining and relaxing constraints. Relaxing constraints (as shown on the right in Figure 4–15), removes those constraints.

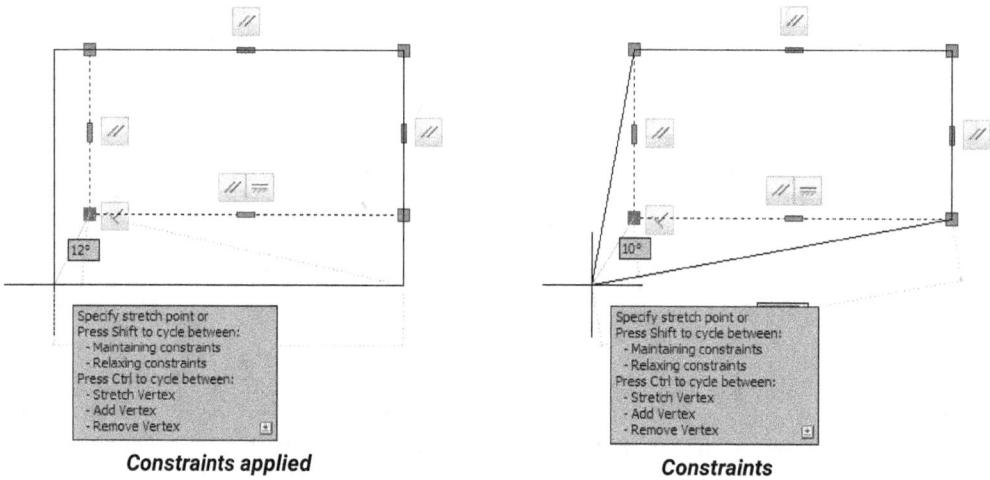

Constraints applied   Constraints

Figure 4–15

* If you modify the location of the grip when the constraints are released, any unfulfilled constraints are automatically deleted.

* You can relax (remove) a constraint by pressing <Shift> while modifying an object.

Deleting Constraints

To delete a constraint, select the constraint in the constraint bar, right-click and select **Delete**, as shown in Figure 4–16. You can also select the constraint and press <Delete>.

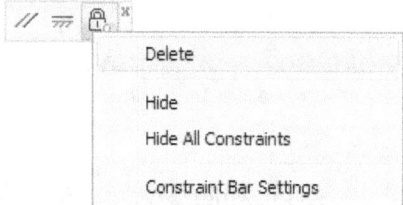

Figure 4–16

* In the *Parametric* tab>*Manage* panel, you can click ⬚⬚ (Delete Constraints) and then select the object from which you want to delete all of the constraints.

Constraint Settings

Click in the *Parametric* tab>*Geometric* panel to open the *Constraint Settings* dialog box in the *Geometric* tab, as shown in Figure 4–17. It contains three tabs: *Geometric*, *Dimensional*, and *AutoConstrain*. The options in these tabs enable you to control how the constraints are displayed and used in the drawing.

Figure 4–17

- The *Geometric* tab enables you to control the constraints that display in the constraint bar and the transparency of the bar.

- The **Show constraint bars after applying constraints to selected objects** controls whether or not constraint bars display when you have applied constraints to objects.

- The **Show constraint bars when objects are selected** controls whether or not the constraint bars display when objects are selected.

- The **Infer geometric constraints** option uses existing constraints to determine whether additional constraints are required as more objects are added to the drawing. The constraints are then automatically added as required. Use **Infer Constraints** in the *Customization* list in the *Status Bar* to toggle the **Infer geometric constraints** option on or off.

- The *AutoConstrain* tab sets the priority in which constraints are applied when **Auto Constrain** is used. You can also control the Tolerance.

4.3 Dimensional Constraints

The dimensional constraints that are created to define a feature's shape are considered parameters. They drive the object's size, distance, and angle and can be changed at any time, causing the features to update automatically.

In the example shown in Figure 4–18, the dimensional value that positions the cut feature has been changed. Therefore, the position of the feature updates to reflect the design change.

The AutoCAD software automatically assigns names (e.g., d1 or d2) to dimensions. You can display the name, name and value, or value of the dimension, as required.

d1=2.0000   d1=1.2500

Figure 4–18

How To: Assign Dimensional Constraints

1. Create the objects that you want to constrain and apply geometrical constraints to them.

2. In the *Parametric* tab>*Dimensional* panel (shown in Figure 4–19), select the type of dimension that you want to place.

Linear   Aligned   Show/Hide   Show All   Hide All

Dynamic Constraint Mode
Annotational Constraint Mode
Dimensional

Figure 4–19

3. Specify the points that you want to dimension and then pick the dimension line location.

4. When the dimension highlights, type a number value, expression, or formula for the dimension.

Types of Dimensional Constraints

All available dimensional constraints are described as follows:

Linear: Constrains the horizontal or vertical distance between two points. The direction depends on the placement of points and dimension line.

Horizontal: Constrains the X distance between two points or objects (in the Linear fly-out).

Vertical: Constrains the Y distance between two points or objects (in the Linear fly-out).

Aligned: Constrains the distance between two points on an object or on two different objects.

Radius: Constrains the radius of a circle or arc.

Diameter: Constrains the diameter of a circle or arc.

Angular: Constrains the angle between two lines or polyline segments, or between three points (vertex, first, and second angle constraint points).

Convert: Turns already existing dimensions into dimensional constraints.

- The dimensional constraints work in the same way as the standard dimension commands.

- For some Dimensional Constraints, you can select entire objects.

- Click (Show/Hide Dynamic Constraints) to toggle the visibility of the selected dimensional constraints on and off. You can also click (Show All Dynamic Constraints) or (Hide All Dynamic Constraints) to toggle all of the constraints on or off.

- Dimensional constraints are dynamic. They display at the same size when you zoom, but they do not plot.

- You can change dynamic constraints to annotation constraints in the *Properties* palette, as shown in Figure 4–20. Annotation constraints use the active annotation scale and dimension style.

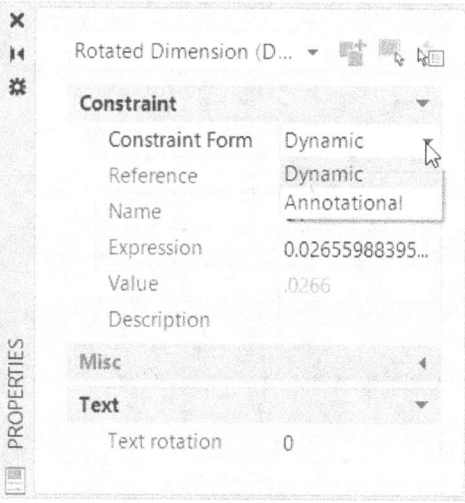

Figure 4–20

- By default, the **Name and Expression** display for dimensional (in both the dynamic and annotation) constraints. This can be changed to **Name** or **Value** in the *Dimensional* tab of *Constraint Settings* dialog box, as shown in Figure 4–21. Open the dialog box by clicking ⬃ in the *Parametric* tab>*Dimensional* panel.

Figure 4–21

How To: Convert Dimensions into Constraints

1. Draw the dimension(s) using standard dimension commands.

2. In the *Parametric* tab>*Dimensional* panel, click 🔲 (Convert).

3. Select the dimension and press <Enter>. The dimension becomes a parameter (dimensional constraint), as shown in Figure 4-22. The parameter value can then be modified.

Figure 4-22

💡 Hint: Best Practices for Dimensional Constraints

When creating dimensions, use the following guidelines:

*   Consider the dimensions that are going to be displayed in drawings and note the resulting feature relationships.
*   Consider changes that might be made to the model in the future and how easily the dimensions facilitate those changes.

Periodically modify dimensions to test *what if* scenarios. This is called *flexing the model* and helps eliminate future problems by verifying that the model behaves correctly.

Modifying Dimensional Constraints

To modify a dimensional constraint, you can double-click on the text and type the new information in the text field, as shown in Figure 4–23.

Figure 4–23

- When dimensional constraints reference one another, **fx:** is added to the beginning of the dimension to indicate that a reference already exists.

You can also modify the constraints in the *Parameters Manager* palette, as shown in

Figure 4–24. Click $f^{(x)}$ (Parameters Manager) in the *Parametric* tab>*Manage* panel.

Figure 4–24

- In *Parameters Manager*, modify the *Expression*. The *Value* updates automatically.

- To remove a dimensional constraint, select it in *Parameters Manager* and click ✕ or press <Delete>.

- By default, all of the parameters in a drawing display. Click 🔻 (Filter) and select **All Used in Expressions** to only display the parameters used in expressions, as shown in Figure 4–25.

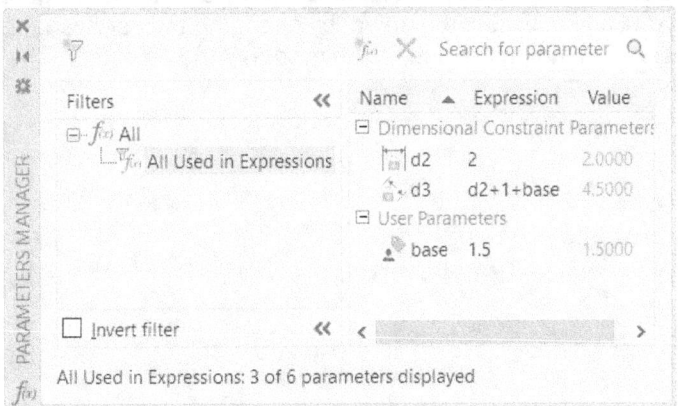

Figure 4–25

- You can search for parameters by typing a value in the *Search for parameter* field in *Parameters Manager*.

Formulas in Constraints

Formulas can be added to dimensional constraints when they are inserted or in *Parameters Manager*.

- Formulas are user-defined mathematical relations that are used to capture and control design intent.

- An equation is created by writing a relation using dimensions or parameters from the model. For example, equations can be used to keep a hole centered on a block, as shown with the dimensions for **d3** and **d4** in Figure 4–26.

Figure 4–26

Creating User Parameters

User parameters can be added to strengthen the formulas. For example, you might have a bolt size that impacts several other parameters in the drawing, as shown in Figure 4–27. By creating a user parameter, you can easily flex the object by changing the user variable and noting how the other objects react. Changing the user value modifies the object.

Figure 4–27

How To: Create a User Parameter

1. In *Parameters Manager*, click f_x (Create User Parameter). A new parameter displays in the *User Parameters* area.

   Note: User parameter names cannot contain spaces, begin with a number, or be over 256 characters.

2. Type a name and an expression.
3. Use the parameter in the expression of other parameters.

Practice 4a
Work with Constraints

Practice Objectives

- Add geometric constraints to the drawing.
- Add dimensional constraints to the drawing.

In this practice, you will add geometric constraints to a drawing using the **Auto Constrain** command. You will then add dimensional constraints to drive an existing model's shape and size, as shown in Figure 4–28.

Figure 4–28

Task 1: Add automatic geometric constraints.

1. In the AutoCAD software, open **Entry-Clamp.dwg** from your practice files folder.

2. In the *Parametric* tab>*Geometric* panel, click ⬚ (Auto Constrain).

3. Select all of the objects in the drawing (use crossing or window selection) and press <Enter>. Many constraints are applied, as shown in Figure 4–29.

- If the constraints were not applied correctly, open the *Constraint Settings* dialog box and check the settings in the *AutoConstrain* tab.

Figure 4–29

4. Select one of the lines and move it by its grip. Note that the object is not constrained enough to keep it from distorting, as shown in Figure 4–30. Press <Esc> twice to exit the selection.

Figure 4–30

5. In the *Geometric* panel, click ⊥— (Coincident).

6. Select the right end point of the bottom arc (as shown on the left in Figure 4−31) and then the left end point of the closest line (as shown on the right in Figure 4−31. The arc and the line is joined.

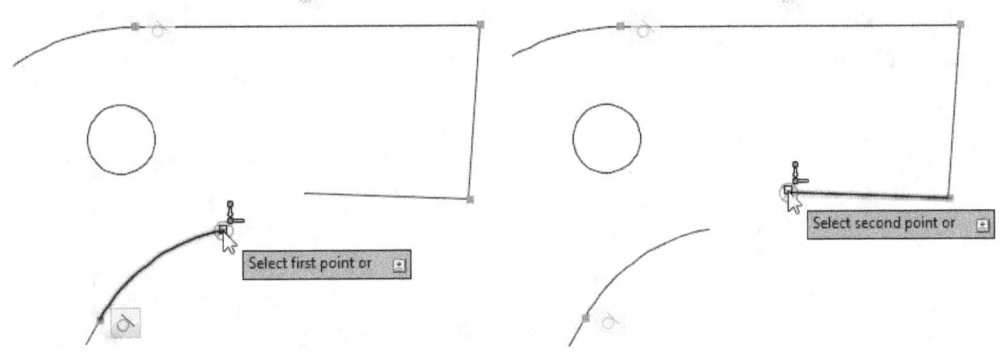

Figure 4−31

7. Add a **Tangent** constraint to the arc and coincident line. In the *Geometric* panel, click

   (Tangent) and select the arc (created in the previous step) and its corresponding line (the line to which you joined it).

   Note: As you add the constraint, its symbol is displayed with the object it is applied to.

8. To make the same line parallel to the line above, click // (Parallel) and select the top line and the bottom line.

9. Click ✕ (Perpendicular). To make the right line (touching the two horizontal parallel lines) perpendicular, select the top horizontal line, and then the right line. The right portion of the object should now be similar to the one shown in Figure 4−32.

Figure 4−32

10. In the *Geometric* panel, click ═ (Equal). Select the vertical line on the right and then the angled line on the bottom left, as shown in Figure 4–33. The two lines become equal in length.

11. Modify one of the lines using grips. Note that the vertical lines automatically adjusts to stay equal in length.

12. Undo the change.

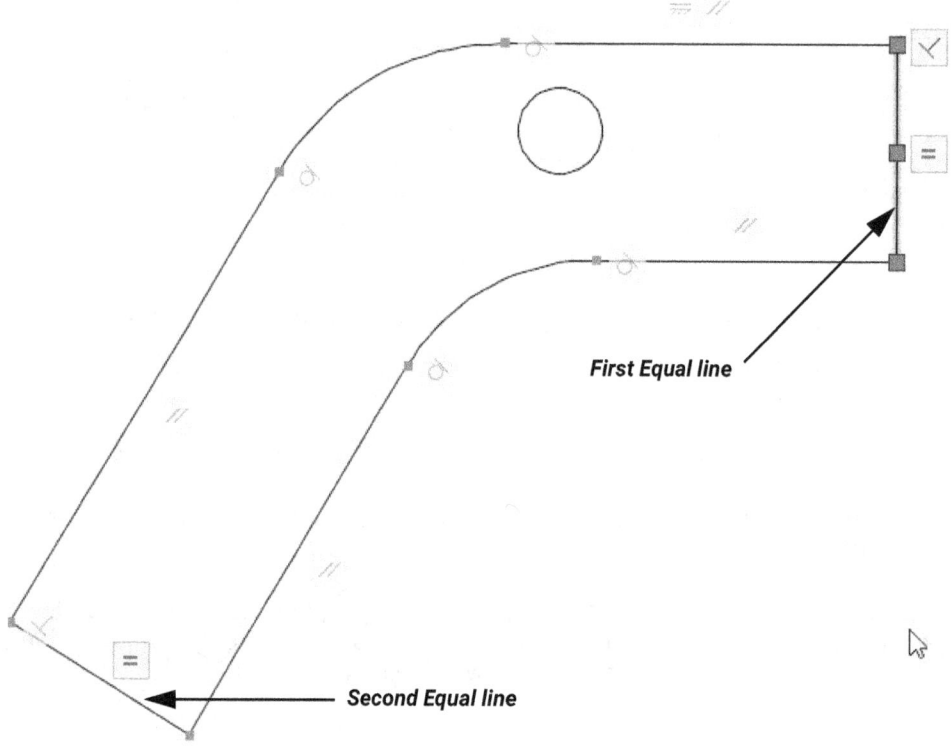

First Equal line

Second Equal line

Figure 4–33

13. Similarly, make the two arcs ═ (Equal). Select the bottom arc and then the top arc.

14. Use ◎ (Concentric) to have the circle and top arc share the same center point by selecting the top arc and then the circle. The circle might move outside the lower arc.

15. Select the bottom left angled parallel line to display its grips. Pull the middle grip slightly down to resize the object so that the circle is inside the lines, as shown in Figure 4–34. Click to resize and press <Esc> to clear the selection.

Figure 4–34

16. In the *Geometric* panel, click ⬚ (Fix). Select the circle to make this a fixed point.

17. Flex the object by moving one of the lines. Note that it is still not fully constrained and needs to be finished with dimensional constraints. Undo the flex action.

18. Click ⬚ (Hide All) to hide the geometric constraints.

Task 2: Add dimensional constraints.

1. In the *Parametric* tab>*Dimensional* panel, click ⬚ (Linear). If the *Annotation Scale* dialog box opens, click **OK**.

2. Press <Enter> to change to the **Object** option.

3. Select the vertical line on the right and then click to the right of it to place the dimensional constraint value field.

4. Type **1** in the *Dimensional constraint* field and press <Enter>. The dimensional constraint is applied, as shown in Figure 4–35.

    - Both the vertical line on the right and the angled line on the bottom left automatically adjust their lengths to the new value because they are equal.

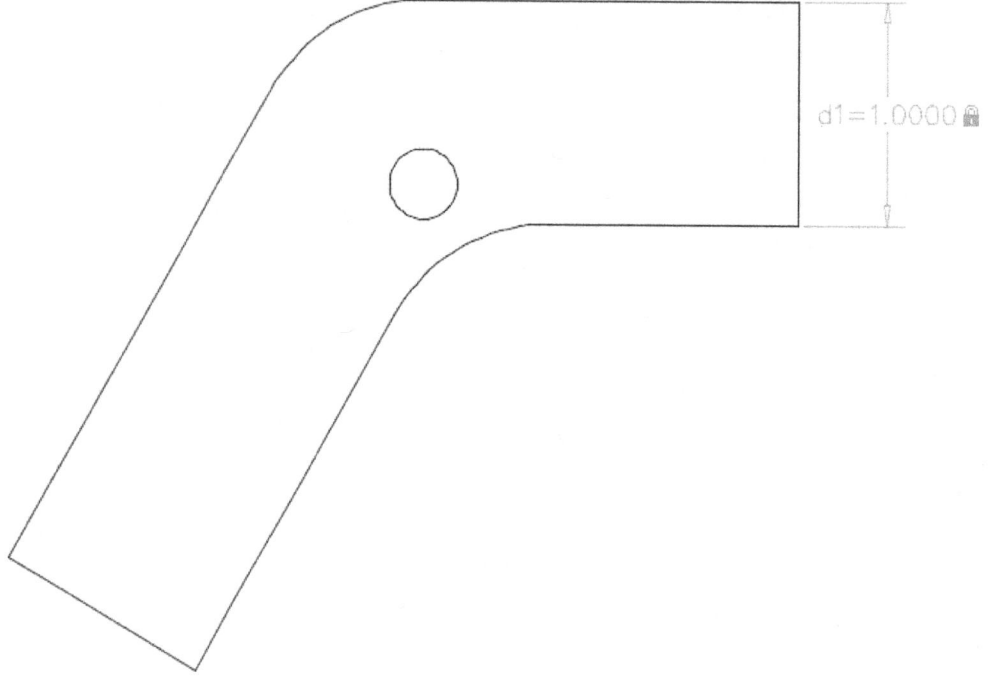

Figure 4–35

*Note: If the dimensional constraint does not display in the format shown in Figure 4–35, set the Dimension name format to **Name and Expression** in the Constraint Settings dialog box (Dimensional tab).*

5. Use ☐ (Linear) with the **Object** option to select the top horizontal line. Set the value of the dimension text to **1**.

6. Use ☐ (Aligned) with the **Object** option to select the top left angled line. Set the value of the dimension text to **d2+1**, as shown in Figure 4–36.

    - If the name of the top horizontal line *Dimensional* constraint is something other than **d2**, type its current name in the formula expression of the Dimensional constraint value field for the angled line in the top left.

Figure 4–36

7. Double-click on the linear dimensional constraint **d2**.

8. Type **2** in the linear *Dimensional constraint* field to change its value and press <Enter>. Both the d2 line and the d3 aligned lines update.

9. In the *Dimensional* panel, click (Radius) and set the bottom arc to the dimension text value of **0.5**.

10. In the *Dimensional* panel, click (Angular). Select the horizontal line at the bottom right and then the angular line at the bottom (left of arc), as shown in Figure 4–37. Set the dimension text value to **120**.

Figure 4–37

Task 3: Modify values in Parameters Manager.

1. In the *Parametric* tab>*Manage* panel, click $f_{(x)}$ (Parameters Manager), if it is not already open.

2. In *Parameters Manager*, under the *Expression* column for *ang1*, change the value to **100** and press <Enter>. The model updates accordingly. Change the same parameter to **150** (as shown in Figure 4–38) and press <Enter> to update the model.

3. At the top of *Parameters Manager*, click (Create User Parameter) to create a new user parameter.

4. Change the name of the new user parameter to **base** and change its *Expression* to **1.5**, as shown in Figure 4–38.

5. In *Parameters Manager*, change the *Expression* for **d3** to **d2+1+base**, as shown in Figure 4–38, and press <Enter>. Note how the model updates.

Figure 4–38

6. Flex the model several times using different values in *Parameters Manager*. Return to the values as specified in Figure 4–38.

7. Hide *Parameters Manager*.

Task 4: Modify constraint settings.

1. In the *Geometric* panel, click (Show All) to display the geometric constraints.

2. In the *Geometric* panel, click ↘ to open the *Constraint Settings* dialog box.

3. Ensure that you are in the *Geometric* tab. In the *Constraint bar display settings* area, clear the **Tangent** option, as shown in Figure 4–39.

Figure 4–39

4. Select the *Dimensional* tab and change the *Dimension name format* to **Value**, as shown in Figure 4–40.

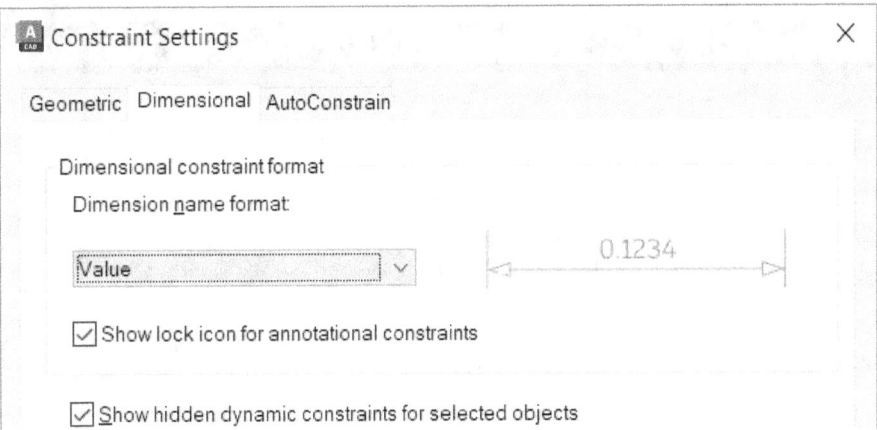

Figure 4–40

5. Click **OK**.

6. The dimensional constraints now only display the value and the *tangent* constraint glyphs are no longer displayed, as shown in Figure 4–41.

Figure 4–41

7. Save the drawing.

End of practice

Chapter Review Questions

1. Which *Geometric* constraint forces two linear objects to take on the angle of the first object?

   a. Symmetrical

   b. Parallel

   c. Vertical

   d. Perpendicular

2. Which of the following can be displayed for the *Dimensional* constraints?

   a. Symmetrical

   b. Tangent

   c. Name and Value

   d. Equal

3. You can convert existing dimensions into *Dimensional* constraints.

   a. True

   b. False

4. How can you add Formulas in the *Dimensional* constraints?

   a. You cannot add Formulas in the *Dimensional* constraints.

   b. When the *Dimensional* constraints are inserted.

   c. Use *Tool Palettes*.

   d. Use *Layer Properties Manager*.

5. The **Auto Constrain** command is best used with the _____object type.

   a. Ellipse

   b. Circle

   c. Rectangle

   d. Arc

6. If you create user parameters, how do they affect the constrained object?

    a. They delete all of the formulas.

    b. They control *Geometric* constraints.

    c. Changing the user value modifies the object.

    d. They remove *Dimensional* constraints.

Command Summary

Button	Command	Location
Constraint Management		
	Delete Constraints	• **Ribbon:** *Parametric* tab>*Manage* panel
	Parameters Manager	• **Ribbon:** *Parametric* tab>*Manage* panel
Dimensional Constraints		
	Aligned	• **Ribbon:** *Parametric* tab>*Dimensional* panel
	Anglular	• **Ribbon:** *Parametric* tab>*Dimensional* panel
	Convert	• **Ribbon:** *Parametric* tab>*Dimensional* panel
	Diameter	• **Ribbon:** *Parametric* tab>*Dimensional* panel
	Hide All Dynamic Constraints	• **Ribbon:** *Parametric* tab>*Dimensional* panel
	Horizontal	• **Ribbon:** *Parametric* tab>*Dimensional* panel
	Linear	• **Ribbon:** *Parametric* tab>*Dimensional* panel
	Radius	• **Ribbon:** *Parametric* tab>*Dimensional* panel
	Show All Dynamic Constraints	• **Ribbon:** *Parametric* tab>*Dimensional* panel
	Show/Hide Dynamic Constraints	• **Ribbon:** *Parametric* tab>*Dimensional* panel
	Vertical	• **Ribbon:** *Parametric* tab>*Dimensional* panel
Geometric Constraints		
	Auto-Constrain	• **Ribbon:** *Parametric* tab>*Geometric* panel
	Coincident	• **Ribbon:** *Parametric* tab>*Geometric* panel
	Colinear	• **Ribbon:** *Parametric* tab>*Geometric* panel

Button	Command	Location
◎	**Concentric**	• **Ribbon:** *Parametric* tab>*Geometric* panel
=	**Equal**	• **Ribbon:** *Parametric* tab>*Geometric* panel
🔒	**Fix**	• **Ribbon:** *Parametric* tab>*Geometric* panel
[✓]	**Hide All Geometric Constraints**	• **Ribbon:** *Parametric* tab>*Geometric* panel
≡	**Horizontal**	• **Ribbon:** *Parametric* tab>*Geometric* panel
//	**Parallel**	• **Ribbon:** *Parametric* tab>*Geometric* panel
✕	**Perpendicular**	• **Ribbon:** *Parametric* tab>*Geometric* panel
[✓]	**Show All Geometric Constraints**	• **Ribbon:** *Parametric* tab>*Geometric* panel
[✓]	**Show/Hide Geometric Constraints**	• **Ribbon:** *Parametric* tab>*Geometric* panel
⤙	**Smooth**	• **Ribbon:** *Parametric* tab>*Geometric* panel
[¦]	**Symmetrical**	• **Ribbon:** *Parametric* tab>*Geometric* panel
⟂	**Tangent**	• **Ribbon:** *Parametric* tab>*Geometric* panel
⫴	**Vertical**	• **Ribbon:** *Parametric* tab>*Geometric* panel

Working with Blocks

You will learn to create local blocks, edit blocks, and remove unused elements by purging. You will also learn to add blocks to tool palettes and modify tool properties in palettes.

Learning Objectives

- Create different types of blocks that can be used in the same drawing or inserted into other drawings.
- Modify block objects using the *Block Editor*.
- Remove unused elements and unreferenced definitions from a drawing.
- Create a new Tool palette and add blocks to it.
- Modify the properties of a tool in the Tool palettes.

5.1 Creating Blocks

The objects that are reused frequently can be saved as a blocks. The blocks you need to use might already exist in your drawings, or you can buy block libraries for almost any type of drawing. You can also easily create your own blocks. A block can be locally defined in a drawing or saved as a drawing file for use in other drawings.

Creating Local Blocks

The **Create Block** command converts a group of selected objects into a single named object or *local block definition* that only belongs to the current drawing.

How To: Create a Block

1. Draw the objects that you want to include in a block.
2. In the *Insert* tab>*Block Definition* panel or *Home* tab>*Block* panel, click ⬚ (Create Block).
3. In the *Block Definition* dialog box (as shown in Figure 5-1), specify the *Name*, *Base point*, *Objects*, *Behavior*, *Settings*, and *Description*.
4. Click **OK**.

Block Settings

When you create a block, you need to specify various parameters in the *Block Definition* dialog box, as shown in Figure 5-1.

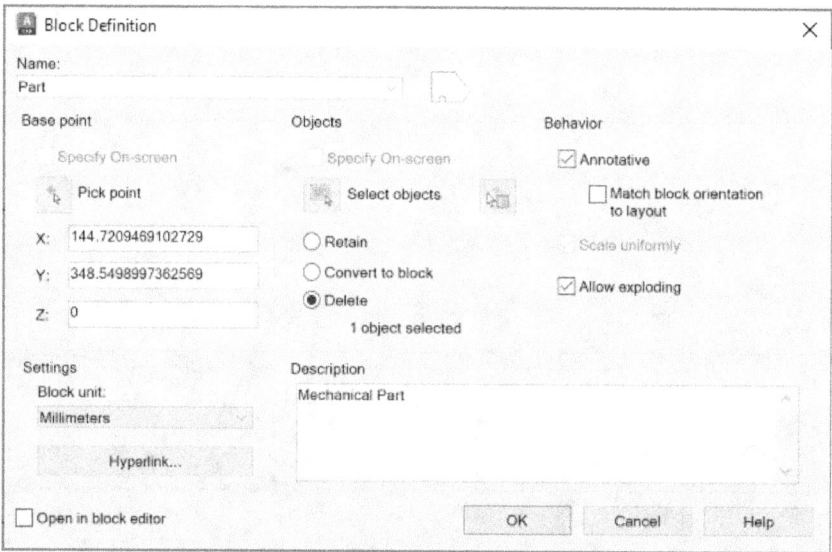

Figure 5-1

Base Point Area

The *Base point* is a critical setting, which controls the handle of the block when it is inserted. A good base point makes a block much easier to insert. In the example shown in Figure 5−2, the block for a door has its base point at the hinge corner, where it attaches to the end of the wall and the block for the manhole cover has its base point at the center of the cover.

Figure 5−2

In the *Base point* area, you can specify the base point by doing one of the following:

• Select **Specify On-screen** to select the base point after you close the dialog box.

• Click ▨ (Pick point) to select a point on the screen and then return to the dialog box.

• Type an exact X,Y,Z coordinate.

Objects Area

• Select **Specify On-screen** to select the objects after you close the dialog box.

• Click ▨ (Select objects) to select objects on the screen and then return to the dialog box.

• Define what you want to do with the objects after you select them. You can retain them, convert them to a block, or delete them.

• Click ▨ (Quick Select) to start the **Quick Select** command, which can be used to filter out objects in your selection as required.

Behavior Area

- Blocks can be annotative, which means they scale appropriately to the sheet of paper when they are plotted. This is used when you are creating annotation blocks, which often include text (such as a section callout bubble or room tags), as shown in Figure 5–3. Use **Annotative** to make the new block annotative.

Figure 5–3

- Create annotative blocks at the correct size for plotting. The Annotation Scale factor of a viewport scales them when they are inserted through the viewport.

- You can also use **Scale uniformly** to force the X- and Y-scaling of the block to be the same when the block is inserted into the drawing.

- Use **Allow exploding** to explode the block into its components after it is inserted into the drawing.

Settings Area

- Select a type of measurement in the *Block unit* drop-down list. This controls the scaling of the block when it is inserted into another drawing that uses a different type of unit. For example, if the unit in the block and the units in the drawing are different, the block is automatically scaled when it is inserted.

- Click **Hyperlink...** to add a link to another file or to a web address.

- Select **Open in block editor** to add dynamic features to the block.

- In the *Description* area, you can type a description of the block or any notes as required.

Creating Drawing Files from Objects (WBlock)

Blocks created with the **Create (Block)** command are stored in the drawing file in which they were created and are only available through that drawing. If you want to select objects and save them as a separate drawing file that can be used globally in other drawings, use the **Write Block (Wblock)** command.

- The **Write Block** command saves a copy of a block definition on your computer as a drawing file. Each use of **Write Block** creates a separate drawing file (.DWG).

- As with any .DWG file, the drawing files created with the **Write Block** command can be inserted into other drawings. Drawings to be used as blocks are often stored in a *block library*, which is a shared network folder containing drawings that are available to everyone in an office.

- You can use **Write Block** to break a large drawing into smaller components.

- To insert a file made with **Write Block** into another drawing, in the *Libraries* tab of the *Blocks* palette, use the navigation tool to the drawing that you want to insert.

- Once you have inserted the file, it creates a local block definition in the drawing. The local block definition is not linked to the DWG file that was made with **Write Block**.

How To: Create a Wblock

1. In the *Insert* tab>*Block Definition* panel, expand the *Create Block* flyout and click (Write Block). The *Write Block* dialog box opens, as shown in Figure 5-4.

Figure 5-4

2. Select an option in the *Source* area:

   - **Block:** Select a block name from the drop-down list to create a Wblock from an existing block in the drawing.

   - **Entire Drawing:** Selects all of the objects in the drawing including any named objects (such as layers and dimension styles that are associated with the objects), and the current layer. Any unused named objects (such as empty layers) are not included. This is a quick way to clean up a file before it is stored.

   - **Objects:** Select the objects using the options in the *Base point* and *Objects* areas.

3. In the *Destination* area, specify the destination filename and path.

4. Also, specify the *Insert units* if they are to be different than the default units.

5. Click **OK**.

5.2 Editing Blocks

You might have a library of standard details, but need to change one of them for your current project. You can change a local block definition in a drawing using the **Block Editor**, as shown in Figure 5–5.

Figure 5–5

- When you open the *Block Editor*, the *Block Editor* contextual tab opens containing the tools that are required to create complex dynamic blocks, including constraints and special parameters. You can use the tools on any of the other tabs as well to create or modify block objects.

- Changing the block definition modifies all of the instances of the block in the drawing.

- The fastest way to start the *Block Editor* is to double-click on the block that you want to edit.

How To: Edit a Block in the Block Editor

1. Double-click on the block that you want to edit. Alternatively, in the *Insert* tab>*Block Definition* panel, click 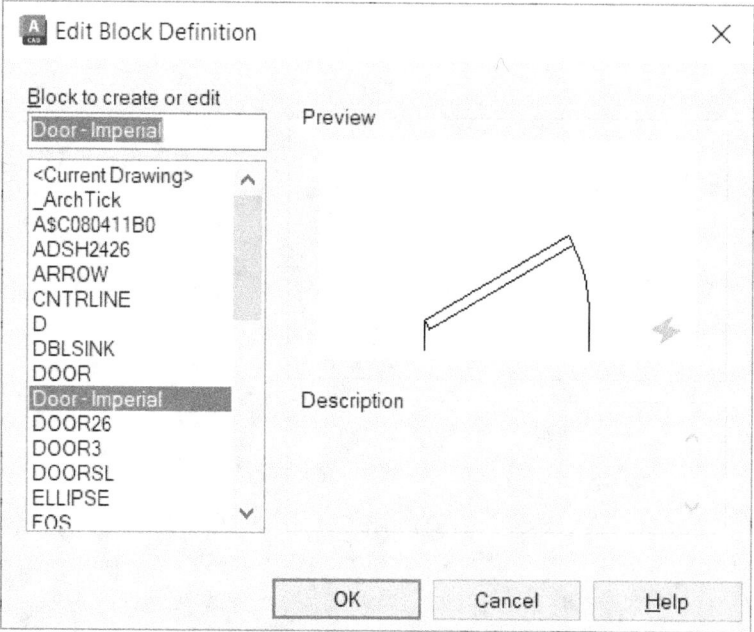 (Block Editor).

2. In the *Edit Block Definition* dialog box (as shown in Figure 5–6), select the block that you want to edit and click **OK**.

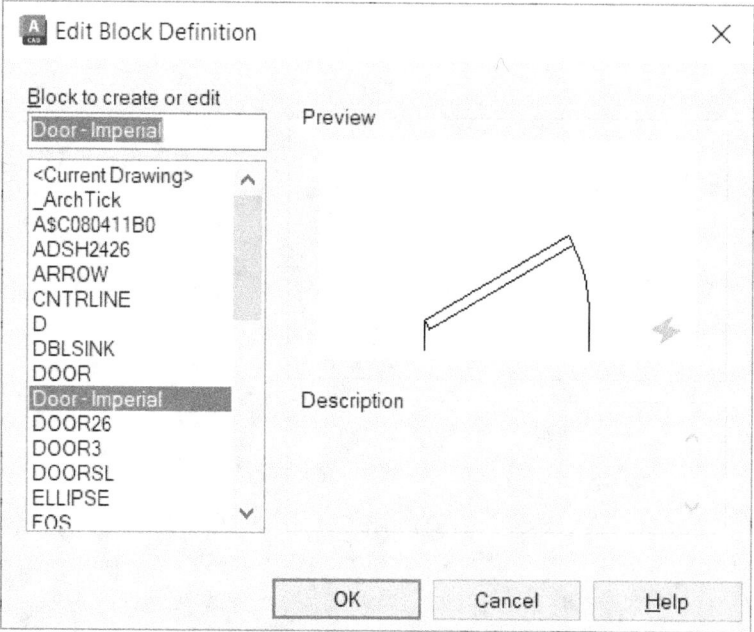

Figure 5–6

3. The *Block Editor* contextual tab opens, the drawing window background changes to gray, the *Block Authoring* Palette displays, and many of the constraint tools display with the selected block.

4. Modify the block.

5. When you are finished, click ✔ (Close Block Editor).

• The selected block displays in the *Block Editor* in its original position, even if you selected an instance that was rotated.

Remaking Blocks

- To modify a single instance of a block (rather than the block definition), you can **Explode** the block into its original raw components, provided that the **Allow Exploding** option was toggled on when the block was created. This command also converts polylines into lines and arcs.

- If the block objects were originally created on layer **0**, they revert to this layer when the block is exploded.

- If you have exploded a block and modified its components, you can use the **Create (Block)** command to make the components into a block again.

- If other instances of the block are in the drawing, select the insertion point that was used for the previous block.

- If you use the same name as the original block when you redefine it, all of the instances of that block in the drawing update to match the new block definition.

Practice 5a
Create and Edit Blocks

Practice Objectives

- Define a block.
- Create a new drawing file from a local block.
- Create a new file and then redefine the block.

In this practice, you will define a block for a couch, first drawing the objects and then using the **Create Block** command. You will then use **Write Block** to create a new drawing file from your local block. You will also use **Write Block** to select part of a drawing and create a new file, and then use **Block Editor** to redefine a block.

Task 1: Create a local block.

In this task, you will define a block for a couch, first drawing the objects and then using the **Create Block** command, as shown in Figure 5−7.

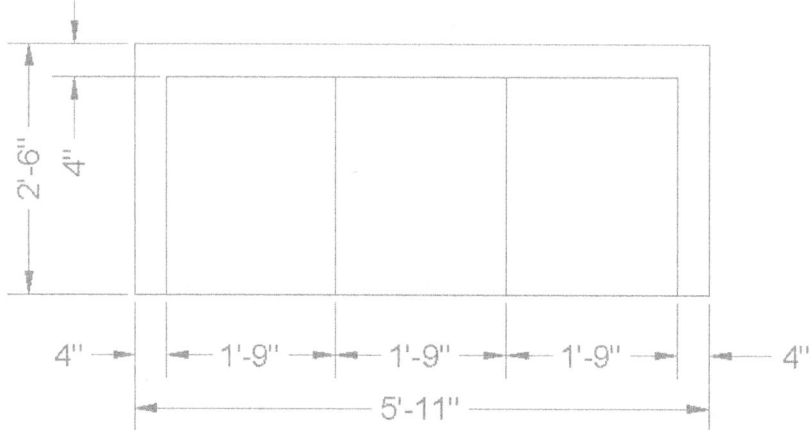

Figure 5−7

1. Open **California House-A.dwg** from your practice files folder.

2. Set the current layer to **Furniture**, if required. (**Hint:** You will draw the block on this layer so that it retains the properties of the layer **Furniture** no matter what layer you insert it on.)

3. Zoom in on any one of the rooms and draw a couch (without the dimensions; they are for reference only), as shown in Figure 5−7.

4. In the *Insert* tab>*Block Definition* panel, click 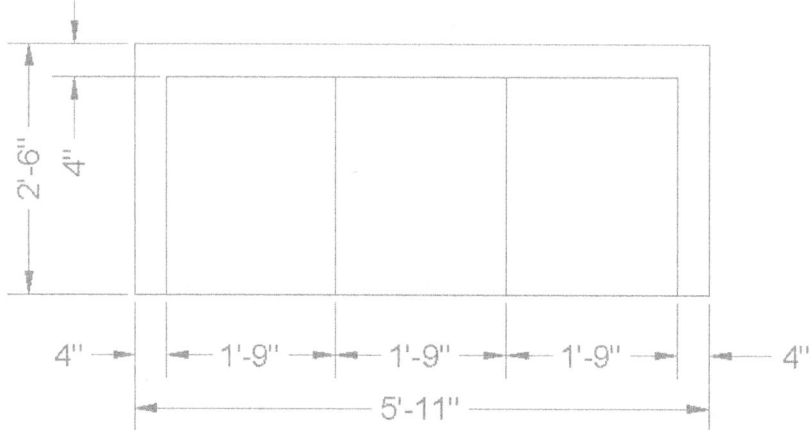 (Create Block). In the *Block Definition* dialog box, name the block **Couch**.

5. In the *Base point* area, click (Pick point) and select the midpoint at the back of the couch as the base point.

6. In the *Objects* area, click (Select objects), select the couch objects, and press <Enter>. Select the **Delete** option.

7. Verify that the *Block unit* is set to **Inches**.

8. Verify that **Open in block editor** is NOT selected.

9. Click **OK**. The block is created and the couch is deleted from the active drawing.

10. Set the current layer to **0**.

11. Open the *Blocks* palette in the *Recent* or *Current Drawing* tab. Using the **Repeat Placement** option, insert a couch in several rooms (note that it is still the color of the layer **Furniture**).

12. Save the drawing with a few couches inserted.

Task 2: Create a drawing file from a block.

1. In the *Insert* tab>*Block Definition* panel, expand the *Block* flyout and click (Write Block).

2. In the *Write Block* dialog box, for the *Source*, select **Block**, expand the drop-down list of local blocks in the drawing, and select **Couch**. You do not need to select the *Base point* or *Objects* because you are using an existing block definition which has all the options already set.

3. In the *Destination* area, use **...** to set the path to your practice folder and the filename to **Couch,** as shown in Figure 5–8. The *Insert units* should be set to **Inches**. Click **OK** to create the new drawing file.

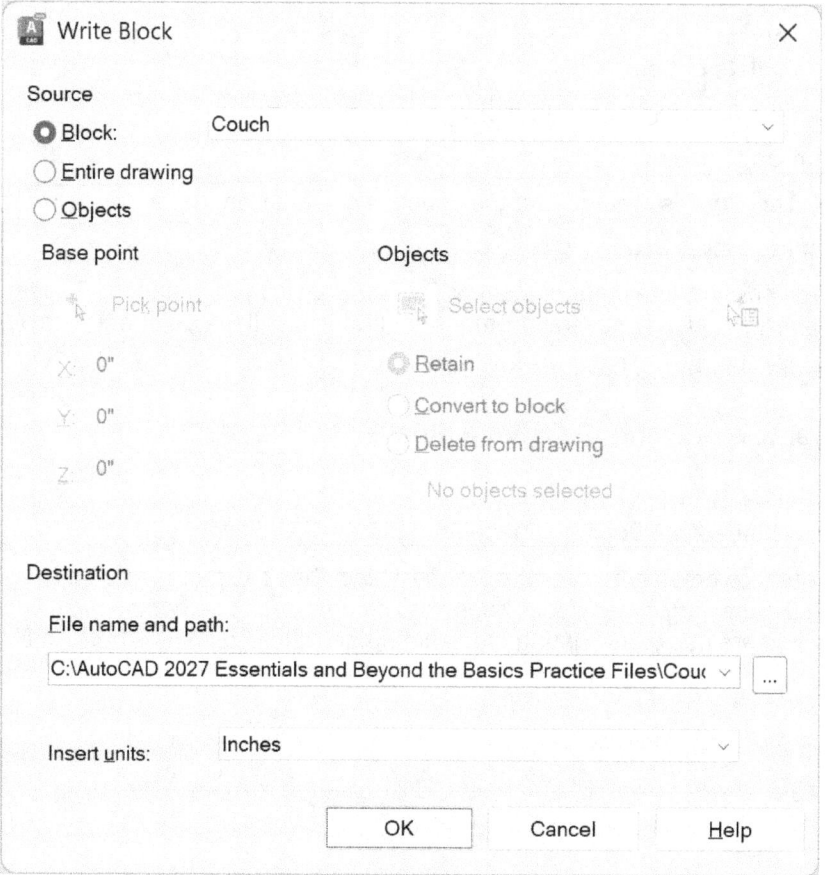

Figure 5–8

4. Open the new drawing **Couch.dwg** from the practice files folder.

5. Use the **Zoom Extents** command to display the couch. Save and close the drawing.

6. Open **Plan1-A.dwg** from your practice files folder.

7. In the *Blocks* palette>*Current Drawing* tab, note the list of blocks displayed. The **Couch** block is not in the graphics list. Open the *Libraries* tab. Click 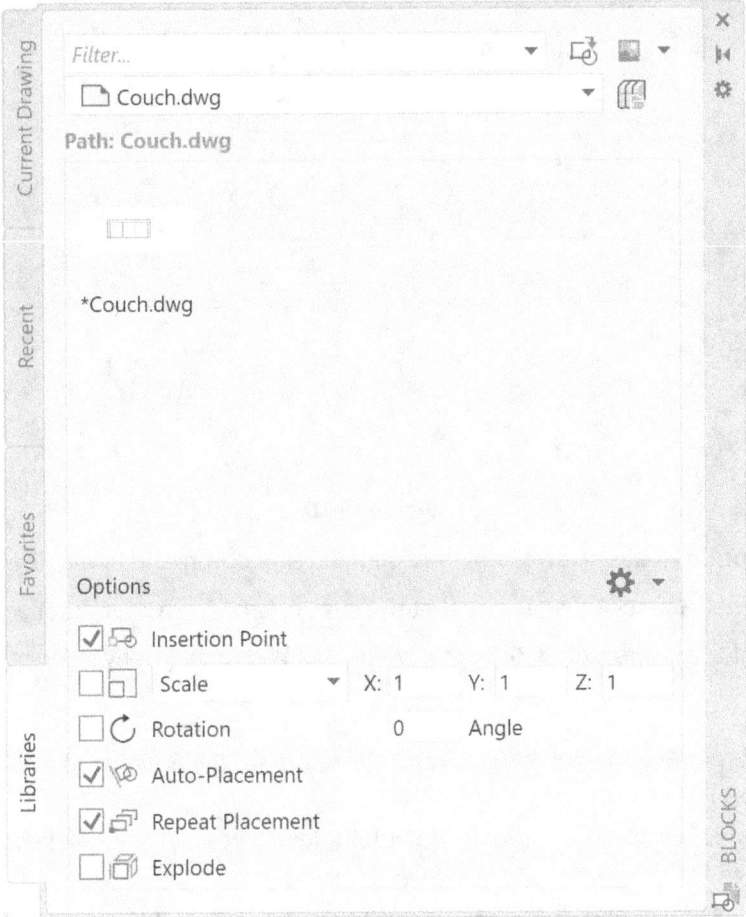 (navigation tool) near the top right corner of the palette to open the *Select a folder or file for Block Library* dialog box. Navigate to your practice files folder and select the **Couch.dwg** file. Click **Open**. Note that it is listed in the *Libraries* tab of the *Blocks* palette, as shown in Figure 5–9.

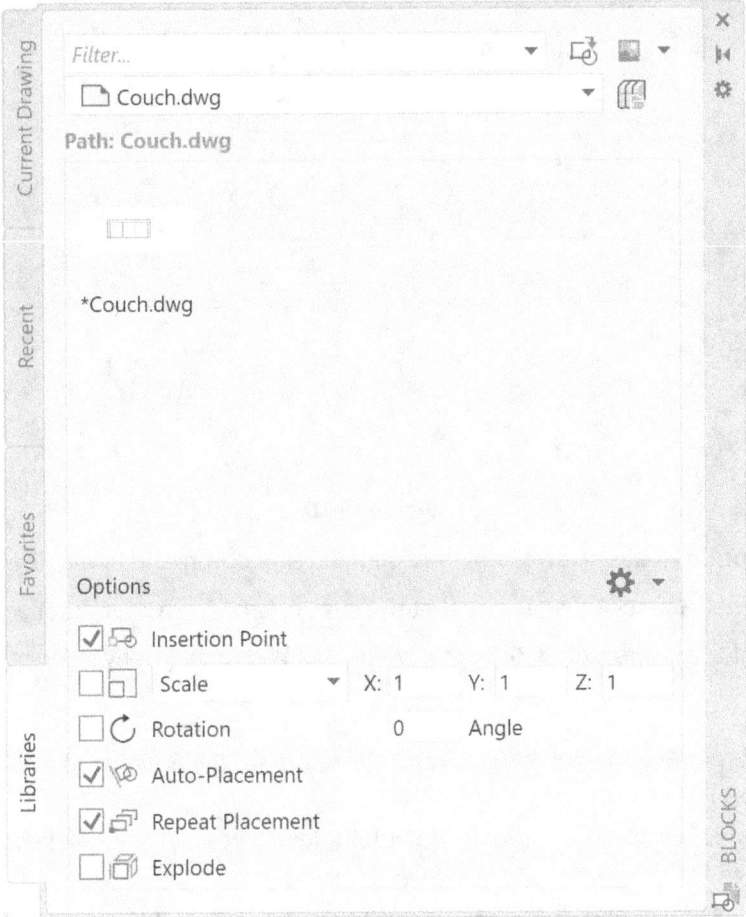

Figure 5–9

8. Insert a couch into one of the rooms. Open the *Current Drawing* tab of the *Blocks* palette and note that it is listed there, which indicates that it is now a local block in the drawing **Plan1-A.dwg**.

9. Save and close **Plan1-A.dwg**.

Task 3: Create a new drawing from part of a drawing.

In this task, you will toggle off most of the layers in a drawing and use **Write Block** to copy the remaining objects to a new file, as shown in Figure 5–10.

Figure 5–10

1. In the **California House-A.dwg**, use the **Zoom Extents** command to display the entire plan.

    - If **California House-A.dwg** is not already open, open it from your practice files folder.

2. Freeze all of the layers except **0**, **Doors**, **Walls**, and **Windows** (many layers are already frozen).

3. Click (Write Block). In the *Write Block* dialog box, in the *Source* area, select **Objects**.

4. In the *Objects* area, click (Select objects) and select all of the visible objects. Right-click or press <Enter> to return to the dialog box.

5. Leave the *Base point* at **0",0",0"**. Set the path to your practice folder and name the file **Floorplan-1.dwg**.

6. Click **OK** to close the dialog box.

7. Close **California House-A.dwg**. Do not save changes.

8. Open **Floorplan-1.dwg**. Only the objects that you selected display along with the layers **0**, **Doors**, **Walls**, and **Windows** (Layer Control).

9. Close the drawing. Do not save changes.

Task 4: Edit a block.

In this task, you will use the **Block Editor** to redefine a block with a new design, as shown in Figure 5–11.

Figure 5–11

1. Open **California House-A.dwg** and thaw the layer **Furniture**. Double-click on one of the **Couch** blocks.

2. In the *Edit Block Definition* dialog box, **Couch** is highlighted with its preview displayed. Click **OK** to continue.

3. The **Block Editor** opens with the block filling the drawing area. Also the background is changed to gray and the *Block Authoring Palettes* displays. Close or hide the *Block Authoring Palettes*.

4. Fillet the back corners of the couch, as shown in Figure 5–11.

5. In the *Block Editor* contextual tab, click ✔ (Close Block Editor) and click **Save the changes to Couch**.

6. Note that all of the instances of the **Couch** block in this drawing are automatically updated to the new style. Insert another **Couch** and note that it has also changed.

7. Save and close the drawing.

End of practice

5.3 Removing Unused Elements

A drawing might contain elements that were defined once but are no longer used. Common examples of this include:

- Blocks that are defined but not inserted anywhere.

- Layers that do not contain any objects.

- Named components that are no longer used.

These unused (or unreferenced) definitions use disk space and can significantly increase the size of your drawing. Use the **Purge** command to remove these items.

The various **Purge** tools are available in the *Manage* tab>*Cleanup* panel, as shown in the Figure 5–12.

Figure 5–12

Use ⊥ (Overkill) to remove duplicate and overlapping geometric objects such as lines, arcs, and polylines. Examples of the changes made by the **Overkill** command include:

- Deleting duplicate line or arc segments.

- Deleting arcs that overlap portions of circles.

- Combining partially overlapping lines drawn at the same angle.

- Deleting zero-length and overlapping polylines.

How To: Purge All Unreferenced Items

1. In the *Manage* tab>*Cleanup* panel, click 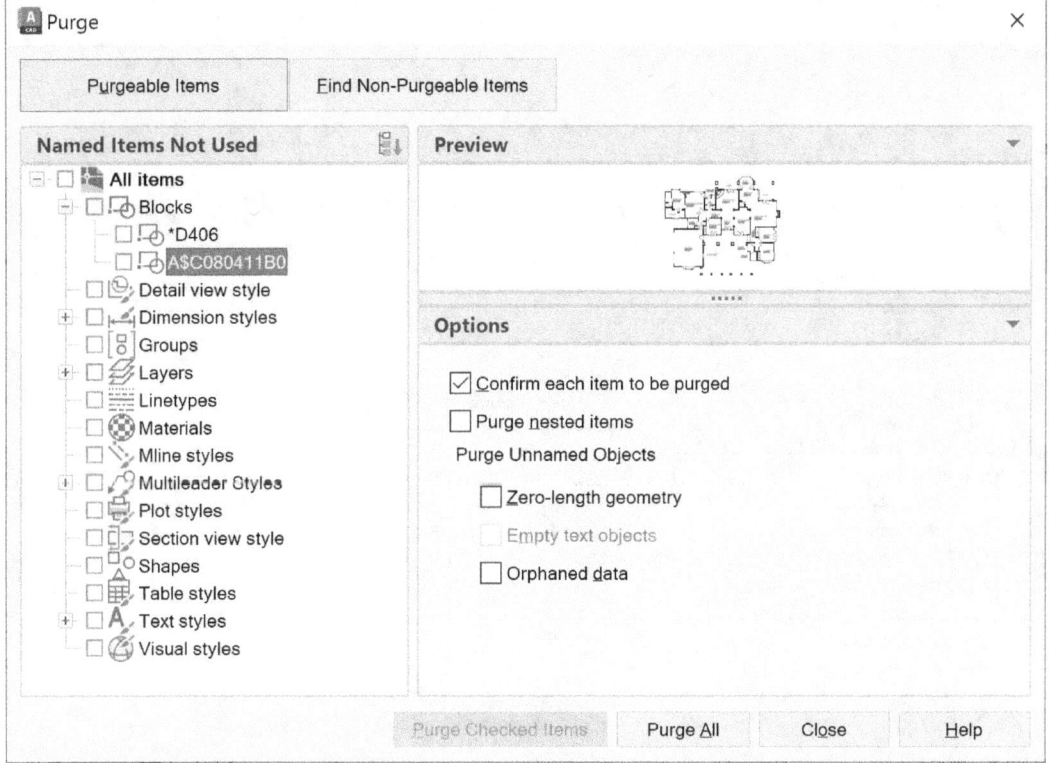 (Purge) or in the Application Menu, select **Drawing Utilities>Purge**. The *Purge* dialog box opens. Click **Purge All** and click **Close** to end the command.

How To: Purge Specific Types of Items or Individual Items

1. In the *Manage* tab>*Cleanup* panel, click (Purge) or in the Application Menu, select *Drawing Utilities>* **Purge**.

2. In the *Purge* dialog box, in the *Named Items Not Used area*, select the category of the item that you want to purge (such as *Blocks*, *Layers*, etc.). You can also expand the list for any category and select individual items to purge, as shown in Figure 5–13. The *Preview* area displays the image of the item to be purged.

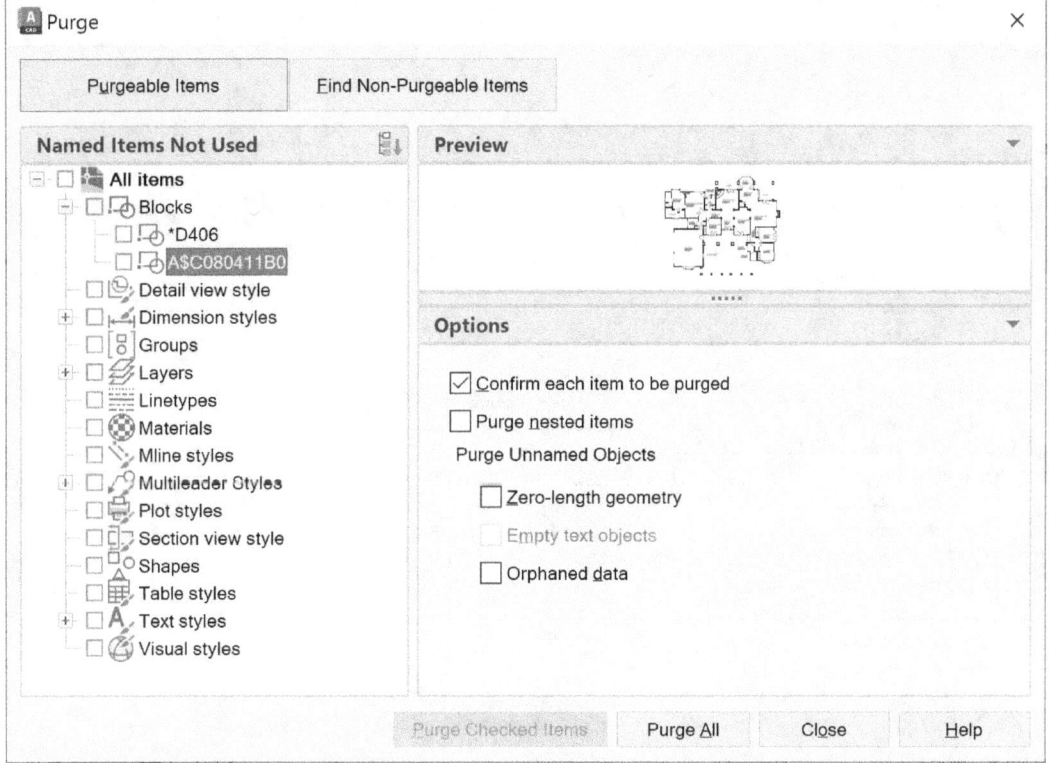

Figure 5–13

3. Click the check boxes of the items to be purged. Click **Purge Checked Items**.

4. Click **Close** when you are finished.

- If the **Confirm each item to be purged** option is selected, you are prompted to verify each item before it is purged.

- To completely purge all of the unreferenced elements in the drawing, select the **Purge nested items** option. For example, this enables you to purge any unreferenced layers that are part of (or *nested in*) an unreferenced block definition.

- The *Purge Unnamed Objects* area provides you with the options of purging **Zero-length geometry** and **Empty text objects** separately.

- Selecting the *Find Non-Purgeable Items* tab in the dialog box displays a list of items that are in use and cannot be purged. (If you are not in the *Purge* dialog box, you can use 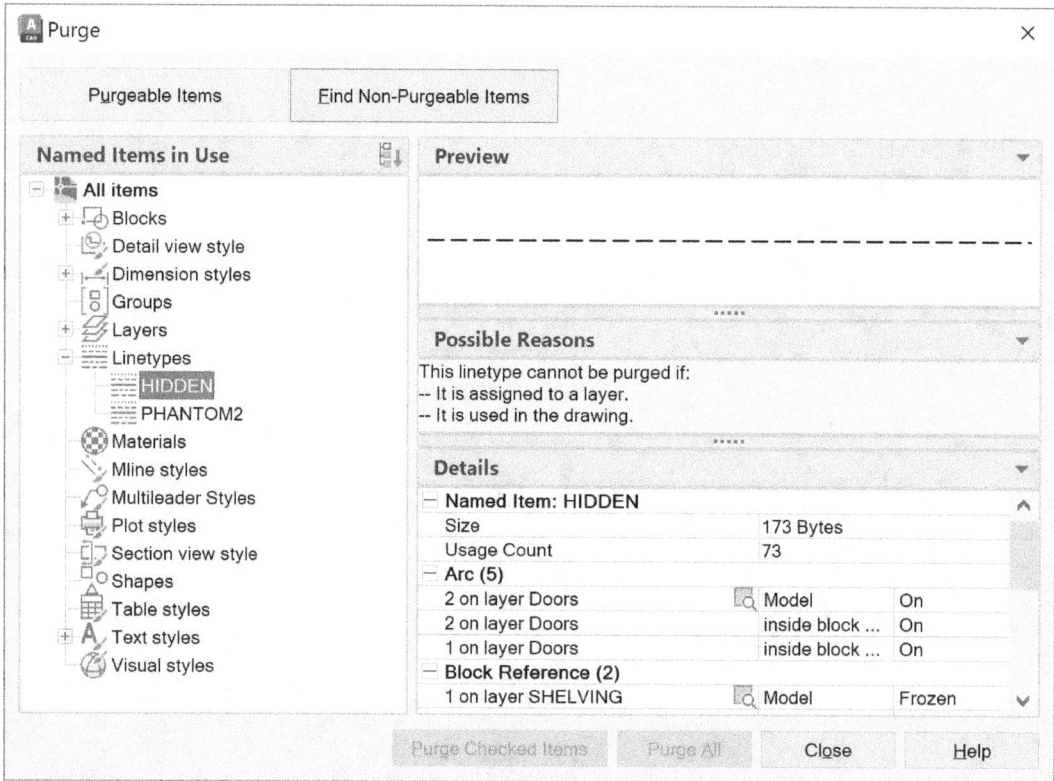 (Find Non-Purgeable Items) in the *Manage* tab>*Cleanup* panel.) Select an item to display the information about why it cannot be purged. A detailed information such as the number of items on each layer and their effect on the size of the file is also provided, as shown in Figure 5–14. You can also click the **Select Objects** button to zoom in to the specific non-purgeable object.

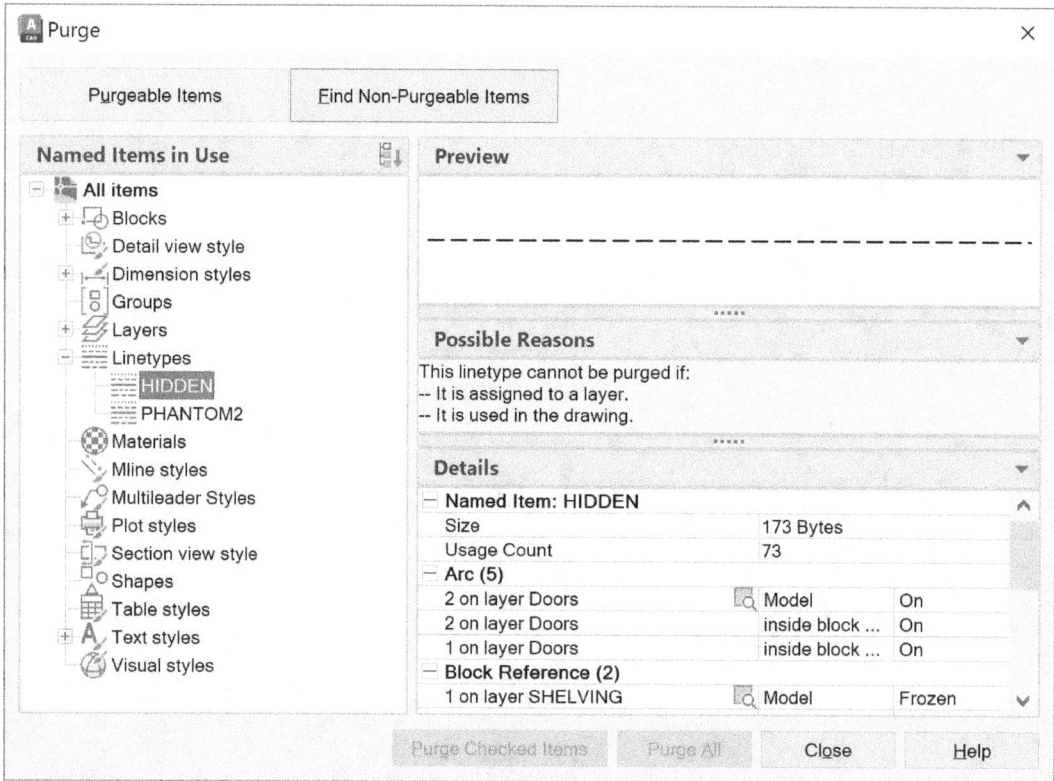

Figure 5–14

Practice 5b
Purge

Practice Objective

- Remove unused block definitions and empty layers.

In this practice, you will remove unused block definitions and empty layers from a drawing using the **Purge** command.

1. Open **Purge-A.dwg** from your practice files folder.

2. Open the Layer Control and review the list of layers.

    - There are more than 25 layers in the list.

3. Expand the **Insert Block** gallery and note that several blocks are defined in this drawing, but are not used.

4. In the *Manage* tab>*Cleanup* panel, click ⬚ (Purge), or in the *Application Menu*, expand *Drawing Utilities* and select **Purge**.

5. In the *Purge* dialog box, expand the **Blocks** category to display the blocks that can be purged, as shown on the left in Figure 5–15.

6. Expand the **Layers** category to display the layers that can be purged.

7. Click **Purge All**. In the *Purge - Confirm Purge* dialog box, select **Purge all checked items**.

8. Most of the unused items are purged, but some still remain. These items were nested in blocks, as shown in the middle in Figure 5–15.

9. Click **Purge All** again and select **Purge all checked items**. All of the unused items are purged, as shown on the right in Figure 5–15.

Figure 5–15

10. In the *Purge* dialog box, click *Find Non-Purgeable Items* tab and expand **Blocks**. Select **_Arch Tick** and note the information about why it cannot be purged. Also note the additional information such as the number of items and their effect on the size of the file, as shown in Figure 5–16.

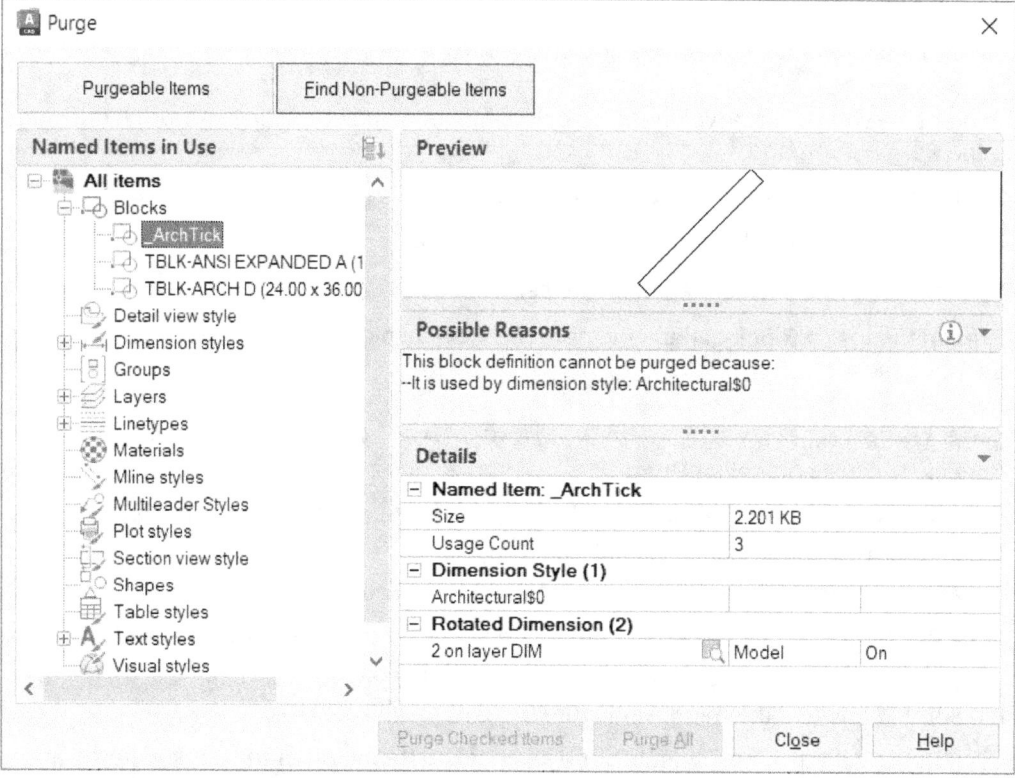

Figure 5–16

11. Close the *Purge* dialog box.

12. Open *Layer Control*. Only a few layers are listed and the unreferenced layers have been removed.

13. Expand the **Insert Block** gallery. The unused blocks have been removed.

14. Save and close the drawing.

End of practice

5.4 Adding Blocks to Tool Palettes

Tool palettes are the easiest way of inserting blocks into your drawing. You can create custom palettes in *Tool Palettes* to organize your blocks into logical categories.

Once the palette has been created, drag and drop blocks into it to create tools for those blocks. Then use the palette tools to insert the blocks into the drawings in which you want to use them, whether or not the block has been defined in the drawing.

How To: Create a New Tool Palette

1. Right-click in the *Tool Palettes* title bar or tab and select **New Palette**.
2. In the *Edit* field, type a name for the palette (as shown in Figure 5–17) and press <Enter>. The new palette does not contain any tools.

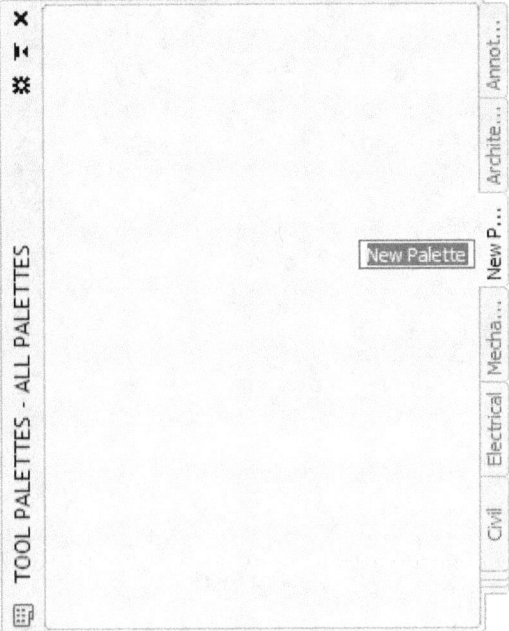

Figure 5–17

- Although you can add tools to the default palettes supplied with the AutoCAD software, creating custom palettes enables you to better organize the tools as you want.

- You can also right-click on the tab and select **Delete Palette** or **Rename Palette** to delete or rename existing palettes.

How To: Add Blocks to a Palette

1. Select a block in the drawing area.

2. Drag and drop it onto the palette, as shown in Figure 5–18.

   Note: The file containing the blocks must be saved before you can add a block to a palette.

Figure 5–18

- Drag the block onto the palette by its *edge*, not by its blue grip. Dragging the grip moves the block in the drawing but does not enable you to drop it into the palette.

- The tool uses the layer, color, and other properties of the object used to create it. Therefore, blocks that you insert with the tool are automatically placed on the same layer as the original block, no matter which layer is current.

- You can rearrange the tools in the palette by dragging and dropping.

- You can also delete individual tools from *Tool Palettes*. Select the tools that you want to delete (use <Shift> or <Ctrl> to select multiple icons), right-click, and select **Delete**.

- You must add blocks to the palette one at a time using this method.

Preparing Blocks for a Tool Palette

- The drawing from which you add the block to a palette becomes the source file for the block tool in the palette. If you move or delete this source drawing file, the palette tool no longer works.

- Create and store your blocks in a library drawing, or several such drawings for different categories of blocks. For example, you can define your furniture blocks in a drawing called *Furniture Library* and then add the blocks to a palette from that drawing.

- Keep your block library drawings in a location from which they cannot be moved or deleted. Make it a network location if everyone needs to access these blocks.

💡 Hint: Creating a Tool Palette from the DesignCenter

The *DesignCenter* offers a quick way of creating a tool palette using the entire set of blocks in a drawing. Right-click on the drawing name in the *DesignCenter* and select **Create Tool Palette**, as shown in Figure 5–19. A palette is created with the same name as the drawing, containing tool icons for all of the blocks defined in that drawing.

Figure 5–19

5.5 Modifying Tool Properties in Tool Palettes

Each tool in a palette can be modified to insert the object using specific properties, such as layer, scale, or rotation. For example, you might need to place a block at two different angles.

- You can create two tools in the palette for inserting the block, each preset to be inserted at the required angle.

- Once a tool has been added to a palette, you can drag and drop it to different places in the palette or to other tabs as required.

Modifying Tool Properties

To modify a tool's properties, right-click on a tool in the palette and select **Properties...**. The *Tool Properties* for a block tool are shown in Figure 5–20. Other types of tools (e.g., for hatching or commands) have different properties.

Figure 5–20

Command Options

Image	The preview image that displays for the tool.
Name	The name that displays with the tool in *Tool Palettes*. By default, this is set to the name of the block.
Description	An optional description for the tool, taken from the block description.

Insert Options

Name	The name of the block in the source file.
Source file	The drawing file used to create this tool in the palette and where the block definition is stored.
Scale	Insertion scale for the block. You can preset a value here. **Auxiliary scale** enables you to scale based on the current dimension scale factor or plot scale factor.
Rotation	Sets the rotation angle for the block when inserted.
Prompt for Rotation	If set to **Yes**, you are prompted for the rotation angle in the Command Line when you insert using the click and pick point method. This has no effect when you insert using the drag-and-drop method.
Explode	If set to **Yes**, the block is inserted as its component pieces, not as a single block object.

General Options

Layer	Sets the layer on which the block is inserted.
Other Options	The other General options (**Color**, **Linetype**, etc.) are normally set to **ByLayer** so that their properties are controlled by the layer.

- If the layer specified in the *Tool Properties* does not exist in the current drawing, it is automatically created when you insert the block.

- If the specified layer is toggled off or frozen, the block is still placed on that layer. However, it does not display until you toggle on or thaw the layer.

Redefining Blocks in Tool Palettes

If the block definition in the source file changes, it does not automatically update in the palette. Open the *Tool Properties* dialog box and select the source file again.

- You can update a block definition in the current drawing to match a block in *Tool Palettes* by right-clicking and selecting **Redefine**, as shown in Figure 5-21.

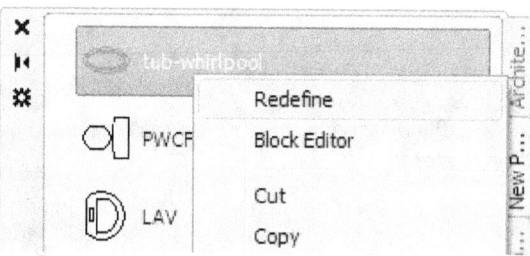

Figure 5-21

- If you open a block in *Tool Palettes* in the *Block Editor*, any changes are saved to the block in the palette and automatically update in the active drawing.

- You can specify an image for a tool palette icon. Right-click on the tool and select **Specify image...**, as shown in Figure 5-22. In the *Select Image File* dialog box, you can select the file you want to use. BMP, JPG, PNG, GIF, and TIF files are all supported image types.

Figure 5-22

Practice 5c
Modify Tool Properties

Practice Objectives

- Create a custom tool palette and add blocks to the palette.
- Copy and modify a block tool.

In this practice, you will create a custom tool palette with blocks and use the palette to insert the blocks. You will then add blocks to the custom tool palette using the drag-and-drop method. You will also modify the properties of the blocks in the tool palette.

Task 1: Add blocks to a custom tool palette.

In this task, you will create a custom tool palette with blocks and use the palette to insert the blocks, as shown in Figure 5–23.

Figure 5–23

1. Open **Fasteners-I.dwg** from your practice files folder. The objects are all defined as blocks in this drawing.

2. In the *View* tab>*Palettes* panel, click ▦ (Tool Palettes) to open *Tool Palettes* if it is not already open. Additionally, keep it as undocked in the drawing window.

3. Right-click in the palette title bar or the tab bar, and select **New Palette**. In the *New Palette* edit field, type **Fasteners** and press <Enter>. A new blank palette with the name **Fasteners** is created and the *Fasteners* tab is active.

    • You can also right-click on the *New Palette* tab and click **Rename Palette**.

4. In the drawing window, select the round Phillips screw and drag and drop it onto the blank open palette (*Fasteners* tab). (Do not select the object by its grip. Select any other highlighted part instead.) An icon and description for the block is added automatically as shown in Figure 5–24.

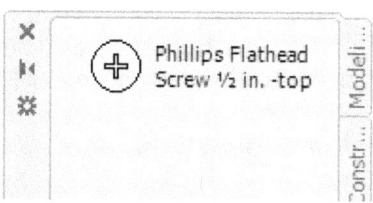

Figure 5–24

5. Repeat Step 4 to add the other bolt and nut blocks to the palette (9 blocks). You must add them one at a time.

6. Close **Fasteners-I.dwg**. Do not save changes.

7. Open **Assembly-I.dwg** from your practice files folder.

8. Set *OSNAP* to **Endpoint** and **Intersection**.

9. Drag and drop the block **Phillips Flathead Screw 1/2 in. -top** to the middle two intersections of the construction lines, as shown in Figure 5–23.

10. Drag and drop the **Hex Bolt 1/2 in. -top** blocks into the drawing, as shown in Figure 5–23.

Task 2: Modify the tool properties.

In this task, you will copy a block tool in the new tool palette and modify the tool properties, as shown in Figure 5–25.

Figure 5–25

1. To make a copy of the **Hex Nut 1/2 in -side** tool, hold <Ctrl> and drag and drop the tool directly below the original one in the palette. The copy of the tool has the same name.

2. Right-click on the new tool icon and select **Properties,** as shown in Figure 5–26.

Figure 5–26

3. In the *Tool Properties* dialog box, change the *Name* to **Hex Nut - Horizontal**. (Do not change the name in the *Insert* rollout properties. Doing so breaks the link to the block definition.)

4. In the *Insert* rollout, change the *Rotation* to **90** to have the hex nut come in horizontally into the drawing. (Note that at the time of release of this content, the image in *Tool Palettes* does not update to display horizontally; however, when you drag it into the drawing window, it comes in horizontally).

   - To display the image horizontally, open it in the *Block Editor*, change it manually and re-save it.

5. In the *General* rollout, verify that the *Layer* is set to **Object**, so that the block is always inserted on this layer. Click **OK**.

6. Insert the **Hex Nut - Horizontal** and the **Hex Nut 1/2 in. -side** along the top and side respectively, as shown in Figure 5-25.

7. Save and close the drawing.

End of practice

Chapter Review Questions

1. When you define a block, you specify a base point. Which of the following is true about the base point?

   a. It is the handle that you use when inserting the block.

   b. It is always at 0,0.

   c. It is always at the center of the block.

   d. It is the point used to select the block objects.

2. Which command creates a separate drawing file from selected objects, that can be used in other drawings?

   a. Make Block

   b. Wblock

   c. Purge

   d. Annotative Block

3. If you change the definition of a block, what happens to any instances of that block that were already inserted in the drawing?

   a. They are automatically renamed.

   b. They are erased.

   c. They change to match the new definition.

   d. Nothing.

4. After adding blocks from a drawing to a Tool Palette, it does not matter if you move or delete the source drawing file.

   a. True

   b. False

5. Which of the following can you set in *Tool Properties* for inserting a block?

    a. Offset

    b. Rotation

    c. Freeze

    d. Flip

6. If a layer that is specified in *Tool Properties* of a block does not exist in the current drawing, what happens when you insert that block into that drawing?

    a. The block is inserted on layer 0.

    b. The block cannot be inserted into that drawing.

    c. You are prompted for a new name for the layer.

    d. The layer is automatically created in the drawing.

Command Summary

Button	Command	Location
	Block Editor	• **Ribbon:** *Home* tab>*Block Definition* panel or *Insert* tab>*Block* panel • **Command Prompt:** bedit or BE
	Create Block	• **Ribbon:** *Home* tab>*Block* panel or *Insert* tab>*Block Definition* panel • **Command Prompt:** block or B
	Find Non-Purgeable Items	• **Ribbon:** *Manage* tab>*Cleanup* panel
	Purge	• **Application Menu:** Drawing Utilities>Purge • **Ribbon:** *Manage* tab>*Cleanup* panel • **Command Prompt:** purge or PU
	Tool Palettes	• **Ribbon:** *View* tab>*Palettes* panel • **Command Prompt:** toolpalettes, toolpalettesclose, or <Ctrl>+<3>
	Write Block	• **Ribbon:** *Insert* tab>*Block Definition* panel, *Create Block* drop-down list • **Command Prompt:** wblock

Projects: Creating and Organizing Blocks

Practice projects are provided for you to gain additional hands-on experience in the topics and commands previously covered. These projects are intended to be self-guided and do not include step-by-step information.

Learning Objectives

- *Mechanical:* Create blocks and insert them into the provided slots of a control panel.
- *Architectural*: Create furniture blocks and insert them to create a floor plan.
- *Civil*: Create blocks and insert and insert them to complete a utility layout.

6.1 Mechanical Project: Control Panel

In this project, you will draw objects to represent components in a control panel, make blocks of those objects, and insert the blocks to complete the drawing, as shown in Figure 6–2.

1. Open **Panel-M.dwg** from your practice files folder.

2. Create the blocks shown in Figure 6–1. All objects should be drawn on layer **0**. Do not create the text captions, dimensions, or center marks.

- Tip: In the CONNECT block, draw the hexagons using the **Polygon** command. Select the **Circumscribed** option with a radius of **2.2**.

Figure 6–1

3. Insert the blocks on the layer **Component** as shown in Figure 6–2.

   • Block objects created on layer **0** use the properties of the current layer. Block objects created on other layers use the properties of those layers, no matter which layer is current when the block is inserted.

Figure 6–2

4. (Optional) Create a tool palette with the blocks from this project, so that you can use it to insert them into the current drawing or other drawings.

6.2 Architectural Project: Furniture Layout

In this project, you will create blocks for office furniture and insert them into a floor plan, as shown in Figure 6–3.

Figure 6–3

1. Open **Office3-A.dwg** from your practice files folder.

2. Create the blocks shown in Figure 6–4. All of the objects should be drawn on the layer **Furniture**, except the door which should be drawn on layer **Doors**. Do not create the text captions and dimensions.

    Note: The objects can be created in either Imperial units (feet and inches) or Metric units (millimeters). In Figure 6–4, Metric units are included in brackets.

Figure 6–4

3. Insert the blocks as shown in Figure 6–3. (Tip: Use the **Array** and **Mirror** commands to help place some of the furniture).

4. (Optional) Create a tool palette with the blocks from this project, so that you can use it to insert these blocks into the current drawing or other drawings.

6.3 Civil Project: Utility Layout

In this project, you will create blocks for a utility layout and insert some of them into an existing plan, as shown in Figure 6–5. The colors have been changed for printing quality.

Figure 6–5

1. Open **Observatory Site-C.dwg** from your practice files folder.

2. Pan to an empty part of the drawing and create the blocks shown in Figure 6–6. All of the objects should be drawn on layer **0**. Do not create the text captions and dimensions.

Figure 6–6

3. Insert the blocks in the drawing as shown in Figure 6–5. Insert the blocks on the appropriate layers.

    • Not all the blocks have been used in the drawing.

4. (Optional) Create a tool palette with the blocks from this project, so that you can use it to insert the blocks into the current drawing or other drawings.

Creating Templates

You will learn to create template drawings, control drawing units and limits, create new layers, set up standard layouts, and save template drawings.

Learning Objectives

- Set standards for creating templates.
- Set the type of drawing units and their precision used in a drawing.
- Create new layers, customize their options, and organize them.
- Create custom page setups and associate them to specific layout tabs.
- Apply a new page setup or an imported page setup to a layout tab.
- Set up layouts to be used in a template.
- Save a drawing as a template file.

7.1 Why Use Templates?

Creating templates is an important step in customizing the AutoCAD® software to your specific work and drawing projects. A template is a drawing that contains the settings that you want to include as the foundation for new drawings. When correctly defined, these settings also establish a set of standards for each project.

Features that should be set in a template include the following (as shown in Figure 7–1):

- Units (coordinates) and limits
- Layers
- Annotation styles for Text, Dimensions, and Multileaders
- Layouts with page setup, border, and title block

Figure 7–1

- Several predefined templates are supplied with the AutoCAD software, some with title blocks and borders at standard sizes. You need to add layers, text styles, and dimension styles if you use these templates.

- Other settings that can be saved in a template are system variables (such as **Global Linetype Scale**), and the Snap and Grid drafting settings. The Object Snap, Polar Tracking, and Object Snap Tracking drafting settings are stored in the AutoCAD system files and cannot be saved in a template.

Drawing Standards

In addition to templates, you should consider the other standards that you might need to add. Creating standards for using with the software enables you to work efficiently and faster without having to search for them when required.

Standards are important in the following key areas:

- **Naming Standards:** Establish a consistent scheme for drawing filenames, folders, and servers.

- **Layer Standards:** Your office or organization should have a standard layer scheme that everyone follows.

    - Your standard layer scheme should be included in your template drawings so that it is available in new drawings. You should rarely need to create a new layer.

    - A logical approach to layer names can simplify layer management. For example, if you name all of the layers related to plumbing with the prefix **P-**, they are grouped together in the Layer Control and are easy to manipulate as a group.

- **Block Standards:** Establish a consistent naming scheme for blocks. Store drawings (that are to be inserted into other drawings) as blocks in a shared network folder that is accessible to everyone who needs them. Alternatively, place sets of related blocks into block library drawings to be accessed using *Tool Palettes* or *DesignCenter*.

- You can also include standard blocks in your template file. (Tool Palettes are not related to templates. When you create custom Tool Palettes, they are available for any drawing).

- **Annotation Styles:** Use text, dimensions, and multileader styles to ensure consistency and minimize the formatting required each time you add text, a table, or dimensions to the drawing.

💡 Hint: Default Template for QNEW

In the *Quick Access Toolbar*, click ⬜ (New) to launch the **QNew** command. **QNew** can be set to use a default template file, so that you are not prompted to select the template when creating a new drawing. You can specify the template along with its path in the **Default Template File Name for QNEW** option in the *Files* tab in the *Options* dialog box, as shown in Figure 7–2.

Figure 7–2

- If a default for **QNew** is set to **None** and has not been specified, the command opens the *Select template* dialog box, similar to the regular **New** command.

The **QNew** template also controls which template is used for the new drawing that automatically opens at startup.

7.2 Controlling Units Display

The first setting you should establish in your template is the type of drawing units to be used. By setting the units in a template, you ensure that any new drawing based on that template automatically starts with the correct units. The **Units** command enables you to specify the type of drawing units used and the precision that the AutoCAD software displays for those units, as shown in Figure 7-3.

Figure 7-3

How To: Set the Drawing Units

1. Open the template drawing that you are creating.

2. In the Application Menu, select **Drawing Utilities>Units**.

3. In the *Length* area, select an option in the *Type* and *Precision* drop-down lists.

4. In the *Angle* area, select an option in the *Type* and *Precision* drop-down lists and set the angle rotation to be **Clockwise** from **0** as required.

5. In the *Insertion scale* area, select an option in the *Units to scale inserted content* drop-down list.

6. In the *Lighting* area, select an option in the *Units for specifying the intensity of lighting* drop-down list (this is only required if you are working in 3D).

7. Click **OK**.

• The *Length Type* options include **Architectural**, **Decimal**, **Engineering**, **Fractional**, and **Scientific**.

• The *Angle Type* options include **Decimal Degrees**, **Deg/Min/Sec**, **Grads**, **Radians**, and **Surveyor's Units**. By default, angles are measured in a counter-clockwise direction. If you need them to go in the other direction, select the **Clockwise** option.

• Note the *Sample Output* area as you modify the settings, as shown in Figure 7–4.

Sample Output	Sample Output	Sample Output	Sample Output	Sample Output
1 1/2",2",0" 3"<45,0"	1.50,2.00,0.00 3.00<45,0.00	1.50",2.00",0.00" 3.00"<45,0.00"	1 1/2,2,0 3<45,0	1.50E+00,2.00E+00,0.00E+00 3.00E+00<45,0.00E+00
Architectural	**Decimal**	**Engineering**	**Fractional**	**Scientific**

Figure 7–4

• Decimal units can stand for many unit types: inches, feet, meters, millimeters, miles, etc.

• The **Insertion scale** controls how blocks created in different units, are scaled when inserted into the drawing. For example, if the block units are inches and the drawing units are millimeters, the AutoCAD software scales the block based on the conversion factor for inches to millimeters (25.4).

• The *Insertion scale* should be set to the unit of measure that each unit is intended to represent (for example, **Meters**, **Feet**, **US Survey Feet**, **Inches**, etc.) regardless of how it is to display. If the inserted content is also set in this way, the scale conversion is going to be correct.

• Changing the precision here only controls the degree of precision that displays and does not affect the size of objects that are drawn. The AutoCAD software still works with its full degree of accuracy, regardless of the precision setting.

• Click **Direction...** to open the *Direction Control* dialog box in which you can set the base angles for **East**, **North**, **South**, **West**, and **Other**. This is usually used in civil engineering drawings.

Hint: Editing the Scale List

The Scale List (used for the Viewport Scale, Annotation Scale, and Plot Scale), is stored in each drawing file and can vary from drawing to drawing. Therefore, if you want to use a standard scale list in each drawing, you should set it in the template drawing as you want it to be displayed.

To edit the scale list, click **Custom...** in the Annotation scale list (as shown in Figure 7–5), or click (Scale List) in the *Annotate* tab>*Annotation Scaling* panel to open the *Edit Drawing Scales* dialog box.

Figure 7–5

You can **Add**, **Edit**, and **Delete** scales, as shown in Figure 7–6. You can also move them up and down in the list so that the most commonly used scales are at the beginning. Click **Reset** to return to the default scale list.

Figure 7–6

Drawing Limits

When you begin drawing, it helps to start with an area of an appropriate size displayed on the screen. For example, a site plan in Engineering units needs to have a larger area displayed than a small mechanical part in the same units.

The *limits* of a drawing define the rectangular area (extents of the area) in which you are going to draw. You can set the limits by selecting a lower left and upper right corner. For example, you might set the upper right limits of a site plan to **1000',500'** while a mechanical part can be set to **12",7"**, as shown in Figure 7−7.

Figure 7−7

How To: Set the Drawing Limits

1. Start the **Limits** command by typing **limits** in the Command Line.

2. Type the coordinates for the lower left corner, which is normally set to **0,0**.

3. Type the coordinates for the upper right corner. They should define an area slightly larger than the objects you are planning to draw.

4. Use **Zoom All** to fit the drawing in the drawing area.

5. Save the drawing.

• Once you set the limits, use **Zoom All**. It zooms to fit the limits of the drawing in the drawing area (if there are objects outside the limits, it displays them as well).

• The limits can be changed at any time without harming your drawing.

7.3 Creating New Layers

A layering scheme is the most important organizing tool in any drawing. A standard layer scheme should be included in your template drawings. Use *Layer Properties Manager* to create new layers and change the properties or status of existing layers, as shown in Figure 7-8.

Figure 7-8

Layer Properties Manager

Layer Properties Manager is a palette and can stay open while you are working in the drawing. It can also be docked and hidden to create space in the drawing area. When layers are modified in *Layer Properties Manager*, the changes are automatically applied to the drawing and listed in the *Layer Control* list in the *Home* tab>*Layers* panel.

* When you create layers, you set their color, linetype, lineweight, and plot or no-plot status, and the plot style (if applicable).

* Layers defined in a template establish a consistent layer standard for all drawings based on that template.

* The icon in the *Status* column indicates whether the layer contains objects (⬜), does not contain objects (⬜), or is the current layer (✓).

How To: Create a New Layer

1. In the *Home* tab>*Layers* panel or in the *View* tab>*Palettes* panel, click 🗐 (Layer Properties).

2. Click 🗏 (New Layer). A new layer is added to the list with the default name **Layer1**.

   - To create several new layers quickly, click 🗏 (New Layer) once and then type the layer names separated by a comma.

3. Type a name for the new layer.

   - Layer names can have up to 255 characters and can include letters, numbers, spaces, and most other special characters (the following symbols are not permitted: < > / \ ? * | , = `.).

4. To set the **Color**, select the color swatch for that layer, select a color in the *Select Color* dialog box (as shown in Figure 7–9), and click **OK**.

   - The *Select Color* dialog box has three tabs: *Index Color*, *True Color*, and *Color Books*. The *Index Color* list (256 colors) is adequate for most needs.

Figure 7–9

5. To set the **Linetype**, select the linetype name for that layer, select a different linetype in the *Select Linetype* dialog box (as shown in Figure 7–10), and click **OK**.

   - Linetypes are set by default to display in a *Paper Space* viewport according to the current viewport scale.

Figure 7–10

6. To set the **Lineweight**, select the lineweight setting for that layer, select a width in the *Lineweight* dialog box (as shown in Figure 7–11), and click **OK**.

Figure 7–11

7. To make the layer non-plotting, click 🖶 (Plot) or 🖶 (No Plot), as shown in Figure 7–12. No *Plot* layers are useful for construction lines, notes, viewports, and other information that is required for drawing construction, but not for the plotted output.

8. If you want to freeze a layer by default in a new viewport, click 🖳 (New VP Freeze), as shown in Figure 7–12. For example, you might want to create a layer that is only displayed in one viewport.

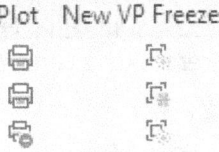

Figure 7–12

9. To add a description, click in the *Description* column and type the description.

• The changes are automatically applied to the drawing.

• If a layer is selected in *Layer Properties Manager* when you click 🗂 (New Layer), the new layer copies the properties of the selected layer.

Sorting Layers by Properties

- You can sort layers in the list according to their properties by selecting any of the column headings at the top of the list. For example, selecting the *Name* column sorts the list alphabetically by name, and selecting the *Freeze* column separates the frozen from the thawed layers. Clicking on a heading again reverses the sort order.

- You can rearrange the display order of columns in *Layer Properties Manager* by dragging the column header to a new location, as shown in Figure 7–13. The new location is saved by the AutoCAD software.

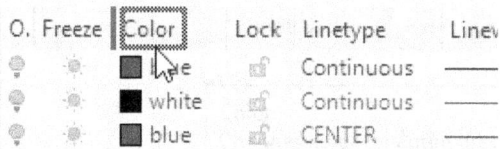

Figure 7–13

- You can resize the width of the columns in *Layer Properties Manager* by dragging the border between the column headings. You can also right-click on a column header and select **Maximize column** to maximize one column, or select **Maximize all columns** to resize all of the columns to the width of their largest cell.

- You can remove any columns that you do not want displayed. Right-click on any column header and select a column name to clear the checkmark and remove it from the display. **Name** is grayed out and cannot be removed, as shown in Figure 7–14.

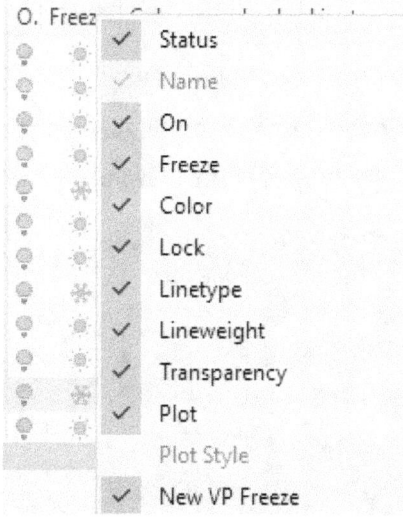

Figure 7–14

- Additional column names display if you are in a layout.

Lineweights

Lineweight refers to how heavy or wide the lines are in an object, as shown in Figure 7–15. Heavier lineweights are used to emphasize parts of the drawing. This becomes important when the drawing is plotted.

Figure 7–15

*   (Show/Hide Lineweight) in the *Status Bar* controls the visibility of lineweights on the screen.
*   Depending on the resolution of your monitor, you might not be able to distinguish between similar lineweights in your drawing. When you print the drawing, the lineweights are easier to differentiate.
*   Plotted lineweight in the AutoCAD software is often controlled by color.

Linetypes

Linetype refers to whether the objects are drawn with dashed, dotted, continuous, or other line styles, as shown in Figure 7–16. Usually, specific types of lines are used for specific types of objects. For example, hidden lines are usually dashed, while most objects are drawn with continuous linetypes.

Figure 7–16

How To: Load a Linetype

The AutoCAD software comes with a wide selection of standard linetypes. If the required style does not display in the *Select Linetype* dialog box, you can load other linetypes into the drawing.

1. In *Layer Properties Manager*, select the linetype name for the layer that you want to modify. The *Select Linetype* dialog box opens.
2. Click **Load...**.

3. In the *Load or Reload Linetypes* dialog box, select the linetype(s) that you want to use. To select more than one, hold <Shift> or <Ctrl> while selecting.

4. Click **OK**. The linetypes are now available for use.

*   The standard linetype definitions are stored in the file **Acad.lin**.

💡 Hint: Linetype Scale

The Linetype Scale controls the length of segments and gaps for all of the linetypes in the drawing. A larger value for the linetype scale places longer segments and gaps. Depending on the size of your drawing, you might need to adjust the linetype scale so that linetypes display and plot at an appropriate size.

*   By default, the linetype scale is set to display in Paper Space viewports so the linetypes are scaled correctly for each viewport.

*   You can type **ltscale** in the Command Line to launch the command.

Other Layer Options

The left panel in *Layer Properties Manager* displays the layer filter tree. Layer filters are an advanced layer management tool that are used to control the layer list and to group layers.

*   One layer filter, **All Used Layers**, is predefined. Selecting this filter only lists layers that contain objects. To return to the full list, select **All** in the Layer Filter tree.

*   If you do not use layer filters, you can hide that portion of *Layer Properties Manager* by clicking « (Collapses Layer filter tree), as shown in Figure 7–17.

Figure 7–17

How To: Delete a Layer

1. Select a layer name in the list.

2. Click (Delete Layer). The layer is removed.

*   You cannot delete layers that contain objects or certain special layers, such as layer **0**.

How To: Rename a Layer

1. In the list, click once on the layer name to select it and then click it again. An edit box displays around the highlighted name (you can also right-click on a Layer name and select **Rename Layer**).

2. Type a new name.

- You cannot rename layer **0** and should not rename the default layer **defpoints**.

How To: Merge Layers

You can select multiple layers in *Layer Properties Manager* and merge their objects into one layer. All of the objects on the selected layers are moved to the merged layer and the selected layers are removed from the drawing.

1. In *Layer Properties Manager*, use <Shift> or <Ctrl> to select one or more layers to merge.

2. Right-click and select **Merge selected layer(s) to...**.

3. In the *Merge to Layer* dialog box, select the layer to which you want to merge the other layers.

4. Click **OK**.

5. In the warning box, click **Yes**.

6. The AutoCAD Text window opens displaying the progress of the merge procedure. The selected layers are merged to the target layer. The selected layers are then deleted.

7.4 Adding Standard Layouts to Templates

You can simplify your day-to-day work by creating layouts in your template files that match the printers and paper sizes that you normally use, as shown in Figure 7–18. These layouts are then ready to use in new drawings based on the templates.

- To create a new layout tab from an existing layout, right-click on the one that you want to use and select **Move or Copy**. In the *Move or Copy* dialog box, select **Create a copy** and select a layout before which the copy is going to be placed. Double-click on the new copied layout tab and enter a new name for the layout.

Figure 7–18

Working in the Page Setup Manager

When you set up template files for your office, you need to be able to specify the layouts that use your office printers and title blocks. To do so, create page setups in *Page Setup Manager* (as shown in Figure 7–19), and then associate standard page setups with the layout tabs.

- In *Page Setup Manager*, you can assign an existing page setup to the current layout tab, create new page setups, modify existing page setups, and import page setups from another file.

Figure 7–19

How To: Create a Page Setup

1. In the *Output* tab>*Plot* panel, click (Page Setup Manager). Alternatively, in the Application Menu, select **Print>Page Setup**.
2. In the *Page Setup Manager* dialog box, click **New**.
3. In the *New Page Setup* dialog box, shown in Figure 7–20, type a name for the setup. Select an existing setup in the *Start with* area if the new setup is similar to an existing one.

Figure 7–20

4. Click **OK**.

5. In the *Page Setup* dialog box (shown in Figure 7-21), select the printer or plotter that you want to use. This determines the paper sizes from which you can select.

Figure 7-21

6. Specify the *Paper size*, *Plot area*, *Plot offset*, *Plot scale*, *Plot style table*, *Shaded viewport options*, *Plot options*, and *Drawing orientation*.

7. Click **Preview...** to display a preview of how the setup is going to print on the sheet.

8. Right-click in the preview and select **Exit**.

9. When the page setup is finished, click **OK** to return to *Page Setup Manager*. The new page setup can now be applied to a layout.

Page Setup Options

Printer/plotter Enables you to select from the list of available printing devices. Check with your CAD manager if the printer/plotter you want to use is not in the list. The AutoCAD software includes several predefined plotter configurations, such as DWF6 e-plot.

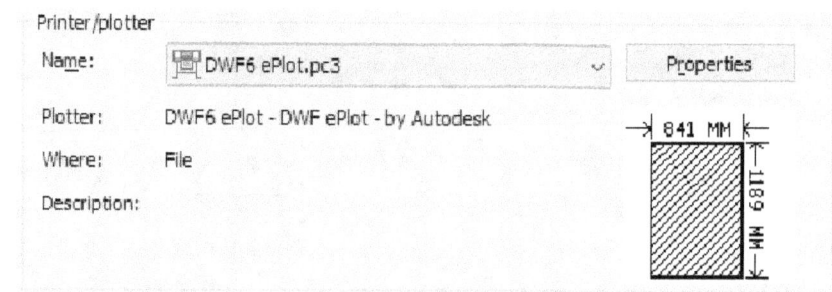

Paper size Enables you to set the size of the layout. The available sizes depend on the selected plotter.

Paper size

ISO expand A0 (841.00 x 1189.00 MM) ⌄

Plot area Sets the printable area. Normally, you use the **Layout** option to plot the entire layout to the extents of the printable area. You can also print the *Extents* of the drawing, the *Display* in the drawing area, a *Window* that you select, or a *View* that has been defined in the drawing.

Plot area

What to plot:

Layout ⌄

Plot offset Controls where the drawing starts to plot on the paper. Depending on your plotter, you might need to set this so that the drawing fits correctly on the paper. The **Center the plot** option is not available when the *Plot area* is set to **Layout**.

Plot offset (origin set to printable area)

X: 0.00 mm ☐ Center the plot

Y: 0.00 mm

Plot scale	Sets the scale when you are printing from a layout. The default scale is 1:1. However, you can set a different scale if you are creating a check plot on a smaller piece of paper.

IMPORTANT: The *Plot scale* for a layout is almost always 1:1 because the layout is created at the actual size required to fit on the piece of paper. The scaling of the model is done using the Viewport Scale.

Plot style table	Coordinates the layer color to pen weight, or sets up other special effects for plotted output. Consult your CAD manager about which one you should use.

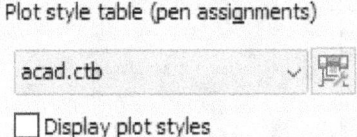

Shaded viewport options	For 3D models, this enables you to set viewports to be hidden or rendered and to control the image quality.

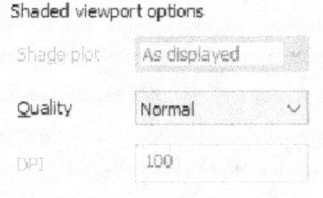

Plot options	Enables you to plot using lineweights or plot styles and to specify how to treat Paper Space objects.

Plot options
- ☑ Plot object lineweights
- ☐ Plot transparency
- ☑ Plot with plot styles
- ☑ Plot paperspace last
- ☐ Hide paperspace objects

| **Drawing orientation** | Sets the paper orientation to **Portrait** (the short edge of the paper is at the top of the page) or **Landscape** (the long edge of the paper is at the top of the page). |

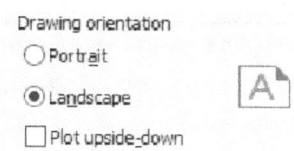

Layout Size: Printable Area

The AutoCAD software displays the *printable* area of the layout as a dashed boundary, as shown in Figure 7–22. Because printers or plotters cannot print to the edges of the sheet, the printable area is smaller than the actual paper size. The size of the margins varies from one printer model to another, and even from one sheet size to another. Ensure that the objects you place on the layout fit in the printable area.

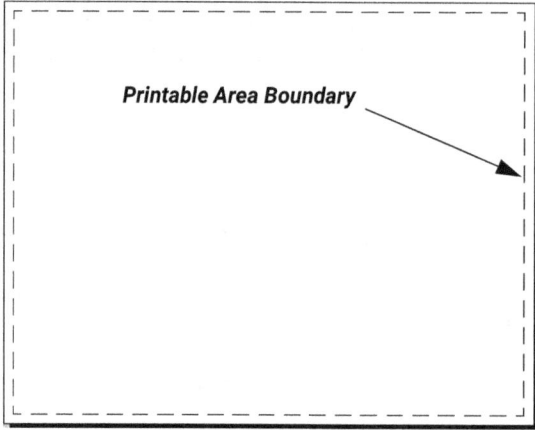

Figure 7–22

How To: Apply a Page Setup to a Layout

1. Right-click on the layout that you want to set and select **Page Setup Manager...**.
2. In *Page Setup Manager*, select a page setup with the required plotter and paper size.
3. Click **Set Current** to apply it to the layout.
4. Click **Close** to close *Page Setup Manager*.

How To: Import a Page Setup from Another File

1. Open *Page Setup Manager*.

2. Click **Import...**.

3. In the *Select Page Setup From File* dialog box, select the file that contains the page setup you want to use and click **Open**.

4. In the *Import Page Setups* dialog box, select the setup that you want to import, as shown in Figure 7–23.

   Note: *If names are not displayed in the list, the drawing might have layouts but they have not been saved as page setups.*

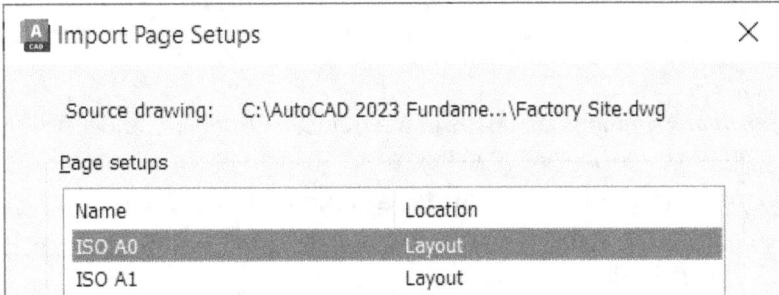

Figure 7–23

5. Click **OK** to complete the process. The imported page setup can now be used in your current drawing.

Setting Up Layouts to Use in a Template

To prepare layouts to be used in a template, specify generic names for the layout tabs, add title blocks, and set up at least one viewport on each Layout.

- Rename new layouts using a generic name. For example, it might be one that reflects the printer and paper size, such as **Printer-ANSI C**. When it is used in a project, you can change the label to match the sheet number and/or sheet name.

- Your company title block should be designed to fit on the paper size specified in the page setup.

- Verify that the viewport is on the layer **Viewport**.

- Repeat the steps for each plotter and paper size required.

7.5 Saving Templates

All of the established settings can be saved in a template file. By saving the settings in a template, you automatically make them available in every new drawing based on that template.

How To: Create a Template

1. Start a new drawing or open an existing drawing.

2. Establish all of the drawing settings as required (e.g., units or layers).

3. In the Application Menu, select **Save As>Drawing Template** to save the drawing as a template.

   *Note: If you use the standard **Save As** command, the dialog box defaults to the **AutoCAD 2018 Drawing (*.dwg)** file type. You should change the file type to **AutoCAD Drawing Template (*.dwt)**.*

4. The *Save Drawing As* dialog box opens in the *AutoCAD Template* folder with **AutoCAD Drawing Template (*.dwt)** selected in the *Files of type* field.

5. Navigate to the required folder, give the file a name, and click **Save**.

6. In the *Template Options* dialog box, in the *Description* area, type a brief description of the template, as shown in Figure 7–24.

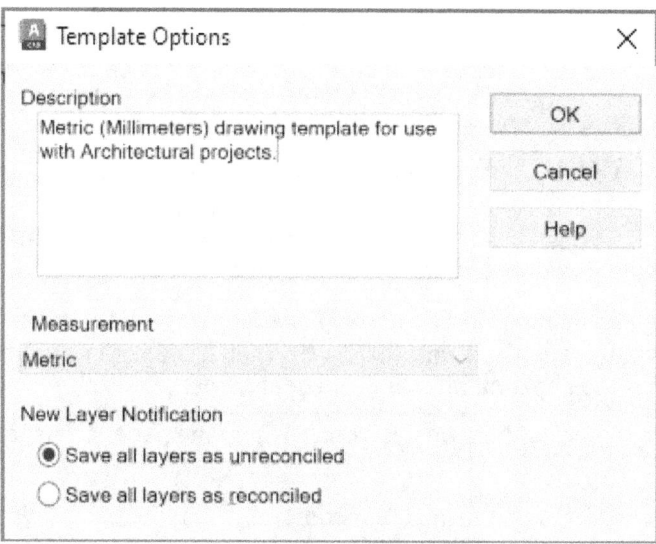

Figure 7–24

7. Select the system of measurement (**Metric** or **English**).

   Note: For more information on reconciled layers, see Reconcile New Layers in the AutoCAD Help system.

8. Select whether to save all of the layers as unreconciled or reconciled.

9. Click **OK**.

- Templates have the file extension .DWT to distinguish them from normal .DWG files.

- Templates should be saved in a separate folder to which everyone has access.

- You can modify an existing template as you would a normal drawing. To open a template, start the **Open** command and select **Drawing Template (*.dwt)** in the expanded *Files of type* drop-down list, as shown in Figure 7–25.

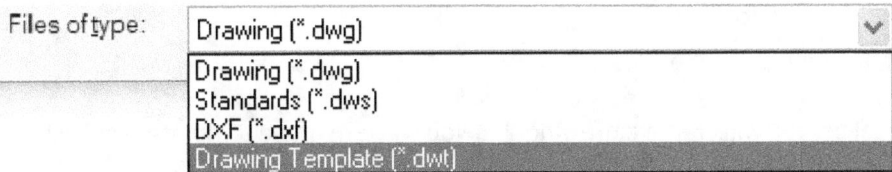

Figure 7–25

Practice 7a
Save a Template

Practice Objectives

- Set the units and limits in a drawing.
- Create a set of layers in a drawing.
- Create a page setup and apply it to a layout tab.
- Add a title block to a layout tab.
- Save the drawing as a template.

In this practice, you will create a drawing that you will turn into a template. You will set the units and test them by measuring distances using grips and use *Layer Properties Manager* to create and modify new layers. You will also create a Page Setup and apply it to a standard layout, and then save the drawing as a template.

Task 1: Control and test the units display.

In this task, you will create a drawing that you will turn into a template. You will set the units and test them by measuring distances using grips, as shown in Figure 7–26.

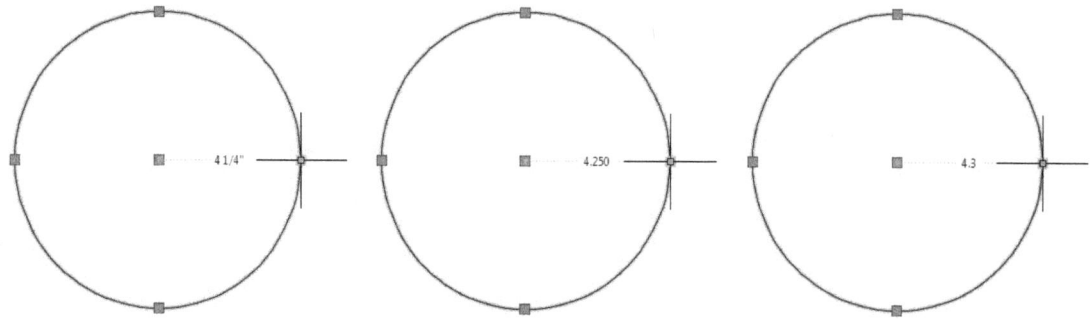

Figure 7–26

1. Start the **QNEW** command and select **acad.dwt** from the default *AutoCAD Template* folder to open a new drawing. Save the new drawing as **AEC-Facilities.dwg** in your practice files folder. Toggle off **Drawing Grid** in the *Status Bar*.

2. In the Application Menu, select **Drawing Utilities>Units**. In the *Drawing Units* dialog box, in the *Length* area, set the *Type* to **Architectural** and the *Precision* to **0'-0 1/16"**.

3. Verify that the *Insertion scale* is set to **Inches**. Click **OK**. Note that the coordinate display in the *Status Bar* changes to display in feet and inches.

4. Draw a **4 1/4"** radius circle (type **4-1/4** for the radius).

5. Use **Zoom Extents** to fill the drawing window with the circle.

6. Select the circle and hover the cursor over one of the outer grips. The radius should be listed as **4 1/4"**.

7. Start the **Units** command again to open the *Drawing Units* dialog box. Change the *Length Type* to **Decimal** and the *Length Precision* to **0.000**. Click **OK**.

8. Select the circle again and hover the cursor on one of the grips. The radius is reported as **4.250**.

9. Start the **Units** command to open the *Drawing Units* dialog box. Change the *Length Precision* to **0.0**.

10. Select the circle and hover the cursor over one of the outer grips. The radius is reported as **4.3**.

11. Start the **Units** command to open the *Drawing Units* dialog box. Set the *Length Type* to **Architectural** with a *Precision* of **0'-0 1/8"**.

12. In the Command Line/Dynamic Input, type **limits**. Set the lower left corner to **0,0** and the upper right corner to **100',75'**.

13. Use **Zoom All** to fit the drawing on the screen. Note that the circle displays very small (almost invisible) in the drawing window.

14. Use **Zoom Extents** to display and fill the drawing window with the circle.

15. Save the drawing.

Task 2: Create new layers.

In this task, you will use *Layer Properties Manager* to create new layers and change their properties, as shown for some of the layers in Figure 7–27.

Figure 7–27

1. Open *Layer Properties Manager* and note that layer **0** is the only layer present.

2. In *Layer Properties Manager*, use (New Layer), create the layers specified in the following table, as shown for few layers in Figure 7–28.

Figure 7–28

*Note: The DASHED linetype is not listed in the Select Linetype dialog box. To load it, select **Load...** and then **DASHED** in the list.*

Layer Name	Color	Linetype	Other
Border	blue	Continuous	
Cabling	cyan	Continuous	
Demolition	red	DASHED	
Dimensions	red	Continuous	
Doors	yellow	Continuous	
Electrical	green	Continuous	
Equipment	green	Continuous	
Furniture	green	Continuous	
HVAC	blue	Continuous	
Notes	cyan	Continuous	
Plumbing	magenta	Continuous	
Titles	blue	Continuous	
Viewports	gray (Index color 8)	Continuous	No plot
Walls	white	Continuous	
Windows	yellow	Continuous	

- If you have a white background then the white color will display as black in the *Select Color* dialog box.
- You are using a color-to-lineweight scheme, in which red is the lightest color and white the heaviest. Gray is used to indicate a no plot layer.
- The layers are automatically added to the Layer Control.

3. Close *Layer Properties Manager* and verify that all of the newly created layers are listed in the Layer Control.

Task 3: Create a page setup.

In this task, you will create a page setup and apply it to a standard layout for the template file, as shown in Figure 7–29.

Figure 7–29

1. Switch to **Layout1**. In the *Status Bar*, right-click on the selected layout tab and select **Page Setup Manager....**

2. In *Page Setup Manager*, click **New**, enter the name as follows (**DWF A (11 x 8.5 in)**) and click **OK**. In the *Page Setup* dialog box set the remaining information from the table below and click **OK**.

Name:	DWF A (11 x 8.5 in)
Printer/plotter:	DWF6 ePlot.pc3
Paper size:	ANSI expand A (11.00 x 8.50 Inches)
Drawing orientation:	Landscape

3. In *Page Setup Manager*, verify that **DWF A (11 x 8.5 in)** is selected and click **Set Current** to apply the setup to *Layout1*. Close *Page Setup Manager*.

4. Rename *Layout1* tab as **A-Sized Landscape**.

Task 4: Add a title block and border.

1. Make the layer **Border** current.

2. In the *Insert* tab>*Block* panel, expand the *Insert Blocks* gallery and use **Blocks from Libraries** to open the *Blocks* palette. Use the ⊞ (navigation tool) in the *Libraries* tab and select **Tblk-Ansi Expanded A (11.00 X 8.50).dwg** from the practice folder. The drawing file gets listed in the *Blocks* palette. Insert the drawing using **0,0,0** for the insertion point. Close the *Blocks* palette.

3. Select the viewport and change it to the layer **Viewports**.

4. Using grips, resize the viewport as required to fit inside the title block such that it does not overlap the title block information.

5. In the *Status Bar*, set the *Viewport Scale* to **1/8"=1'-0"**.

6. The layout displays similar to that shown in Figure 7–30.

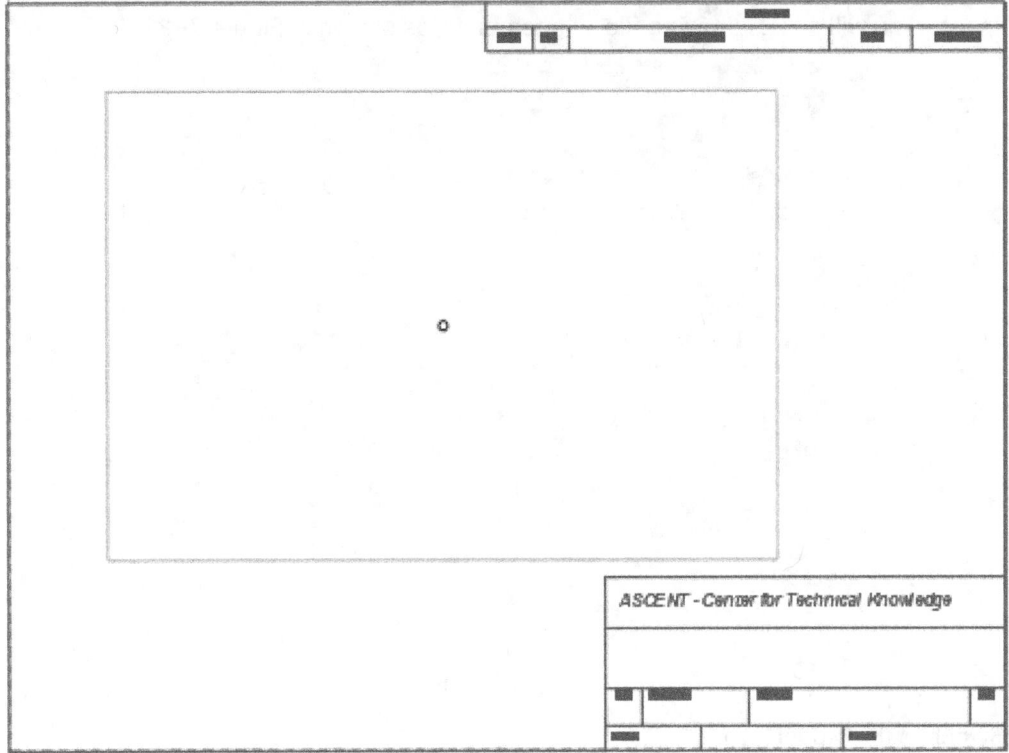

Figure 7–30

7. Save the drawing.

Task 5: Save a template.

In this task, you will save a drawing file as a template, as shown in Figure 7–31.

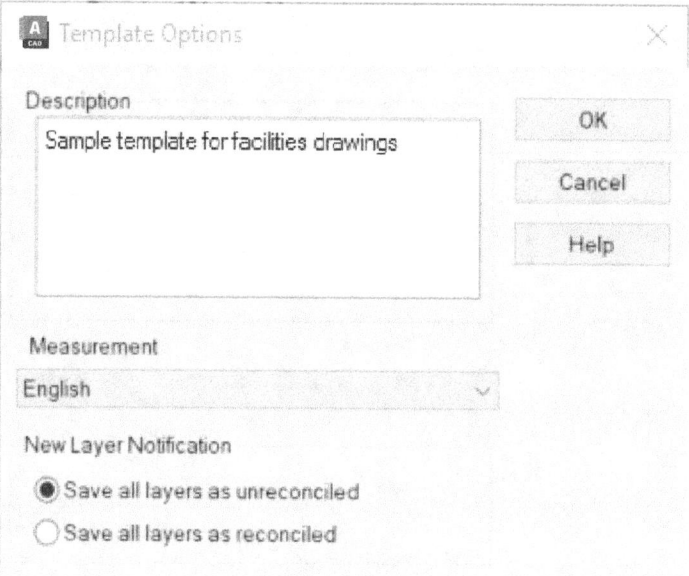

Figure 7–31

1. Switch to the **Model** layout.

2. Erase everything in the drawing, zoom all, and set the current layer to **Walls**.

3. In the Application Menu, select **Save As>Drawing Template**. In the *Save Drawing As* dialog box, note that the *Files of type* is set to **AutoCAD Drawing Template (*.dwt)**. Navigate to your practice files folder. For the name, verify that **AEC-Facilities.dwt** is already displayed. Click **Save** to continue.

4. In the *Template Options* dialog box, enter the description **Sample template for facilities drawings** and verify that **English** is selected as the *Measurement*. Click **OK** to finish.

5. Close the template file.

6. Start a new drawing based on **AEC-Facilities.dwt**, which you saved in the practice files folder.

7. Verify that the settings you built into the template (units, layers, and layouts) are working in the new drawing.

8. Close the file without saving changes.

End of practice

Chapter Review Questions

1. Which objects should be set in the template file?

   a. Layers

   b. Polygons

   c. Constraints

   d. Polylines

2. Which of the following is controlled by the Drawing Limits?

   a. The drawing precision.

   b. The extents of the area where you intend to draw.

   c. The scale of the drawing.

   d. The maximum number of objects added in the drawing.

3. Changing the Units Precision in a drawing changes the size of objects that you have drawn.

   a. True

   b. False

4. When creating a template file, you want to add custom layouts. Which of the following commands enables you to define the printer, paper size, and plot scale for a layout?

   a. Page Setup

   b. Plotter Setup

   c. Layout Setup

5. Which command enables you to create a template file?

   a. Template

   b. New

   c. Save As

   d. Open

Command Summary

Button	Command	Location
	Layer Properties Manager	• **Ribbon:** *Home* tab>*Layers* panel or *View* tab>*Palettes* panel • **Command Prompt:** layer or LA
N/A	**Limits**	• **Command Prompt:** limits
	New	• **Quick Access Toolbar** • **Command Prompt:** qnew
	Page Setup Manager	• **Ribbon:** *Output* tab>*Plot* panel • **Application Menu:** Print>Page Setup • **Shortcut Menu:** (*right-click on Model tab or Layout tab*) Page Setup Manager • **Command Prompt:** pagesetup
	Save As	• **Application Menu:** Save As • **Command Prompt:** saveas
	Scale List	• **Ribbon:** *Annotate* tab>*Annotation Scaling* panel • **Command Prompt:** scalelistedit
0.0	**Units**	• **Application Menu:** Drawing Utilities>Units • **Command Prompt:** units or UN
	Zoom All	• **Ribbon:** *View* tab>*Navigate 2D* panel • **Navigation Bar:** Zoom All • **Command Prompt:** zoom+a or ZA

Working with Layouts

You will explore working with named views, create multiple viewports, create additional viewports, add layer overrides in viewports, and modify annotative scales.

Learning Objectives

- Create viewport configurations and named views of specific areas in a drawing.
- Modify a viewport by removing portions so that it displays more clearly in the layout.
- Override layer properties in a viewport.
- Control the display of objects in viewports by modifying the annotative scales.

8.1 Creating and Using Named Views

Named views are areas of a drawing that are stored under specific names and can be accessed as required. In a large or complex drawing, named views provide a faster method of display control than the **Zoom** command.

- You can create named views by either using the **New View** command or *View Manager*. These can be accessed in the *View* tab>*Named Views* panel, as shown in Figure 8–1.

Figure 8–1

- Once the named views have been created, you can access them in the *Unsaved View* list, as shown in Figure 8–2.

Figure 8–2

How To: Create a Named View Using View Manager

1. In the *View* tab>*Named Views* panel, click 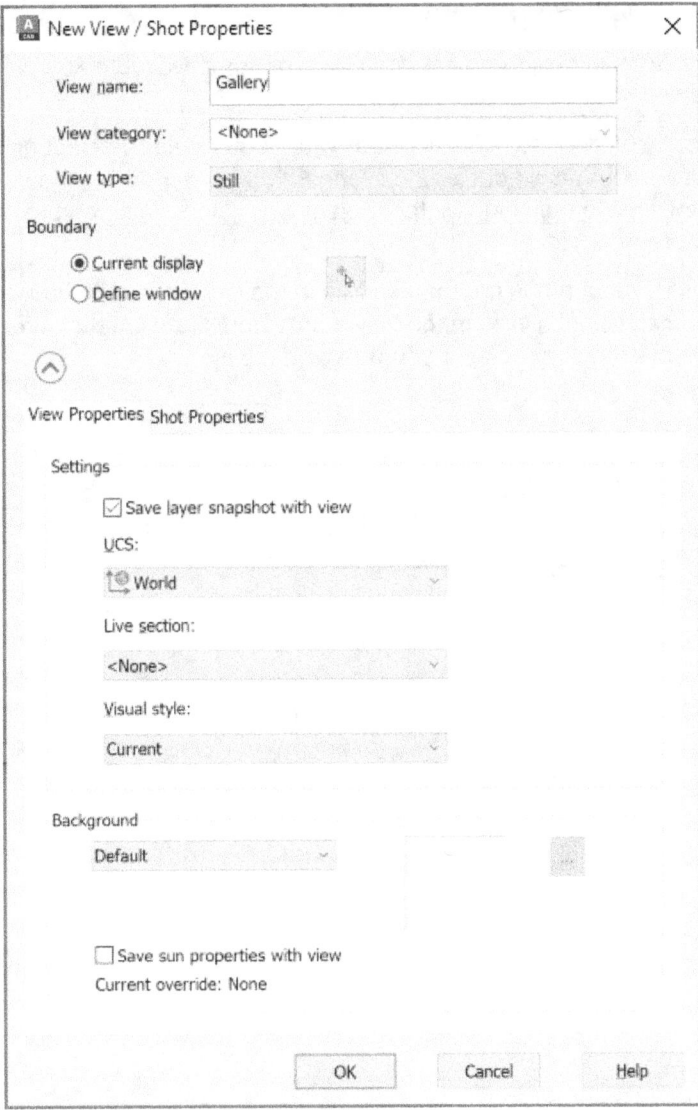 (View Manager) to open the *View Manager* dialog box, and then click **New**.

2. In the *New View / Shot Properties* dialog box, type a name in the *View name:* field, as shown in Figure 8-3.

3. The *View type* should be set to **Still**, as this option is typical for 2D views. The other *View type* options relate to 3D features.

Figure 8-3

4. In the *Boundary* area, select the **Current display** option to save the current screen view, or select the **Define window** option to define a different view by clicking 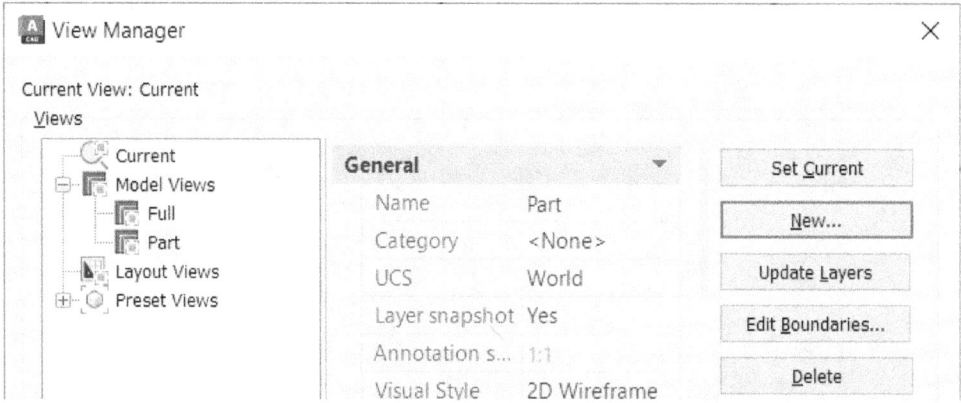 (Define view window).

5. In the *Settings* area, select whether to save the layer snapshot with the view.

6. Click **OK** to create the view.

• The view can be defined to store the current layer settings (On/Off, Freeze/Thaw, etc.), so that these layers are automatically displayed when the view is restored.

Additional View Manager Options

In the *View Manager* dialog box, there are additional options available for you to control and modify named views.

• After a view has been defined, you can modify its boundaries by selecting it in the *Views* area, under the **Model Views** node and clicking **Edit Boundaries**, as shown in Figure 8–4. The current view area is then highlighted. Select two points on screen to define a new area and press <Enter>.

• Views that store layer settings are marked **Yes** in the *Layer snapshot* under *General* properties. You can select a view in the *Views* area and click **Update Layers** (as shown in Figure 8–4) to save the current layer settings with the view.

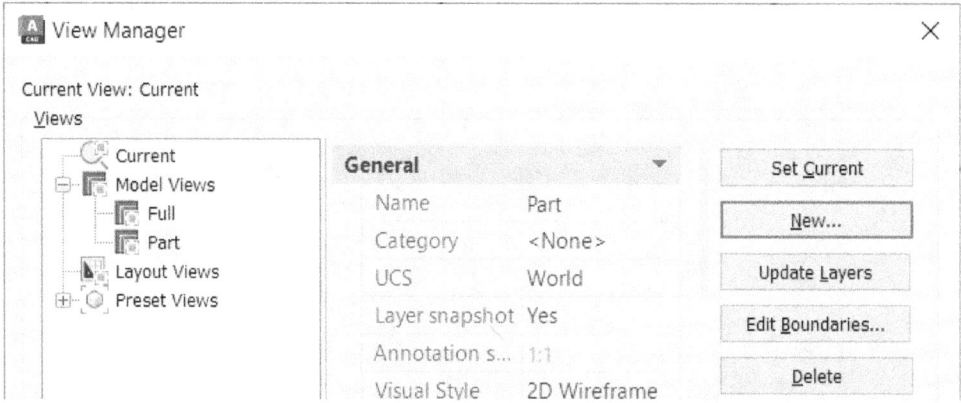

Figure 8–4

8.2 Advanced Viewport Options

To be more efficient in the creation of layouts, you can use previously created named views of your model as the basis for Viewports in a layout. You can also modify the shape of existing viewports, as shown in Figure 8–5.

Figure 8–5

Creating Viewports from Named Views

Once a named view has been created, you can insert it as a viewport in a layout. You can create viewports from named views using the *Layout* tab>*Layout Viewports* panel. (For the *Layout* tab to display in the ribbon, you must be in one of the layouts.)

- The (Insert View) drop-down menu displays all of the named views that you have created in a gallery. Once you insert a view, use the various grip options to size, move and scale the view and the layout viewport.

- The *Viewports* dialog box enables you to select named views to create single or multiple named view viewports at the same time.

How To: Create Viewports Using the Viewports Dialog Box

1. Verify that you are in an active layout.

2. Set the layer to which you want to add the viewports to be current.

3. In the *Layout* tab>*Layout Viewports* panel, click 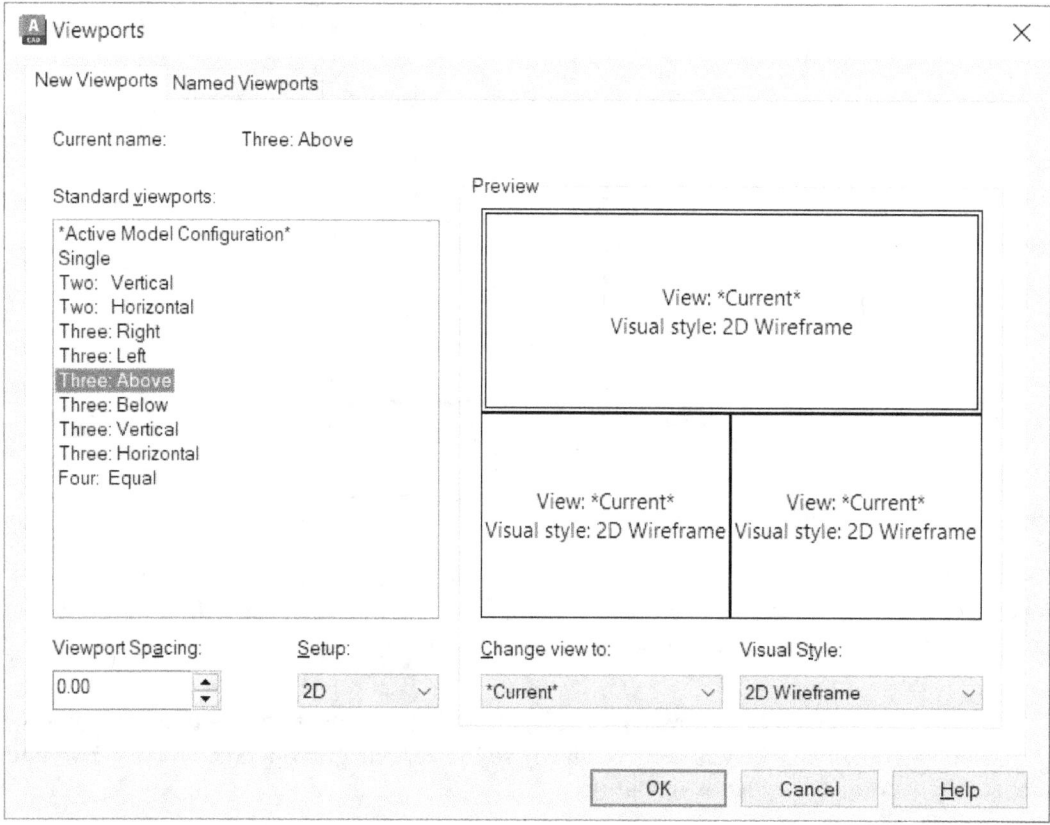 (arrow).

4. In the *Viewports* dialog box, select the *New Viewports* tab.

5. In the *Standard viewports* area, select the standard viewport configuration that you want to use. If required, set the **Viewport Spacing**.

6. In the *Preview* area, select one of the Views as shown in Figure 8–6. The *Preview* view is highlighted and, by default, the current view is displayed in all of the viewports.

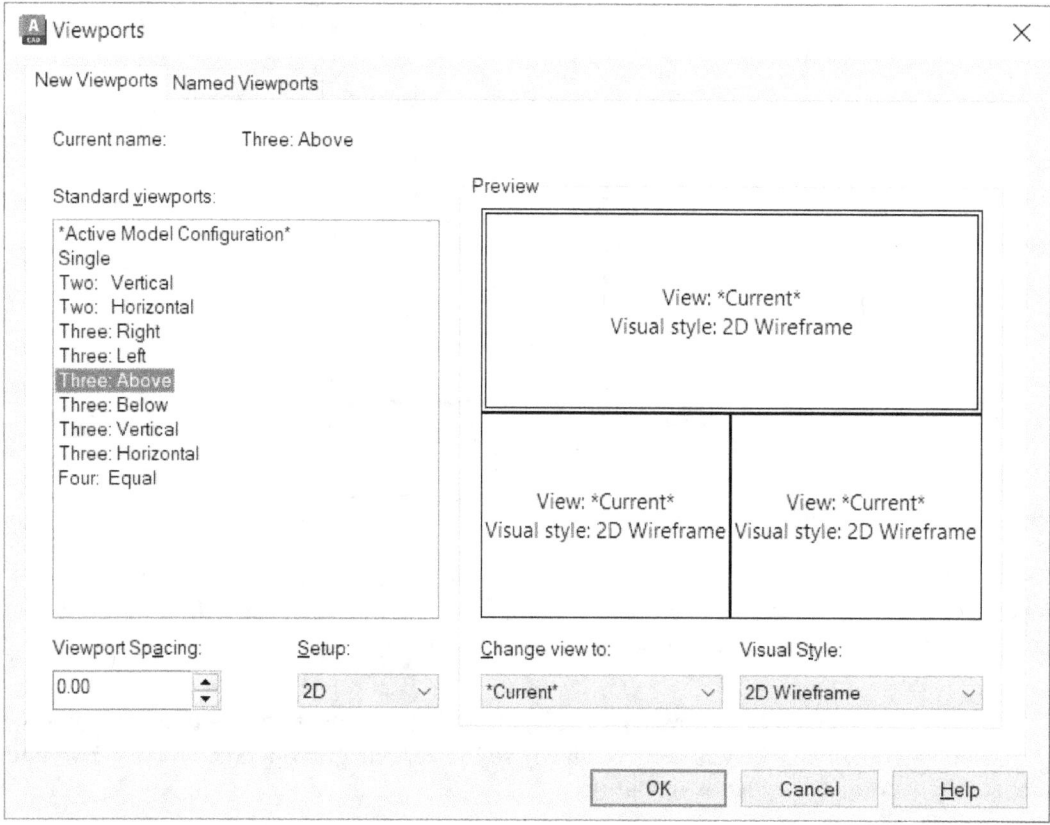

Figure 8–6

7. In the *Change view to* drop-down list, select a named view (if any have been saved), as shown in Figure 8–7, to display in that Viewport location.

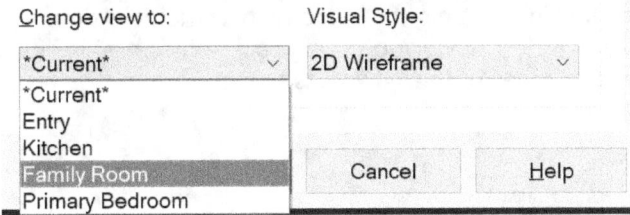

Figure 8–7

8. The view name displays in the *Preview* area, as shown in Figure 8–8.

Figure 8–8

9. The Visual Style can be preselected if you are working in 3D.

10. Click **OK** to continue.

11. If you are working in a layout, you are prompted to select two corners or to use fit to place all of the viewports on the sheet.

*   By default, **2D** puts the current view in all of the viewports. **3D** puts standard 3D views (Top, Front, and SE Isometric) in the new viewports.

*   The *Named Viewports* tab enables you to restore the saved configurations of Model Space viewports. However, the configuration of viewports in a layout cannot be saved.

*   The *Viewports* dialog box works in both Model Space (for *tiled* viewports) and Paper Space or Layout mode (for *floating* viewports).

💡 Hint: Model Space Viewports

Model Space can also be divided into viewports, but only for viewing. For example, if you have a very complex drawing you might need to display multiple close-up views at the same time as shown in Figure 8–9. The viewport that is currently active is highlighted with a blue border. You can drag the edges of the viewports to resize them.

Figure 8–9

In Model Space, you can use **Named** in the *View* tab>*Model Viewports* panel to create a new viewport configuration. However, it is easier to expand ⬚ (Viewport Configuration) in the *View* tab>*Model Viewports* panel and select the required arrangement, as shown in Figure 8–10.

Figure 8–10

Clipping Viewports

You can remove any portions of a viewport that are not required, or make its shape fit better in the available layout space. This is most effective if you have already created the viewport with the correct scale and view of the drawing.

How To: Clip a Viewport

1. In the *Layout* tab>*Layout Viewports* panel, click ⊡ (Clip).

2. Select the viewport that you want to clip.

3. Select a clipping object (which has already been created) or press <Enter> to draw a polygonal object, as shown in Figure 8–11.

Figure 8–11

- Use the **Delete** option to remove the clipping boundary and restore the original viewport.

- If the clipping boundary extends outside the current viewport boundary, the viewport is extended in that direction.

- You can reclip a viewport without needing to delete the old clip boundary first.

- You can also change the shape of a polygonal viewport (without clipping) by using grips to stretch the vertices to new locations.

8.3 Layer Overrides in Viewports

When you are working in viewports, you might want to modify the layers that display in the various viewports, as shown in Figure 8–12. You can modify layers per viewport and change their color, linetype, lineweight, and plot style using *Layer Properties Manager*. To create the viewport specific changes, you need to be working in a layout tab.

Figure 8–12

Overriding Layer Properties in Viewports

You can use *Layer Properties Manager* to change layer properties (such as color, linetype, and lineweight) in a single viewport without the change being made in other viewports. The changes only affect the current viewport and not the model or other viewports, as shown in Figure 8–13.

Figure 8–13

- Viewport specific settings include **New VP Freeze**, **VP Freeze**, **VP Color**, **VP Linetype**, **VP Lineweight**, **VP Transparency**, and **VP Plot Style**. As the name specifies, the **VP Freeze** can be used to freeze/thaw a layer in only one viewport. Similarly, **VP Color** enables you to change the color of a layer in a single (current) viewport. The **New VP Freeze** tool can be used to freeze/thaw a layer in any subsequent viewport that you might create and does not affect the current viewport.

- To create these changes, you must be in a layout tab and working through a viewport.

How To: Modify Layer Properties in a Viewport

1. In a layout tab, double-click in a viewport to enter Model Space.

2. Open *Layer Properties Manager* and modify the viewport properties as required. Their icon changes to and the changes are highlighted as they are modified, making it easy to see the changes (the (Toggle Override Highlight) should be toggled on), as shown in Figure 8–14.

    *   You might need to extend *Layer Properties Manager* to display all the columns.

Figure 8–14

3. These changes are immediately and automatically reflected in the viewport.

    *   The layers also highlight in the Layer Control in the *Layers* panel as shown in Figure 8–15.

Figure 8–15

- The *Viewport Overrides* layer filter is automatically created when you use viewport overrides. Selecting **Viewport Overrides** displays only those layers that contain viewport overrides, as shown in Figure 8–16.

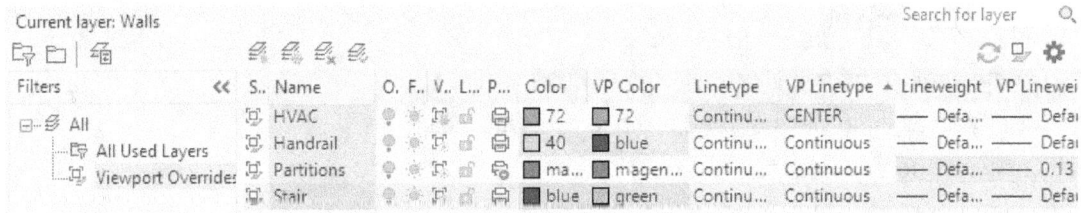

Figure 8–16

Freezing Layers in Viewports

The **VP Freeze** tool is also available in the *Layer Control* for easily freezing a layer in a viewport.

In the *Layer Control*, use ⌁ (Freeze or Thaw in current viewport) to freeze/thaw a layer in only one viewport.

> **Note:** *If you freeze a layer or toggle it off using the standard tools, it becomes hidden in all of the viewports.*

How To: Freeze a Layer in a Viewport

1. Make the viewport active in which you want to freeze the layer.

2. In the *Layer Control*, click ⌁ (Freeze or thaw in current viewport) so that it displays ⌁ for the required layer.

3. Repeat for any other layers that you want to freeze in the current viewport.If you use this tool when you are in a layout but not in a viewport, it freezes a layer in the layout without affecting other layouts. It does not affect the layer display in any viewports when used this way.

Practice 8a
Viewports and Named Views

Practice Objectives

- Create and use named views.
- Modify an existing viewport and remove a viewport clip.
- Apply viewport overrides.

In this practice, you will create and use named views using *Viewport Manager* and the **Viewports** command. You will set up multiple viewports based on named views. You will remove a viewport clip using the **Clip** command. You will also freeze layers in individual viewports and apply layer overrides to the color settings for layers in a viewport.

Task 1: Create and use named views.

In this task, you will create and restore views in a drawing.

1. Open **Office-M.dwg** from your practice files folder.
2. Zoom in on the stairway in the upper right corner, as shown in Figure 8–17.

Figure 8–17

3. In the *View* tab>*Named Views* panel, click (View Manager). The *View Manager* dialog box opens.
4. Click **New...** to open the *New View / Shot Properties* dialog box.
5. In the *View name* field, type **Stairs** and select the **Save layer snapshot with view** option (*View Properties* tab in the details section, which might need to be expanded), if required.

6. Accept the other default settings and click **OK**. Click **OK** to close the *View Manager* dialog box.

7. Zoom extents to display the entire drawing. Toggle off the layer **HVAC**.

8. In the *View* tab>*Named Views* panel, click (New View).

9. In the *New View / Shot Properties* dialog box, type **Elevators** for the view name.

10. Verify that the **Save layer snapshot with view** option is selected.

11. In the *Boundary* area, click (Define view window). The drawing area displays with the prompt to specify the first corner point for window selection.

12. Without clicking anywhere, use **Zoom** and **Pan** to display the two elevators in your drawing window. Then click two corner points of a window to define the view, as shown in Figure 8–18, and press <Enter> to return to the dialog box.

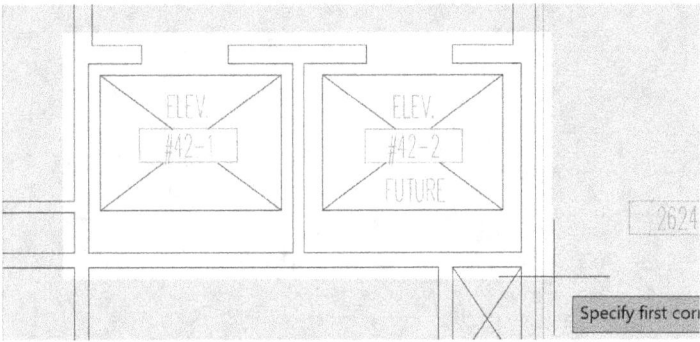

Figure 8–18

13. Click **OK** to close the *New View / Shot Properties* dialog box.

14. In the *View* tab>*Named Views* panel, use the *View* list (where it displays *Unsaved View*) to select the view **Stairs**, as shown in Figure 8–19. The drawing zooms in to the stairs area. Zoom out and note that the **HVAC** layer is toggled on (green HVAC components display).

Figure 8–19

15. In the *View* list, select the view **Elevators**. You are zoomed in to the elevators area. Zoom out and note that the layer **HVAC** is toggled off.

Task 2: Create multiple viewports from named views.

In this task, you will create multiple viewports based on named views using the *Viewports* dialog box, as shown in Figure 8-20.

Figure 8-20

1. Switch to the **A-401 Detail Plans** layout and set the current layer to **Viewports**.

2. In the *Layout* tab>*Layout Viewports* panel, click ↘ (arrow). In the *Viewports* dialog box, verify that you are in the *New Viewports* tab. In the *Standard viewports* area, select **Three: Left**, and set the *Viewport Spacing* to **10** (distances in this drawing are in millimeters).

3. In the *Preview* area, click in the top right viewport. In the *Change view to* drop-down list, select **Stairs**. Click in the bottom right viewport and change the view to **Elevators**, as shown in Figure 8−21. Click **OK** to close the *Viewports* dialog box.

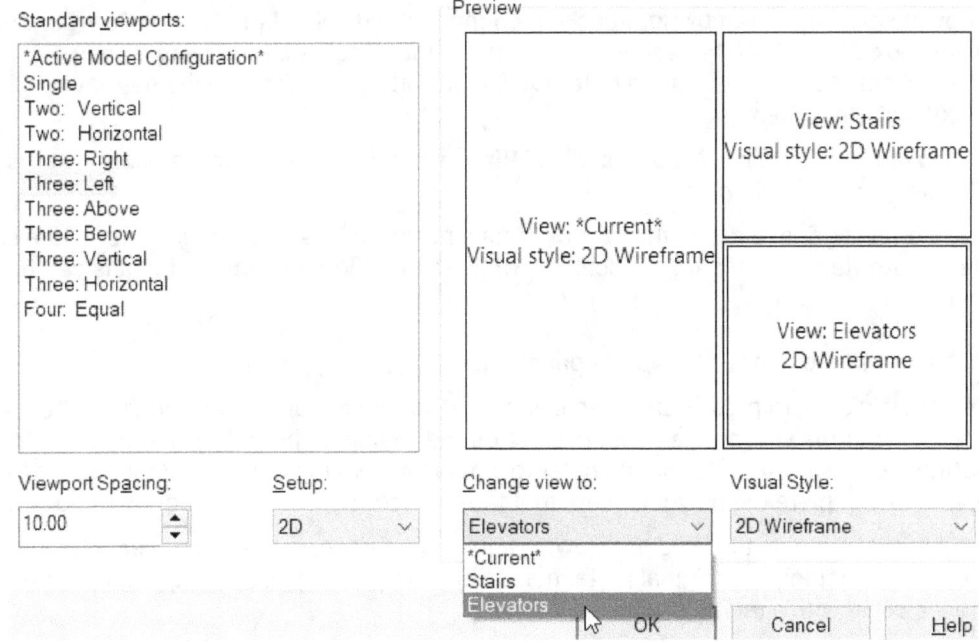

Figure 8−21

4. Select two corners to place the three viewports near the center of the layout, as shown in Figure 8−20.

5. Activate the top right viewport. In the *Status Bar*, change the scale to **1:20**. Use **Pan** to display the stairs fully inside the viewport, as shown in Figure 8−20. Use viewport grips to make the viewport wider to accommodate the stairs completely. Verify that the scale is still **1:20** and lock the viewport.

6. Similarly set the scale of the Elevators viewport to **1:20**. Use **Pan** and viewport grips to center the elevators and match the width of the Stairs viewport, as shown in Figure 8−20. Verify that the scale is still **1:20** and lock the viewport.

7. Activate the viewport on the left and change the scale to **1:30.** Pan to display the restrooms and locate them closer to the right edge of the viewport. Use viewport grips to make the viewport narrower to only display the restrooms, as shown in Figure 8−20. Verify that the scale is still **1:30** and lock the viewport.

8. Using viewport grips, move the three viewports as required to center them better in the layout, as shown in Figure 8−20.

Task 3: Clip a viewport.

In this task, you will clip an existing viewport using the **Polygonal** option.

1. Copy the existing layout by right-clicking on the tab and selecting **Move or Copy**. In the dialog box, select **A-401 Detail Plans** and select the checkbox for **Create a copy**. Click **OK**. The copy of the layout is placed before **A-401 Detail Plans.** Rename the new layout as **A-201 1st Floor Plan**.

2. If required, switch to the **A-201 1st Floor Plan** layout. Delete the two viewports (**Stairs** and **Elevators**) on the right side.

3. Use viewport grips to resize the narrow remaining viewport so that it fills most of the sheet. Unlock the viewport and set the scale at **1:50**. Pan the floor plan such that it is centered in the viewport.

4. In the *Layout* tab>*Layout Viewports* panel, click ⌐ (Clip).

5. Select the viewport, press <Enter> to select the **Polygonal** option. Starting from the lower left corner of the viewport, select points to define a clipping boundary that cuts out the bottom right portion of the view, similar to what is shown in Figure 8–22. Select the **Close** option to complete the polygon. Note that the right corner of the viewport is removed.

6. Double-click outside the irregular viewport. In Paper Space, in the cleared area that was created by clipping the original rectangular viewport (i.e., the bottom-right corner area), draw a circle with a *radius* of **150**.

7. In the *Layout* tab>*Layout Viewports* panel, expand ⌐ (Viewports flyout) and click

    ⌐ (Viewports, Object) and select the circle. Double-click inside the circular viewport and set its viewport scale to **1:30**. Pan to display any one room of the plan, similar to what is shown in Figure 8−22.

Figure 8−22

Task 4: Remove viewport clip and apply viewport overrides.

In this task, you will remove a viewport clip, freeze layers in individual viewports, and apply layer overrides to the color settings for layers in a viewport, as shown in Figure 8–23.

Figure 8–23

1. Copy the **A-201 1st Floor Plan** layout and rename it as **H-201 1st HVAC Floor Plan**.
2. Switch to the **H-201 1st HVAC Floor Plan** layout, if required.
3. Delete the circular viewport.
4. Select the large irregular viewport boundary. If a *Selection* dialog box displays, select **Polyline**. In the *Layout* tab>*Layout Viewports* panel, click ⌐⌐ (Clip).

5. At the *Select clipping object* prompt, press <Down Arrow> and select the **Delete** option (as shown in Figure 8–24) to remove the clipping boundary. Note that it becomes a rectangular area again.

Figure 8–24

6. Double-click inside the rectangular viewport. Open *Layer Properties Manager* and for layer **HVAC**, toggle the (VP Freeze) option, as shown in Figure 8–25. Note that the HVAC components do not display in this viewport only.

7. Change the *VP Color* for the layer **Stair** to **Green** (as shown in Figure 8–25) and note that the stairs become green in this viewport only. Note that the regular layer color is still blue.

Figure 8–25

8. Switch to the **A-201 1st Floor Plan** layout. It should display differently from the **H-201 1st HVAC Floor Plan** layout. The objects on the **HVAC** layer should be visible and the stairs should be blue.

9. Save and close the drawing.

End of practice

8.4 Annotative Scale Features

The Annotation Scale is connected to the Viewport Scale. Therefore, annotative objects, such as dimensions and text, display in viewports that have the same scale. You can add Annotation Scales to objects, enabling them to display in viewports of different scales. This ensures that all of the relevant information always displays at the correct scale and in the required viewports. For example, for the drawing shown in Figure 8–26, you might want the room names to display in each view, and to display different dimensions for each view.

Figure 8–26

- When you change a Viewport Scale, the annotation objects displayed in the viewport change as well. The display of objects depends on what the annotation visibility is set to and whether or not the scale is automatically added to the object.

 Annotation Visibility (Show annotation objects - At current scale): When toggled **Off**, only annotative objects with the current scale display. It is recommended that you use this option most of the time. It is what is plotted.

 Annotation Visibility (Show annotation objects - Always): When toggled **On**, annotative objects for all of the scales display. Use when you need to add or remove an annotative object to the current scale.

 Add scales to annotative objects when the annotation scale changes: When toggled **Off**, annotation scales are not automatically added to objects in the viewport.

 Add scales to annotative objects when the annotation scale changes: When **On**, annotation objects in the drawing update to match the new annotation scale.

- When you add a scale to an object, a scale representation is created. When you select an annotative object that has more than one scale, all of its scale representations display, as shown in Figure 8–27. There is no limit to the number of scales that can be added to an object, but too many scales can be confusing when you try to grip edit the object.

Figure 8–27

- If you modify the information contained in the annotation, it updates in all of the scale representations.

- You can grip edit each scale representation separately in its associated viewport so that it fits the location.

Modifying Annotative Object Scales

When you add annotative objects to a viewport, they automatically use the scale of the viewport. If you need to change the scale or move annotative objects out of a viewport, you can modify the scales associated with the objects or with the viewport.

- These tools are available in the *Annotate* tab>*Annotation Scaling* panel, or when you right-click on an annotative object, as shown in Figure 8–28.

Figure 8–28

- To display an annotative object in several viewports that use different scales, right-click on

    an annotative object, select **Add/Delete Scales** or click (Add/delete Scale), and then select an annotative object. This opens the *Annotation Object Scale* dialog box (shown in Figure 8–29), where you can click **Add** to set the other annotative scales that are used in each viewport.

Figure 8–29

- You can change the locations of individual scale representations, but you might need to

    have them all return to one position. In the *Annotation Scaling* panel, click (Sync Scale Positions) to move all of the related representations to the same location as the selected item.

- If you do not want an annotative object to display in the current viewport, but do want it to be

    visible in a viewport at a different scale, click (Delete) to delete the current scale.

Practice 8b
Annotative Scale Features

Practice Objectives

- Create annotative styles and annotative hatching.
- Control the visibility of annotation objects.

In this practice, you will specify annotative styles for text, dimensions, and multileaders. You will create annotative hatching using the Hatch command. You will then create viewports at different scales and add annotative objects to them, as shown in Figure 8–30.

Figure 8–30

Task 1: Define annotative text and dimensions.

1. Open **Service-A.dwg** from your practice files folder.

2. In the *Annotate* tab, set the *Dimension style* to **Architectural** (an annotative style), as shown in Figure 8–31.

3. Set the *Text style* to **Hand** (an annotative style), as shown in Figure 8–31.

4. Set the *Multileader style* to **Annotative**, as shown in Figure 8–31.

Figure 8–31

5. Switch to the *D-Sized* layout tab, which contains four viewports.

6. Select each viewport in Paper Space by clicking on the viewport border. Confirm the Annotation Scales:

   - *Service*: **1/4"=1'-0"**
   - *Vestibule*: **3/8"=1'-0"**
   - *Bathroom*: **1/2"=1'-0"**
   - *Stairs*: **3/4"=1'-0"**

7. Click 🔒 (Lock/Unlock Viewport) to lock the Viewport Scales for each viewport.

8. Set the layer **Dimensions** to be current. Double-click inside the viewport that displays the Service area and add the dimensions and text shown in Figure 8–32. They only display in the current viewport.

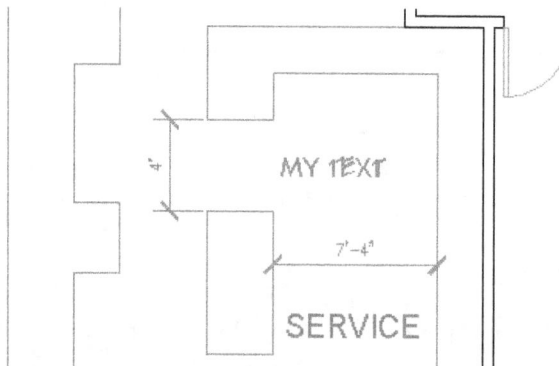

Figure 8–32

Task 2: Define the annotative hatching.

1. Continuing in the Service viewport, set the layer **Hatching** to be current.

2. Start the **Hatch** command.

3. In the *Hatch Creation* contextual tab>*Options* panel, click ▲ (Annotative).

4. Set the *Hatch Pattern* to **ANSI 31** and the *Hatch Pattern Scale* to **1**. Add hatching to the three counter areas inside the Service area viewport.

5. Close the *Hatch Creation*. In the *Vestibule* viewport, note that the portion of the counter area in the upper-right corner does not display any hatch. In the *Stairs* viewport, note that the portion of the counter area, near the upper horizontal viewport boundary, does not display any hatch. The hatching displays in the current viewport only.

Task 3: Add annotative scales.

1. Select the hatch object that you just created.

2. Right-click on the selected hatching and select **Annotative Object Scale>Add/Delete Scales**. The *Annotation Object Scale* dialog box opens. Only the current Annotation Scale displays, which is **1/4"=1'-0"**.

3. Click **Add...** to add the other scales. The *Add Scales to Object* dialog box opens.

4. Select the *scales* **3/8"=1'-0"** and **1/2"=1"-0"**. Doing so will enable the annotative hatch object to display in the Vestibule viewport and the Stairs viewport.

5. Click **OK**. The scales display in the *Annotation Object Scale* dialog box.

6. Click **OK**. Note that the annotation objects (hatches) now display in the Vestibule and Stairs viewports.

Task 4: Change the annotation object display.

1. Switch to the *Model* tab and note how the annotative objects (text, dimensions, hatch) display.

2. Click ▲ (Show annotation objects - At current scale) to toggle it off. Note that the annotative objects no longer display.

3. Save and close the drawing.

End of practice

Chapter Review Questions

1. What is the purpose of *View Manager*?
    a. To create layouts using different areas of a drawing.
    b. To create a new block using selected objects.
    c. To create a new drawing file using selected objects.
    d. To store areas of a drawing under specified names.

2. It is possible to create a single or multiple named view viewports at the same time.
    a. True
    b. False

3. What does the ⧈ (Clip) command do?
    a. Fillets the corners of an existing viewport to make it circular.
    b. Removes the portions of a viewport that are not required.
    c. Joins multiple viewports to create a single one.
    d. Breaks a viewport to create multiple viewports.

4. How can you change the color of a layer in a single (current) viewport?
    a. In *Layer Properties Manager*, change the *VP Color* property.
    b. In *Layer Properties Manager*, change the *New VP Freeze* property.
    c. In the viewport, switch to Model Space and change the color of the layer.
    d. Create a new layer and move the objects to the new layer.

5. If you want to display an annotative object in several viewports that use different scales, what should you do?
    a. Create separate layers for each viewport and put the objects on each layer.
    b. Create annotative styles (dimension, text, etc.) for each viewport.
    c. Use **Add/Delete Scales** to add the scales for each viewport.
    d. Lock each viewport.

Command Summary

Button	Command	Location
	Add/Delete Scales	• **Ribbon:** *Annotation* tab>*Annotation Scaling* panel • Right-click menu
	Add Annotation Scales Automatically	• Status Bar
	Annotation Visibility	• Status Bar
	Clip	• **Ribbon:** *Layout* tab>*Layout Viewports* panel • **Command Prompt:** vpclip
	Named (Paper Space)	• **Ribbon:** *Layout* tab>*Layout Viewports* panel • **Command Prompt:** viewports or vports
	Named (Model Space)	• **Ribbon:** *View* tab>*Model Viewports* panel • **Command Prompt:** viewports or vports
	New View	• **Ribbon:** *View* tab>*Named Views* panel
	Sync Scle Positions	• **Ribbon:** *Annotation* tab>*Annotation Scaling* panel • Right-click menu
	View Manager	• **Ribbon:** *View* tab>*Named Views* panel • **Command Prompt:** view or V
	Viewport Configuration Control	• **Ribbon:** *View* tab>*Model Viewports* panel

Annotation Styles

You will learn how to create various annotation styles which includes text styles, dimension styles, and multileader styles.

Learning Objectives

- Create and modify text, dimension, and multileader styles.
- Create sub-styles of existing dimension styles.

9.1 Creating Text Styles

When you add text to your drawing, it uses the properties (e.g., height, font, etc.) of the current *text style,* as shown in Figure 9–1. Text styles should be created in the template file so that everyone on the same project uses the same styles. You can create a new style by assigning the height, width, and slant to a text font, or to a typeface design.

Figure 9–1

- There are two default styles: **Standard** and **Annotative**. You can create other styles as required.

- A variety of font files are available for creating different styles of text. There are two different types of fonts: Truetype fonts (used by most Microsoft Windows software) and AutoCAD® shape fonts. You can use the fonts that the AutoCAD software installs or the other Truetype fonts that were installed with Windows.

How To: Create a Text Style

1. In the *Annotate* tab>*Text* panel>*Text Style* list, select **Manage Text Styles...**.

   - You can also open the dialog box by clicking ⬃ (Panel Arrow) in the *Annotate* tab>*Text* panel.

   - You can also open the dialog box by clicking A⁄ (Text Style) in the *Home* tab>expanded *Annotation* panel.

2. In the *Text Style* dialog box (shown in Figure 9–2), click **New....** The new style takes on the attributes of the current text style.

Figure 9–2

3. In the *New Text Style* dialog box, type a new name and click **OK**.

4. Expand the *Font Name* drop-down list, select a font (a preview of the font displays in the *Preview* area). For some fonts, you can also specify a *Font Style* (such as bold or italic).

5. Select the **Annotative** option if you want the text style to scale per viewport. You can also set a default height for the style, but this is typically left at **0** so that you can use one style for different sizes of text.

6. In the *Effects* area, set up the required properties.

7. Click **Apply** to continue working in the dialog box or **Close** to close the dialog box. The style that was created is now the current style.

• You can change the current style in the Text Style Control in the *Home* tab>expanded *Annotation* panel, the *Annotate* tab>*Text* panel, or the *Text Editor* contextual tab>*Style* panel when you have started the **Multiline Text** command.

• You can change the style of existing text by selecting the text object and then selecting a style in the *Home* tab>*Annotation* panel or *Annotate* tab>*Text* panel.

• If you modify an annotative style, you need to use **annoupdate** to update any existing objects to match the revised annotative style.

Style Effects

The style effects make a text style different from a standard font. You can define several text styles that use the same font but differ in width, oblique angle, etc.

Width Factor	Defines the character width relative to the height. A width factor of **1** is the default. Numbers greater than one increase the width and numbers less than one decrease the width. Typical width factors are in the range of 0.8 to 1.5.
Oblique Angle	Enables you to slant the lettering. Positive values incline the top of the text to the right and negative values slant it to the left. Typical obliquing angles range from +10 to -10. Angles of +30 and -30 are commonly used to label isometric drawings.

- Text is normally placed horizontally in a drawing. Vertical, upside-down, or backward text orientation can also be defined when creating text styles.

Notes on Text Styles

- The *Preview* displays an image of how your text style is going to be displayed when used in the drawing. All of the effects of a text style are previewed except the height.

- To rename a text style, double-click on the style name. In the edit box, type the new name.

- To delete a text style, highlight it in the list and click **Delete**. It is only deleted if it is not in use.

- Some TrueType fonts can be filled or outlined. To have them filled in your drawing, you need to set the **textfill** system variable to **ON** (textfill = 1).

- **Match Properties** (in the *Home* tab>*Properties* panel) enables you to copy the style from one text object to another in your drawing. It is also available in the *Text Editor* contextual tab.

Practice 9a
Create and Use Text Styles

Practice Objective

- Create several new text styles.

In this practice, you will define several new text styles using the **Text Style** command, as shown in Figure 9–3. The color of the text in Figure 9–3 has been changed to black for printing clarity.

The Standard Style | Hand lettering Style
Title Text Style | Dimensions Style

Figure 9–3

1. Open **AEC-Facilities1-A.dwg** from your practice files folder. It is a blank file.

2. Make the layer **Notes** current. In the *Annotate* tab>*Text* panel, note that the active text style is **Standard**.

3. Switch to one of the layouts. Start the **Multiline Text** command. Note that the preview text (abc) is not currently visible with the cursor. Zoom in until it displays. Place the text **The Standard Style** anywhere in the drawing.

4. In the *Annotate* tab>*Text* panel, in the *Text Style* list, select **Manage Text Styles**, or click

   ↘ (Panel Arrow) in the *Annotate* tab>*Text* panel to open the *Text Style* dialog box. Modify the **Standard** text style by changing the *Font Name* to **romans**. Click **Apply** and **Close**. Note how the text you just entered has updated.

5. Open the *Text Style* dialog box again and click **New**.

6. Create a new style named **Title2**. Set the *Font Name* to **Arial**, the *Font Style* to **Bold**, and the *Width Factor* to **1.5**. Click **Apply** to save the changes.

7. Create another new text style named **Hand2**. For the *Font Name*, select **CityBlueprint**. Set the *Width Factor* to **1.5**. Click **Apply** to save the changes.

8. Create another new text style named **Dimensions**. For the *Font Name*, select **romans**. Set the *Width Factor* to **0.8**. Click **Apply** to save the changes and click **Close**.

9. Make each style current and then add text to the drawing using a text string to test the styles.

10. Set the current style to **Hand**. Erase all of the text and save the drawing.

End of practice

9.2 Creating Dimension Styles

The dimension style controls all aspects of how your dimensions display (type and size of arrows, type of units displayed, text specifications, text placement, etc.). You might need to have several styles in a drawing to display different information, as shown in Figure 9–4. For example, in mechanical drawings you might have one style with decimal units that displays two decimal places of precision, another that displays three decimal places, and a third that displays both English and Metric units at the same time.

Figure 9–4

- You can set the current dimension style in the Dimension Style Control in the *Home* tab>*Annotation* panel or *Annotate* tab>*Dimensions* panel.

- There are two default styles: **Standard** and **Annotative**. You can create other styles as required.

How To: Create a Dimension Style

1. In the *Annotate* tab>*Dimensions* panel>*Dimension Style* list, select **Manage Dimension Styles...**.

   - You can also open the dialog box by clicking ⬊ (Panel Arrow) in the *Annotate* tab>*Dimensions* panel.

   - You can also open the dialog box by clicking ⊢⫞⊣ (Dimension Style) in the *Home* tab>expanded *Annotation* panel.

2. Click **New...** in *Dimension Style Manager,* as shown in Figure 9-5.

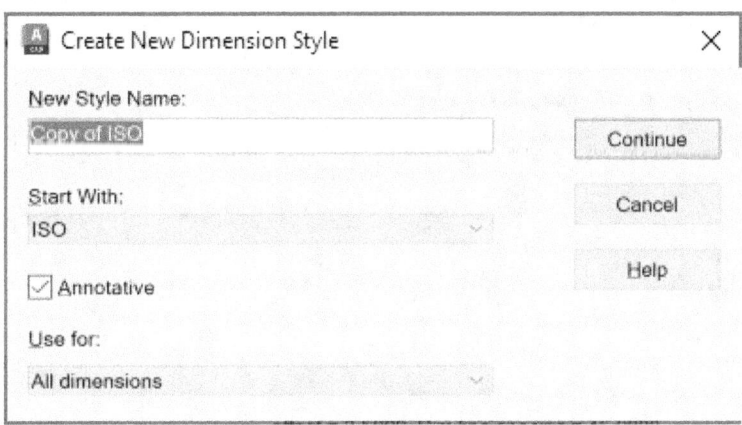

Figure 9-5

3. The *Create New Dimension Style* dialog box opens, as shown in Figure 9-6. In the *Start With* drop-down list, select a style to use as a template. In the *New Style Name* field, type a new style name and then select the **Annotative** option as required. Click **Continue**.

Figure 9-6

4. Modify the tabs as required and click **OK**.

5. If you want to make the new style current, double-click on its name in the *Styles* area or select it and click **Set Current**.

6. Click **Close**.

- All of the distances and sizes specified for the dimension style should be at their final plotted distance or size.

Modifying Dimension Styles

In *Dimension Style Manager,* click **Modify** to open the *Modify Dimension Style* dialog box.

Dimension Style Lines Tab

The *Lines* tab controls the appearance of the dimension lines and extension lines, as shown in Figure 9–7.

Figure 9–7

- *Color* and *Lineweight* are set to **ByBlock** by default. This is essentially the same as **ByLayer**. The dimension elements use the color and linetype of the current layer.

- *Extend beyond ticks* only applies if ticks are used rather than arrowheads.

- *Baseline spacing* is used for baseline dimensions that are applied with the **Baseline** or **Quick Dimension** commands.

- *Offset from origin* controls the size of the gap between the object and the start of the extension line.

- *Fixed length extension lines* controls how far the line reaches from the dimension line toward the dimensioned object.

Dimension Style Symbols and Arrows Tab

The *Symbols and Arrows* tab controls the size and style of the arrowheads on the dimension lines and leaders, and other symbols, such as Center marks (for circles and arcs) or the Arc length symbol, as shown in Figure 9–8.

Figure 9–8

- The *Leader* can have a different arrow style from the dimension lines.

- *Center marks* are used with Radius and Diameter dimensions and the **Center Mark** command.

Dimension Style Text Tab

The *Text* tab controls the placement and appearance of the dimension text, as shown in Figure 9–9.

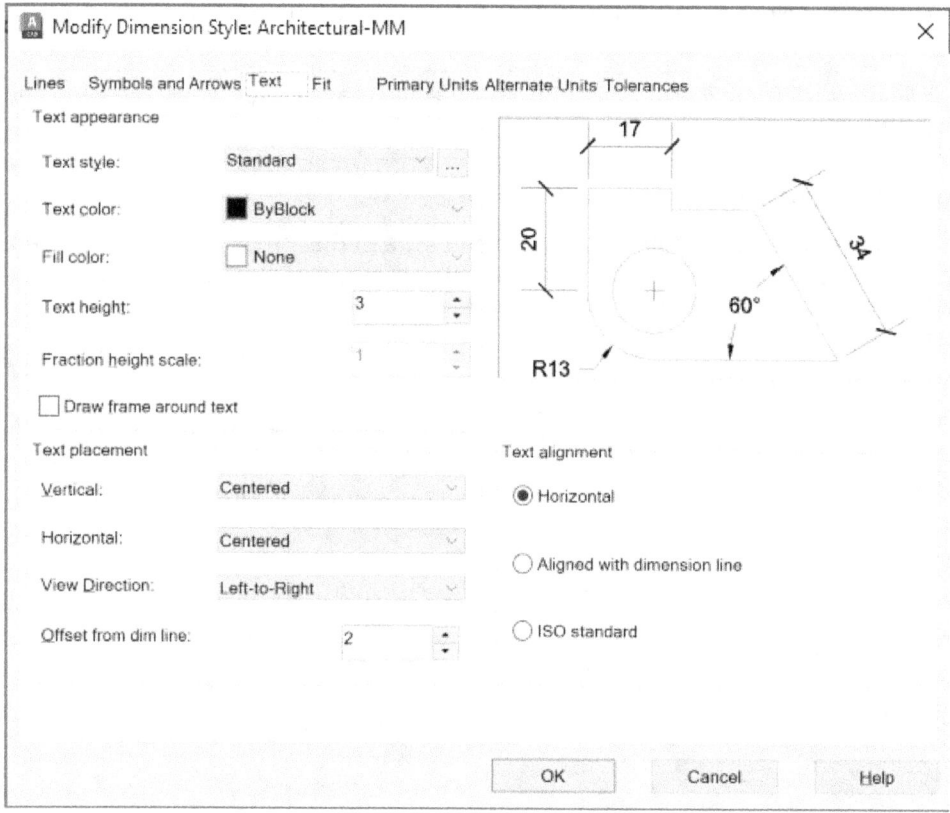

Figure 9–9

- You can specify a text style in the *Text style* drop-down list. If you have not defined one, you can click ⊡ (Browse) to open the *Text Style* dialog box to create a new style. The text height should be set to the required plotted height.

- Do not set a height in text styles to be used for dimensioning. Use the dimension style to control the height.

- If you want the text to plot at a heavier weight than the rest of the dimensions (a standard drafting technique), set the text color to be a color that plots to a medium weight and leave the rest of the dimension elements with the *Text color* set to **ByBlock**. You can set the layer **Dimensions** to be a lightweight color.

- The *Fill* color can be set to **Background** or another color so that the text masks any objects behind it.

- In the *Text placement* area, you can set the text placement to **Vertical** and **Horizontal** dimensions.

- *Offset from dim line* controls the size of the gap between the text and dimension lines. This applies when the text is centered on the line and above the line.

- *View Direction* displays the dimension text **Left-to-Right** or **Right-to-Left**.

Dimension Style Fit Tab

The *Fit* tab controls the positions of arrows, text, leader lines, and the dimension line, as shown in Figure 9–10. It also controls the scale for dimension features.

Figure 9–10

- When you set the *Scale for dimension features* to **Annotative**, the other options are grayed out. The dimensions are scaled according to the scale of the viewport through which they are inserted.

- If you are not using Annotative dimensions, you can use **Scale dimensions to layout** to display the objects in all viewports. You can also select **Use overall scale of** to dimension directly on the model when you are plotting from Model Space.

Dimension Style Primary Units Tab

The *Primary Units* tab controls the format of the primary units in the dimension text, as shown in Figure 9–11. This is independent of the type of units that are used in the drawing.

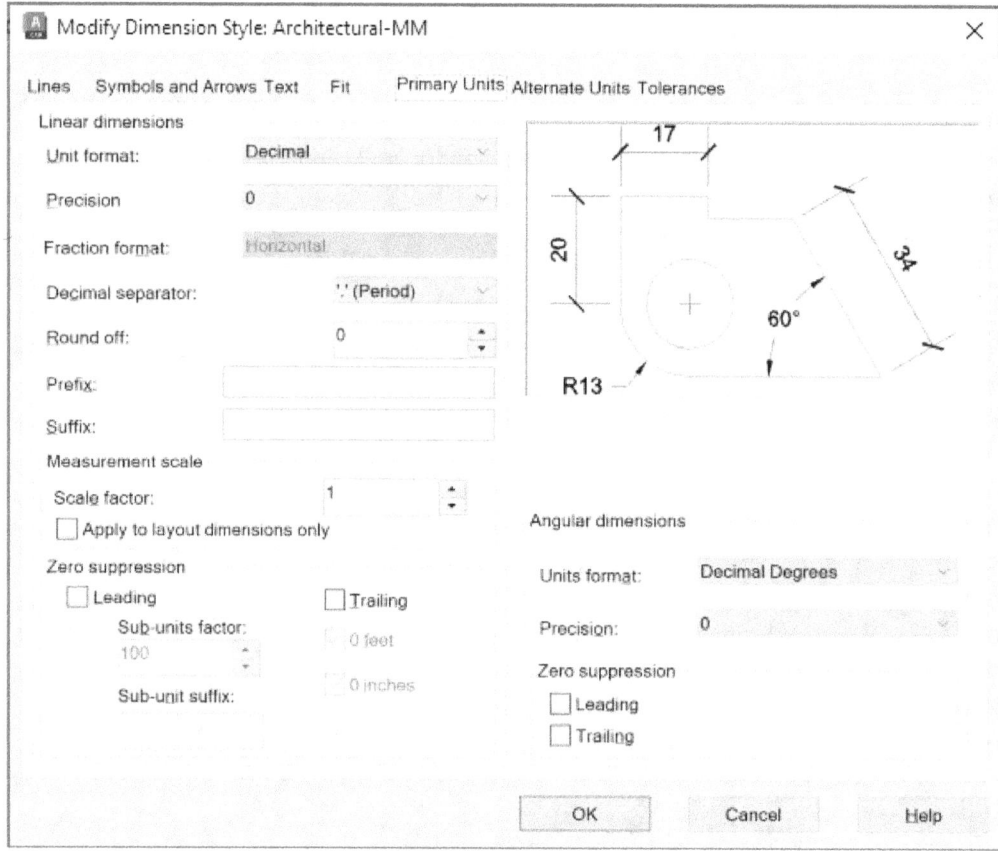

Figure 9–11

- You can set the required type of units for dimensioning, the number of decimal places, and other information to define the appearance of the text.

- A default *Prefix* and *Suffix* can be added in front or after all of the dimension values (for example, a suffix of mm for millimeters).

- The *Scale factor* multiplies the actual dimension value. For example, if the actual distance is 5 and the scale factor is 2, the value that displays in the dimension text is 10. If objects are drawn at full size, the scale should normally be set to 1.

- The *Sub-units factor* eliminates the leading zeros in dimension values by specifying that any measurement less than one primary unit be dimensioned in a smaller unit of measure. The *Sub-unit suffix* automatically appends a different dimension suffix to such dimensions.

Dimension Style Alternate Units Tab

The *Alternate Units* tab is very similar to the *Primary Units* tab.

- *Multiplier for alt units* is the conversion factor between the units in which your drawing was created and the units you want to use for alternative dimensions. For example, if the Primary Units are decimal inches and the Alternate Units are millimeters, *Multiplier for alt units* should be **25.4** (1 inch = 25.4mm).

Dimension Style Tolerances Tab

The *Tolerances* tab is usually used in mechanical design to indicate the degree of precision required in manufacturing.

- *Method* determines how the tolerance is calculated and displayed. The options are **None**, **Symmetrical** (equal bilateral), **Deviation** (unequal bilateral), **Limits**, and **Basic** (places a box around the dimension and is used with Geometric Dimensioning & Tolerancing).

Creating Dimension Sub-Styles

You might need to use a slightly different style for a specific type of dimension. For example, you might want linear dimensions to use tick marks instead of arrows and to always be forced above the dimension line. You can create a style that uses arrows, and then create a sub-style that is only used for linear dimensions, as shown in Figure 9–12. When using that style, all of the dimensions that you place have arrows, except for the linear dimensions.

Figure 9–12

How To: Set Up a Dimension Sub-Style

1. Open *Dimension Style Manager*.

2. Click **New...**.

3. In the *Create New Dimension Style* dialog box, in the *Start With* drop-down list, select the style to use as a template.

4. In the *Use for* drop-down list, select a dimension type for the sub-style (linear, angular, etc.) that you are creating, as shown in Figure 9–13.

Figure 9–13

5. Click **Continue**.

6. In the *New Dimension Style* dialog box, define the sub-style as required with settings for lines, arrows, text, fit, etc.

7. When all of the settings have been adjusted, click **OK**. The new sub-style is listed in *Dimension Style Manager* under the main style.

💡 Hint: Modifying a Single Dimension

Select a dimension and use the *Properties* palette to modify the style of a single dimension without changing the style definition. In the *Properties* palette, all of the dimension style settings are listed. Each setting can be changed for the selected dimension.

Practice 9b
Create Dimension Styles (Architectural)

Practice Objectives

- Change the dimension style of various dimensions.
- Create a new dimension style and a related sub-style.

In this practice, you will test existing dimension styles and change them as required. You will also create a new dimension style with a related sub-style, as shown in Figure 9–14.

Figure 9–14

Task 1: Test the existing dimension styles.

1. Open **AEC-Facilities2-A.dwg** from your practice files folder. It is a blank drawing.

2. Switch to the **Model** layout.

3. Change the current layer to **Walls** and draw a **50'-0" x 25'-0"** rectangle with a **10' radius** circle at its center.

4. Switch to the **A-Sized Landscape** layout.

5. Double-click in the viewport to activate it. Pan in the viewport to display the rectangle and the circle. Set the *Viewport Scale* to **1/8"=1'-0"**. (You can pan the drawing to place it centrally). Lock it.

6. Set the current layer to **Dimensions**. Using the **Standard** dimension style, add a linear dimension for the top length (horizontal) line and a radial dimension for the circle. The dimension text and arrows are not displayed because this dimension style is not annotative.

---

7. Using the *Properties* palette for each of the dimensions, change the *Dim style* to **Annotative**. The dimension information is now available, but it is not designed to work with architectural dimensions.

   • Use grips to move the dimensions to the required location, as shown in Figure 9-14.

Task 2: Create a new dimension style.

1. In the *Annotate* tab>*Dimensions* panel, expand the *Dimension Styles* list and select **Manage Dimension Styles**, or click ⬎ (Panel Arrow) to open *Dimension Style Manager*. Click **New....**

2. In the *Create New Dimension Style* dialog box, set the *New Style Name* to **Architectural**. In the *Start With* drop-down list, select the **Standard** style to use as a template. Select **Annotative** (as shown in Figure 9–15) and click **Continue**.

Figure 9–15

3. In the *New Dimension Style* dialog box, set the following options and click **OK**:

Symbols & Arrows tab	*Arrowheads* area	First, Second, and Leader: **Right angle**
Text tab	*Text appearance* area	Text style: **Dimensions**
Fit tab	*Scale for dimension features* area	Annotative (checked)
Primary Units tab	*Linear dimensions* area	Unit format: **Architectural**

4. Select **Architectural** and click **Set Current** in the *Dimension Style Manager*. Click **Close**.

5. Using the new style, add linear dimensions for the left and bottom edges of the rectangle. Add radial dimensions to the circle and angular dimensions to the left corner of the rectangle. Note the differences from the dimensions in the previous style.

Task 3: Create a dimension sub-style.

1. In the *Dimension Styles* list, select **Manage Dimension Styles...**.
2. In *Dimension Style Manager,* select the new **Architectural** style and click **New...**.
3. Delete **Copy of Architectural** and leave the *New Style Name* blank.
4. In the *Use for* drop-down list, select **Linear dimensions** and click **Continue**.
5. Modify the options as follows:

Symbols & Arrows tab	*Arrowheads* area	First and Second: **Oblique**
Text tab	*Text alignment* area	Aligned with dimension line
Text tab	*Text placement* area	Vertical: **Above**

6. Click **OK** and **Close** to exit *Dimension Style Manager*. Note that the linear dimensions update to display the new format, as shown previously in Figure 9–14.
7. Erase all of the dimensions.
8. Double-click outside the viewport to return to Paper Space.
9. Save the drawing.

End of practice

Practice 9c
Dimension Styles (Mechanical)

Practice Objective

* Create dimension styles and apply them to dimensions.

In this practice, you will create two dimension styles and then apply dimensions with those styles, as shown in Figure 9–16 and Figure 9–17.

1. Open **Dim-I.dwg** from your practice files folder.

2. Create the two dimension styles (**Tolerance** and **English_Metric**) based on the settings listed in the tables. Start with the **Standard** style, make each style **Annotative**, and use the default settings for options that are not specified.

	Tolerance	English_Metric
Lines tab		
Baseline spacing	0.38	0.5
Symbols and Arrows tab		
Arrowheads	Right angle	Closed filled
Center marks	Line	Line
Text tab		
Text style	Standard	Standard
Text color	ByBlock	Magenta
Text height	0.18	0.125
Vertical Placement	Centered	Above
Horizontal Placement	Centered	Centered
Text alignment	Horizontal	Aligned with dimension line
Primary Units tab		
Unit format	Decimal	Architectural (Fraction format: Horizontal)
Precision	0.00	0'-0 1/16"

	Tolerance	English_Metric
Alternate Units tab		
Alternate units	None	Decimal, precision 0
		Multiplier 25.4
		Suffix mm
Tolerances tab		
Method	Limits	None
Upper value	0.02	
Lower value	0.03	
Scaling for height	0.75	

3. For **English_Metric**, create the **Angular dimensions** and **Diameter dimensions** sub-styles.

   - To create a sub-style, in *Dimension Style Manager*, select **English_Metric** and click **New**. In the *Use for* drop-down list, select **Angular dimensions**, and then set the options below. Repeat this for **Diameter dimensions**.

	Angular dimensions	Diameter dimensions
Text tab		
Vertical text placement	Centered	Centered
Text alignment	Horizontal	Horizontal

4. Use the new dimension styles to dimension the objects shown in Figure 9–16 and Figure 9–17.

- Set the layer **Dimensions** to be current.
- A layout is prepared for each style. The scale of the viewport in the **B-Sized Eng-Met** layout is 1:1 and the scale of the viewport in the **C-Sized Tol** layout is 2:1. Lock the viewports so that you do not change the scale by mistake.

Tolerance

Figure 9–16

English_Metric

Figure 9–17

End of practice

9.3 Creating Multileader Styles

Multileaders are used to point to objects in your drawing with text or symbols. Use *Multileader Style Manager* to create styles that control the display options for different multileaders. The styles can be annotative or a specified scale, and have different arrowheads, text styles, colors, linetypes, etc., as shown in Figure 9–18. You can create styles for specific uses and then use *Multileader Style Manager* to update them as required. This ensures accuracy throughout the drawing and makes it easy to modify multileaders.

Figure 9–18

How To: Create a Multileader Style

1. In the *Annotate* tab>*Leaders* panel>*Leader Style* list, select **Manage Multileader Styles...**. The *Multileader Style Manager* dialog box opens, as shown in Figure 9–19.

    *   You can also open the dialog box by clicking ⌄ (Panel Arrow) in the *Annotate* tab>*Leaders* panel.

    *   You can also open the dialog box by clicking ⌁ (Multileader Style) in the *Home* tab>expanded *Annotation* panel.

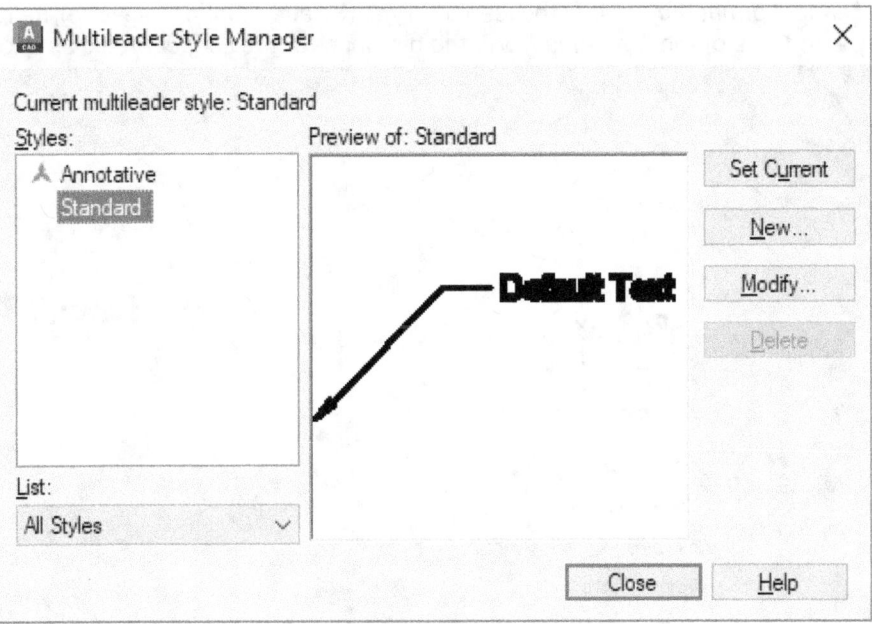

Figure 9–19

2. Click **New...**.

3. In the *Create New Multileader Style* dialog box, type a *New style name*, expand the *Start with* drop-down list and select a style, and select or clear the **Annotative** option, as shown in Figure 9–20.

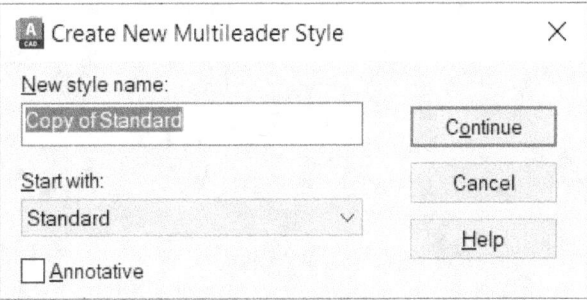

Figure 9–20

4. Click **Continue**. The *Modify Multileader Style* dialog box opens.

5. In the *Leader Format* tab, specify the leader's *Type* (**Straight**, **Spline**, or **None**), its formatting, the style and size of the *Arrowhead*, and the distance for the *Leader break*, as shown in Figure 9–21.

Figure 9–21

6. In the *Leader Structure* tab, specify how you want the leader to work, as shown in Figure 9-22. For example, the default leader style has the *Maximum leader points* set to **2** and *Landing Settings* toggled on. Select **Annotative** if you are using the annotative scaling tools.

- If you are creating a spline leader style, you might need to clear the **Constraints** and **Landing Settings** options.

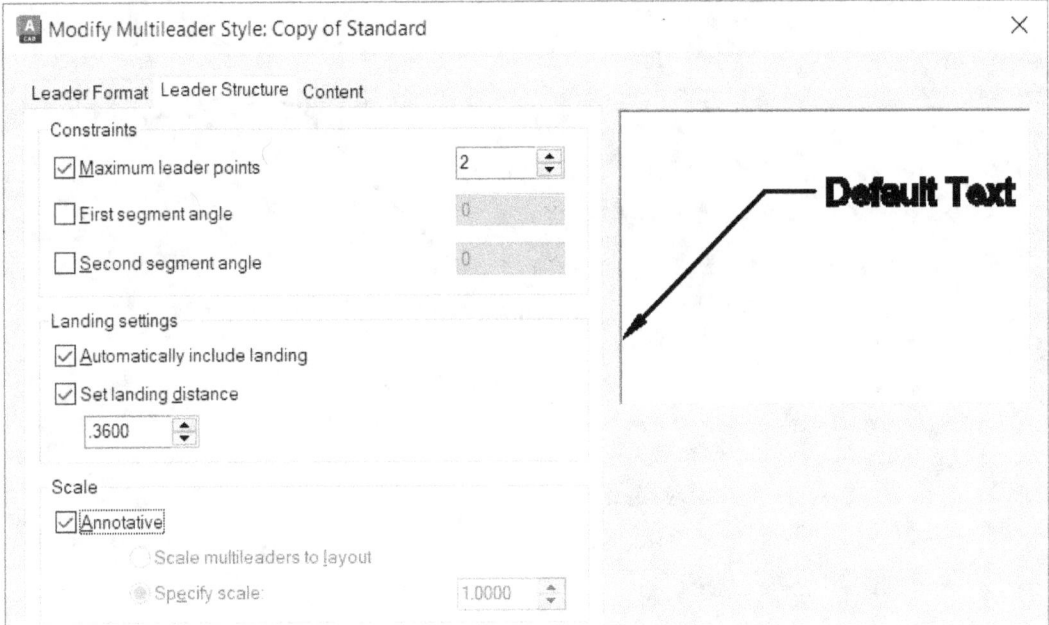

Figure 9-22

7. In the *Content* tab, you can specify whether you want the multileader content to be **Mtext**, **Block**, or **None**. Once you set the *Multileader type*, the rest of the options vary according to the selection. The **Mtext** option is shown in Figure 9–23.

- When you have selected text, you can set the attachment to be **Horizontal** or **Vertical**.

Figure 9–23

8. When you use the **Block** *Multileader type*, you can select from a variety of preset blocks with attributes or use your own custom blocks, as shown in Figure 9–24.

Figure 9–24

9. When you are satisfied with the style, click **OK**. In *Multileader Style Manager*, select the new style and click **Set Current**.

10. Click **Close**.

• If you need to make a change to a style, open *Multileader Style Manager*, select the style that you want to change, and click **Modify**.

• If you need to delete a style, open *Multileader Style Manager*, select a style, and click **Delete**.

• You can also create style overrides for the Leader, Content, and Workflow by selecting **Options** in the **Multileader** command.

Practice 9d
Create Multileader Styles

Practice Objective

- Create a multileader style.

In this practice, you will create a multileader style using a spline and a block, as shown in Figure 9–25.

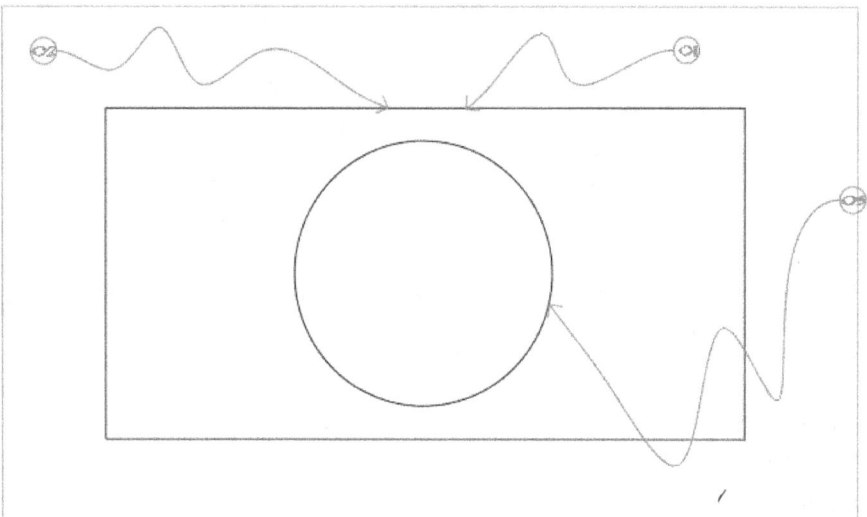

Figure 9–25

1. Open **AEC-Facilities3-A.dwg** from your practice files folder. Note that the drawing opens in the **A-Sized Landscape** layout.

2. In the *Annotate* tab>*Leaders* panel, click ⬎ .

3. In *Multileader Style Manager*, click **New...**.

4. In the *Create New Multileader Style* dialog box, name the new multileader **Keynote**. Start with the **Standard** style and make it **Annotative**. Click **Continue**. The *Modify Multileader Style* dialog box opens.

5. In the *Leader Format* tab, in the *General* area, set the *Type* to **Spline**. In the *Arrowhead* area, set the *Symbol* to **Right angle**.

6. In the *Leader Structure* tab, clear **Maximum leader points** (this enables you to make as many points on the spline as required).

7. In the *Content* tab, change the *Multileader type* to **Block**. In the *Block options* area, set the *Source block* to **Circle**. Click **OK**.

8. In *Multileader Style Manager*, select **Keynote** and click **Set Current**. Click **Close**.

9. Start the **Multileader** command to test the new multileader style by clicking several points to create a zig zag leader. Press <Enter> to stop selecting points along the spline.

10. In the *Edit Attributes* dialog box, enter a tag number (01, 02, 03, etc.) for the keynote. Click **OK**.

11. Erase the leaders, switch to Model Space, and save the drawing.

End of practice

Chapter Review Questions

1. If you change the font of a text style, what happens to existing text that uses that text style?

   a. The text is moved to a new layer.

   b. The text remains the same.

   c. The text is deleted.

   d. The text updates with the new font.

2. What are dimension sub-styles used for?

   a. To override the dimension style settings for a particular type of dimension, such as angle or radius.

   b. To automatically dimension specific objects, such as rectangles and circles.

   c. To link dimensions to specific layers.

   d. To copy dimension styles between drawings.

3. You have a dimension style that uses decimal units and you want to change it to use fractional units. What do you do?

   a. Modify the *Alternate Units* in the dimension style.

   b. Modify the *Primary Units* in the dimension style.

   c. Edit the text of the dimension and change the value.

   d. Edit the *Fit* settings in the dimension style.

4. While creating a multileader style, which of the following are available options for the *Type* of the leader? (Select all that apply.)

   a. Straight

   b. Curved

   c. Polyline

   d. Spline

5. You cannot use custom blocks with Multileader.

   a. True

   b. False

6. When creating a Text Style, Dimension Style, or Multileader Style, you want the size of the text and other objects to scale automatically according to the scale of the viewport in which they are used. In the related Style Manager, which of the following options would you set?

   a. Text Size

   b. Alternate Units

   c. Scale Text

   d. Annotative

Command Summary

Button	Command	Location
	Dimension Style	• **Ribbon:** *Home* tab>expanded *Annotation* panel or the Panel Arrow in the *Annotate* tab>*Dimensions* panel • **Command Prompt:** dimstyle
	Multileader Style	• **Ribbon:** *Home* tab>expanded *Annotation* panel or the Panel Arrow in the *Annotate* tab>*Leaders* panel • **Command Prompt:** mleaderstyle
	Text Style	• **Ribbon:** *Home* tab>expanded *Annotation* panel or *Annotate* tab>**Text** panel>*Text Styles* list>Manage Text Styles or the Panel Arrow in the *Annotate* tab>*Text* panel • **Command Prompt:** style or ST

Projects: Drawing Setup and Utilities

Practice projects are provided for you to gain additional hands-on experience in the topics and commands previously covered. These projects are intended to be self-guided and do not include step-by-step information.

Learning Objectives

- *Mechanical:* Create a template file that contains features such as layers, limits, and text. Additionally, create dimension and text styles to be used for electronic schematics and part designs.
- *Civil:* Create a template that contains features such as layers, limits, text, and multileader styles to be used for interior design and mapping projects.

10.1 Interiors Project

In this project, you will create a new template drawing for use with Interior Design projects. You will establish units, limits, layers, a text style, and a multileader style, as shown in Figure 10−1.

Figure 10−1

1. Start a new drawing based on **AEC-Imperial.dwt**, which is located in your practice files folder.

2. Verify that the units are **Architectural**. Set the *Limits* to **75',45'**.

3. Add the following new layers: **Existing**, **New**, and **Demo**.

4. Add a text style named **Room Names**.

5. Create a new multileader style named **Keynotes** using the **Circle** block and any type of leader, as shown in Figure 10−1.

6. Save the drawing as a template named **AEC-Interiors.dwt**. Ensure you save it as a DWT file and add a description as required.

7. Start a new drawing using your template and test some of the settings.

10.2 Mechanical/Schematic Project

In this project, you will create a new template drawing for use with electronic schematic diagrams. You will establish units, limits, layers, a text style, and a multileader style, as shown in Figure 10–2.

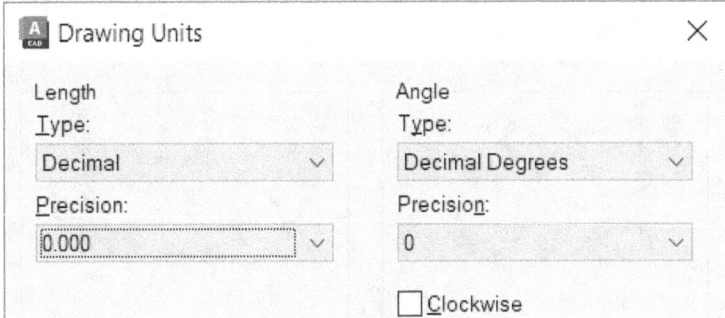

Figure 10–2

1. Start a new drawing based on **Mech-Inches.dwt**, which is located in your practice files folder.

2. Verify that the *units* are **Decimal** and set the *Precision* to **3** decimal places, as shown in Figure 10–2. Set the *Limits* to **36,24**. This drawing is in decimal inches.

3. Toggle on **Snap** and **Grid** and set them to **0.125**.

4. Add the following new layers: **Resistor**, **Transistor**, and **Capacitor**.

5. Add a text style named **Wiring**.

6. Create a new multileader style named **Keynotes** using the **Circle** block and any type of leader.

7. Save the drawing as a template named **Elec-Inches.dwt**. Save it as a DWT file and add a description as required.

8. Start a new drawing using your template to test some of the settings.

10.3 Civil/Map Project

In this project, you will create a new template drawing for use with mapping. You will establish units, limits, layers, a text style, and a multileader style, as shown in Figure 10–3.

Figure 10–3

1. Start a new drawing based on **Civil-Feet.dwt**, which is located in your practice files folder.

2. Change the *Units* to **Decimal**, with the *Precision* set to **whole units**. This drawing is in decimal feet. Set the *Limits* to **10000,7000**.

3. Add the following new layers: **City Line**, **County Line**, and **District Line**.

4. Add a text style named **Road Names**, as shown in Figure 10–3.

5. Create a new multileader style named **Keynotes** using the **Circle** block and any type of leader.

6. Save the drawing as a template named **Civil-Mapping.dwt**. Ensure you save it as a DWT file and add a description as required.

7. Start a new drawing using your template to test some of the settings you have established.

10.4 Mechanical Project: Dimension Styles

In this project, you will create dimension styles and dimension the part, as shown in Figure 10–4.

Figure 10–4

1. Open **Dimplate-I.dwg** from your practice files folder.

2. Based on the dimensions shown in Figure 10–4, create two dimension styles: **Normal** and **Tolerance**. Use **Annotative** style as the base for your new dimension styles.

- The **Normal** style should have sub-styles for angular and radial dimensions.

   (Hint: The **Fit** option in the angular dimensions needs to be adjusted to move the text outside the lines first, and set the *Text Placement* option to **Over dimension line, without leader**. The **Fit** option in the radial dimensions needs to be set to **Draw dim line between ext lines** for *Fine Tuning*.)

- The **Tolerance** style, for the toleranced dimensions, uses a deviation style tolerance. Ensure the following values are set:

  - *Precision*: **0.000**
  - *Upper value*: **0.030**
  - *Lower value*: **0.010**

- *Scaling for tolerance* text height: **0.75** (75% of the other dimension text)

3. Make the layer **Dimensions** current and dimension the part as shown in Figure 10−4. You will need to draw the arc that displays the placement of the five small holes, and the lines from the center of those holes to the large hole.

External References

You will explore how to attach drawing, image, DWF, DGN, and PDF reference files and how to open reference files from within a host drawing. You will also learn methods to detach, unload, and reload reference files, clip reference files, manage drawing reference-specific information, edit drawing reference files, and bind external references.

Learning Objectives

- Attach other drawing files along with DWF, DGN, image, and PDF files to a drawing.
- Set the attachment options of externally referenced files.
- Open, modify, detach, and unload referenced files.
- Clip the referenced file to control the part that is visible.
- Set a drawing reference file to be an attachment or an overlay.
- Bind blocks, layers, dimensions styles, etc., from a reference drawing into a host drawing.
- Control how much of a drawing reference file is loaded into the host file.

11.1 Attaching External References

When you insert one drawing into another as a block, the graphics are merged and no link remains between the two files. External References enable you to combine files and retain the link, as shown in Figure 11−1. This serves two main purposes: it controls the file size because objects in the referenced drawing do not become part of the host drawing, and objects modified in the reference file are automatically updated in the host drawing because the files are linked.

Figure 11−1

- Reference files enable members of a design team to share common source files and still have the most current information.

- External reference files can be managed through the *External References* palette.

- When you open a drawing that contains an external reference file that cannot be found, a *References - Not Found Files* warning box opens, as shown in Figure 11–2. Here you can directly open the *External References* palette, which enables you to check for the missing file and resolve the issue, or ignore the unresolved reference file.

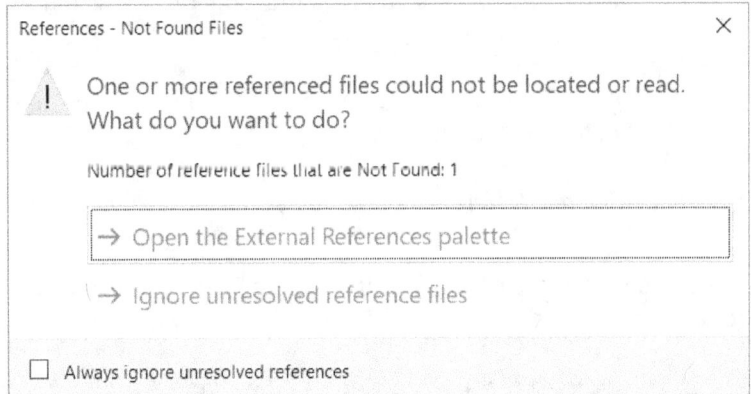

Figure 11–2

- When you open the *External References* palette, unresolved files display the 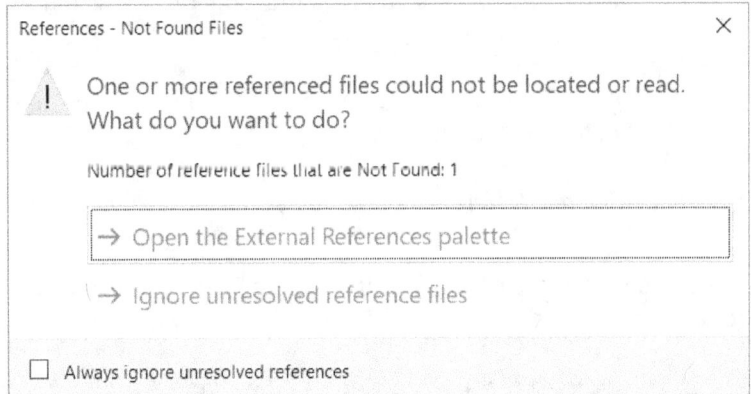 warning symbol file icon, and the ⚠ warning symbol displays beside the file with **Not Found** in the *Status* column.

Several file formats can be used as external references:

AutoCAD® drawing files (DWG)	Also known as Xrefs, they are connections to other drawings that you can edit in-place or externally, while retaining the link. You can turn layers on and off in the host drawing.
Raster image files	Various types of graphic files, such as GIF, JPG, and PNG. They can be renderings or scanned images that can be used as a reference as you trace over existing drawings.
DWF underlays	Non-editable files that include vector information that can be displayed in the DWF viewer and incorporated as an underlay in any drawing file.
DGN underlays	Files that come from the MicroStation platform. You can also import and export to DGN files.
PDF Underlays	Attach PDF files as underlays one page at a time.
Point Clouds	Attach RCS or RCP files to AutoCAD drawings. The point cloud is automatically scaled to match the unit type in the host drawing.
Coordination Model	Attach Autodesk Navisworks (NWD or NWC) files to AutoCAD drawings. The coordination model is automatically scaled to match the unit type in the host drawing.

External References Palette

You can use the *External References* palette (shown in Figure 11–3) to attach, unload, reload, and detach reference files. You can open a reference file in an appropriate software to make modifications to the original file and can also change the location in which the original file is saved if it is moved.

- You can open the *External References* palette by clicking in the *Insert* tab>*Reference* panel or by typing **Xref** in the Command Line.

- You can also open the *External References* palette by clicking ⬜ in the *View* tab>*Palettes* panel.

- If you have a reference file in the drawing, you can right-click on it and select **External References** to open the palette.

- When you have external references in a drawing, ⬚ (Manage Xrefs) displays near the right end of the *Status Bar*. Click it to open the *External References* palette. ⬚ (Manage Xrefs) does not display in the *Status Bar* until the drawing contains at least one Xref.

- The *External References* palette is similar to other palettes and can be either floating, docked, or hidden.

Figure 11–3

The *External References* palette is divided into two panes.

Top Pane

In the top pane, a list of file references displays, as shown in Figure 11–4.

- By selecting the appropriate column heading, you can sort the files in the list according to name, status, size, date, and saved path.

Figure 11–4

- ☰ (List View) displays all of the attached external references and detailed information including: size, date, and saved path.

- ⛫ (Tree View) switches to an hierarchical view that displays nested reference files (i.e., drawings that are attached to referenced drawings). Double-click on a reference filename in Tree View to display or hide the nested reference files below it.

Bottom Pane

In the bottom pane, a list of details about a selected file or a preview of the file displays, as shown in Figure 11–5.

Figure 11–5

- 🗋 (Details) displays information about a selected file and enables you to modify the name of the reference. If the file is a drawing file, it enables you to modify the type of attachment.

- 🖼 (Preview) displays a small image of the selected file.

How To: Attach a Reference File

1. In the *View* tab>*Palettes* panel, ▢ click (External References Palette).

    *   You can also open the *External References* palette by clicking the *Reference* panel arrow in the *Insert* tab of the ribbon.

2. In the *External References* palette, click on the arrow with 🖼️ ▾ (Attach DWG) to open the file list, as shown in Figure 11–6, and select a file format to attach.

Figure 11–6

3. In the *Select Reference File* dialog box, select the file that you want to attach and click **Open**.

4. In the *Attach External Reference* dialog box, set the options as required, as shown in Figure 11–7.

    •   The options and title of the dialog box (External Reference, Image, or Attach DWF Underlay) vary depending on the type of file selected. Several options are used in every situation.

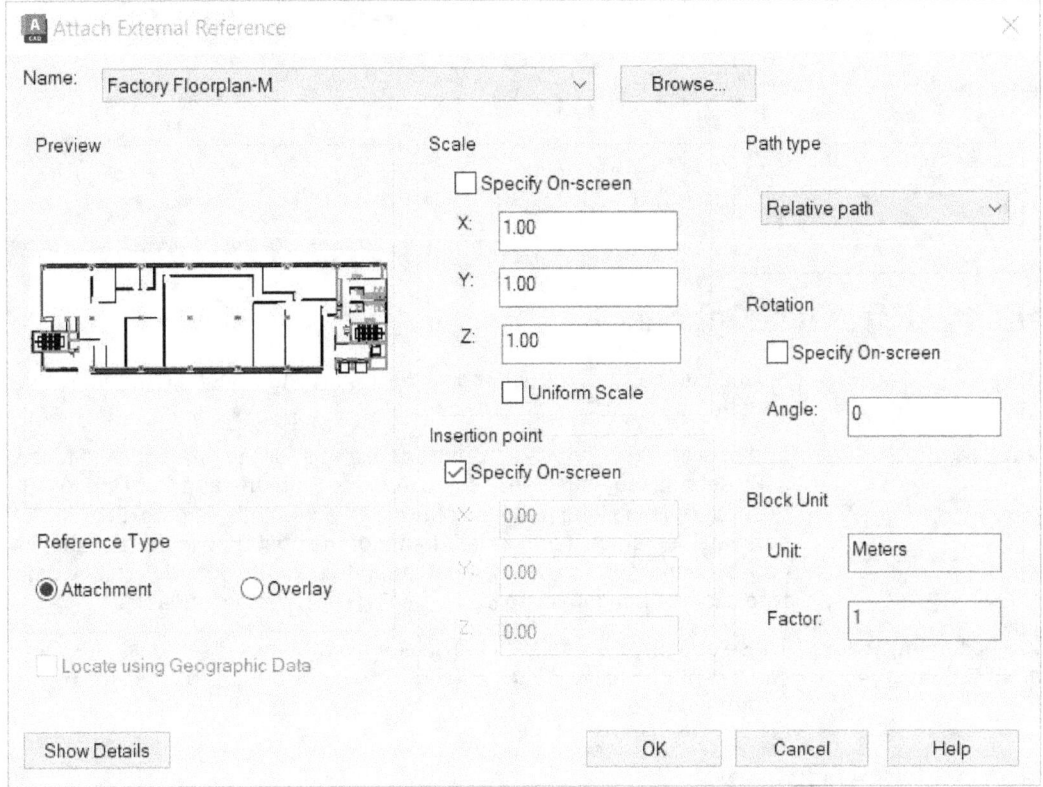

Figure 11–7

5. Click **OK**.

6. If you used the **Specify On-screen** option for *Insertion Point*, *Scale*, and *Rotation* in the dialog box, then specify them in the drawing window.

- You can use the Reference tools in the *Insert* tab>*Reference* panel to attach or modify various types of externally referenced files, as shown in Figure 11–8.

Figure 11–8

General Attachment Options

Name	Select a name from the list or click **Browse...** and select a different file to attach.
Path type	Controls how the AutoCAD software searches for the reference file to load it. By default, the Path type is set to **Relative Path**. It starts from the folder of the host drawing. **Full path** uses the entire path. With **No path**, the AutoCAD software searches in the current folder of the host drawing, and in the project paths, support paths, and *Start-in* folder. The default **Relative path** type can be changed using the REFPATHTYPE system variable.
Insertion Point, Scale, and Rotation Angle	These options are similar to the selections for block insertions. The values can be entered in the *Attach External Reference* dialog box or in the Command Line.

Shortcut Menu Options

In the *External References* palette, right-click on an Xref file to open a shortcut menu that contains various options for the attached Xref file.

- When a drawing has an external reference that has been moved and cannot be found, the shortcut menu offers you options to find the file, as shown in Figure 11–9. The **Select New Path** option enables you to fix the missing path by selecting the file from the new location. Once the reference file's new location has been selected, the software prompts you to use the new path for the other missing references or leave the rest of the paths as is. The **Find and Replace** option opens the *Find and Replace* dialog box, which enables you to find the current path and replace all of its instances with the new path, all at once.

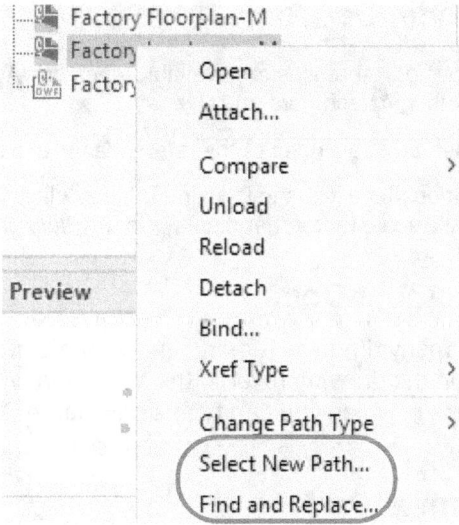

Figure 11–9

- The shortcut menu also provides you with the option of changing the path type by selecting **Change Path Type**. If the path type option of the selected reference file is grayed out and cannot be selected, it indicates that it is the current path type. Figure 11–10 shows an example of the referenced file using the **Relative Path** type, which is grayed out to indicate that the path type is currently used.

Figure 11–10

Xref Specific Attachment Options

Reference Type	Two types of references are available when one AutoCAD drawing is inserted into another: **Attachment** and **Overlay**.
Block Unit	The Insertion Scale units of the reference file and host drawings (expand Application Menu, expand Drawing Utilities, click 0.0 (Units)) control the automatic scale factor that displays in the *Block Units* area.

Image Specific Attachment Options

You can attach an image as many times as required in the same drawing file. If a raster image by that name already exists in the drawing (even if the extension type is different) a *Substitute Image Name* dialog box opens in which you can type a new name. This name displays in the External References palette.

DWF Specific Attachment Options

Select one or more sheets	If you are using a multi-sheet DWF file you can select any of the sheets to insert into the host drawing.

- When you insert a DWF as an underlay, you have the option of selecting the units. If you set the *scale factor* to **Specify on Screen** then, at the *Specify Scale Factor or [Unit]:* prompt, right-click and select **Unit** to provide you with a list of units. Select the unit of the existing drawing and have the software automatically scale the DWF file to those units. For example, if you are working in a drawing whose insertion scale units are set to **Meters** and the DWF file is in Architectural units, it automatically scales the DWF file by 0.0254. The default insertion scale unit is set to the current drawing units.

- You can insert multiple copies of a DWF file using the same sheet or different sheets in a multiple sheet file.

DGN Specific Attachment Options

MicroStation DGN file units are set up in *Master units* and *Sub units*. When you insert a DGN as an underlay, you need to specify the units that you want to convert. For example, if you attach a mechanical drawing that is created with *Master units* of millimeters and *Sub units* of thousandths of millimeters, you would convert the *Master units*. However, if you are working with a file that has *Master units* of feet and *Sub units* of inches and you want to insert it into an AutoCAD Architectural unit file (which uses inches as its default units), you would convert the *Sub units*.

PDF Specific Attachment Options

Select one or more pages	If you are using a multi-sheet PDF file, you can select any sheet(s) to insert into the host drawing.

- All the supported objects in the PDF file are converted into 2D geometry, raster images, and TrueType text.

- Once you have attached the PDF file as an overlay, you can modify how the PDF objects are converted using (Import as Objects). In the *External References* palette, select the attached PDF file. It opens the *PDF Underlay* contextual tab. In the *PDF Import* panel, click (Import as Objects) and then click **Settings** in the Command Line. The *PDF Import Settings* dialog box opens and you can set the import options for the PDF file, as shown in Figure 11–11.

Figure 11–11

- In the *PDF data to import* area, select the types of data to import, as follows:

  - **Vector geometry:** Lines that touch become connected polylines.

  - **Solid Fills:** Joins 2D solids with coincident edges to create hatch objects.

  - **TrueType text:** Converts TrueType fonts to text objects. If the PDF file contains SHX fonts, these are converted to separate geometric representations, which can be converted to multiline text objects using the **Recognize SHX Text** tool in the *Insert* tab>*Import* panel (**PDFSHXTEXT** command).

  - **Raster images:** Extracts images to PNG files, which are then attached to the drawing as reference files.

- In the *Layers* area, set which layers the attached objects are added to.
- In the *Import options* area, set options that are used as geometry is imported:
  - **Import as block:** Creates a single block rather than separate lines.
  - **Join line and arc segments:** Creates polylines from connected objects.
  - **Convert solid fills to hatches:** Joins 2D solids with coincident edges to create hatch objects.
  - **Apply lineweight properties:** Assigns a lineweight to the imported geometry according to its thickness in the PDF.
  - **Infer linetypes from collinear dashes:** Creates a single polyline from collinear dash and dot segments.

11.2 Modifying External References

When you have attached external references to your drawing, you can modify the way they function in the drawing.

- You can **Open**, **Unload**, **Reload**, and **Detach** individual references, as shown in Figure 11–12.

Figure 11–12

- All of the reference file formats can be clipped to display part of the reference. You can make changes to a selected reference in the *Properties* palette.

- You can use standard AutoCAD® commands, such as **Move**, **Rotate**, and **Scale** on references. Raster images can also be used to trim or extend to another object.

Opening Reference Files

You can modify a reference file in the software in which it was created and then reload it into the drawing. You can open a reference file from within the host drawing. Select the file in the *External References* palette, right-click, and select **Open**.

- A drawing reference file opens the drawing in the AutoCAD software.

- Image files open the image in the software with which the file format is associated.

- Autodesk® Viewer (https://viewer.autodesk.com/) is a free online file viewer that enables you to view DWF files.

- DWF files also open in the Autodesk® Design Review software, if it is installed. DGN files cannot be opened with the AutoCAD software.

- You can also open drawing reference files by picking the reference in the drawing window, right-clicking and selecting **Open Xref**, as shown in Figure 11–13.

Figure 11–13

Detaching and Unloading Reference Files

There are two ways of removing a reference file from your drawing: **Unload** and **Detach** (as shown in Figure 11–14).

Figure 11–14

Detaching Files

Use **Detach** to permanently remove a reference file from your drawing.

- It severs the link between the current drawing and the external reference drawing.

- To get the reference back after detaching it, you need to re-attach it.

- If you have attached multiple copies of a DWF file, **Detach** removes all of them.

Unloading and Reloading Files

Use **Unload** to temporarily remove a reference file.

- When you unload a reference file, the AutoCAD software hides the reference geometry. However, it keeps the file in the *External References* palette list and remembers its insertion point, scale, and other attachment information.

- Unloading references that are not currently required causes a drawing to open and perform faster.

- To display an unloaded reference again, it must be reloaded using the **Reload** option.

- You can use the **Open** option in the shortcut menu to quickly open the unloaded reference file.

- Reloading loads the most recently saved version of the reference.

- All of the references reload automatically when you open the host drawing.

- Renaming the unloaded reference file in the *External References* palette does not automatically reload the renamed file. You have to explicitly reload it, as it remains unloaded until then.

- **Refresh** synchronizes information stored in memory when used with the Autodesk® Vault software.

- **Reload All References** (shown in Figure 11–15) updates all of the references in a drawing so that you are using the most up-to-date versions that have been saved.

Figure 11–15

Comparing Xrefs

Once you have made changes to an Xref, you can now compare the original and the modified Xref. By comparing the two Xrefs, you can now identify the modifications that were made to the drawing file that is attached as an external reference in the current drawing. The differences in the changed Xref are highlighted by a revision cloud. The comparison can be started by selecting **Compare** in right-click menu as shown in Figure 11–16.

Figure 11–16

- When a drawing which is referenced in a drawing is changed, a alert balloon is displayed in the *Status Bar*, as shown in Figure 11–17. Select the link in the balloon to reload the reference and also to compare the changes. This message also displays when someone else changes a reference while you have the host file open.

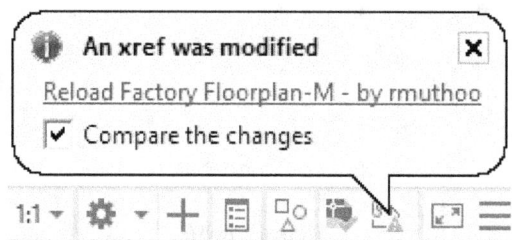

Figure 11–17

- When you start the **Xref Compare** command, the drawing opens in a *Compare* window which is indicated by drawing being enclosed in a blue border and the *Xref Compare* toolbar displayed along the top of the drawing window, as shown in Figure 11–18. The changes are highlighted in a revision cloud as shown in Figure 11–18.

Figure 11–18

- You can expand the *Compare* toolbar to toggle the various display options, change the color and shape of the revision clouds, and zoom to the previous and next comparison in the drawing, as shown in Figure 11–19. Use **X** to end the comparison.

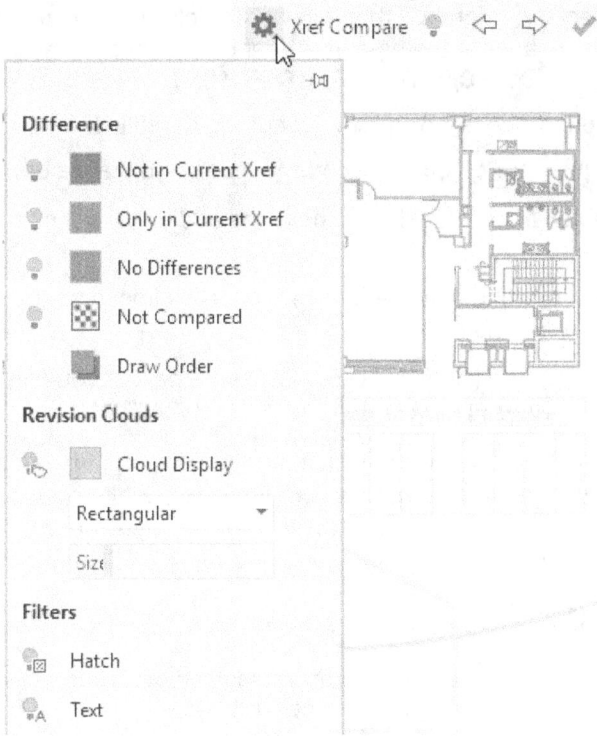

Figure 11–19

Clipping Reference Files

When you attach an external reference to your drawing, the entire reference file displays. However, you might not want the entire file to display, even in Model Space. You can control which part of the referenced file is visible by clipping it, as shown in Figure 11–20.

Figure 11–20

How To: Clip a Reference File

1. In the drawing, select the reference that you want to clip, right-click and select the appropriate **Clip** command for the type of reference selected. (Drawings: **Clip Xref**; Images: **Image>Clip**; DWF files: **DWF Clip**; DGN files: **DGN Clip**.)

2. Enter a **Clipping** option. Press <Enter> to accept the default **New boundary** option.

3. Select the **Rectangular** or **Polygonal** boundary option and draw a boundary.

    *   If you have selected a drawing file, you have the additional option of selecting an existing polyline as the boundary.

4. Specify the points or existing polyline. The reference is clipped so the reference information outside the boundary is invisible.

*   You can only clip one image (.DWF or .DGN file) at a time, but you can clip multiple drawing files.

*   Drawing reference files have an additional clip option: **Invert Clip**. Instead of masking everything outside the boundary it covers everything within the boundary. This can be very useful if you are working on a renovation project in which you are moving interior walls but not changing other parts of the building.

Other Clip Options

On/Off	Turns the clip boundary on or off without removing it from the reference. If the boundary is off the entire reference displays.
Clipdepth	Controls the front and back clipping planes in the Z-direction of the clip. Drawing reference files only.

Delete	Removes the clipping boundary from the reference files. You cannot use the **Erase** command to remove the clipping boundary.
Generate Polyline	Creates a polyline at the location of an existing clip boundary. This is a separate entity from the boundary. Drawing reference files only.

- If you run the command on a file that already has a boundary, the AutoCAD software prompts you to delete the current boundary first.

- To modify the clip boundary, start the associated **Clip** command. You can toggle the **Clip Boundary** on or off or delete it.

Clip Frames

The lines around clipped references are called *Clip Frames*. They can be toggled on or off for all of the references in a drawing using system variables that are related to each reference type: **xclipframe** for drawing references, **imageframe**, **dwfframe**, **pdfframe**, and **dgnframe**, as shown in Figure 11–21.

Frame ON   Frame OFF

Figure 11–21

- **Frame Boundaries** have three options. When set to **0**, the boundary is invisible. When set to **1**, the boundary is visible. When set to **2**, the boundary is visible but does not plot.

- When the boundary is visible, you can select the external reference by selecting the boundary or any visible part of the reference file.

Modifying References

When you select the border of a reference file, a contextual tab displays according to the type of reference file that was selected.

- A *DWF underlay* contextual tab has panels for *Adjust*, *Clipping*, *Options*, and *DWF Layers*, as shown in Figure 11-22. PDF and DGN underlays are the same. You can also right-click on the DWF object in the drawing window and select many of the options from the shortcut menu.

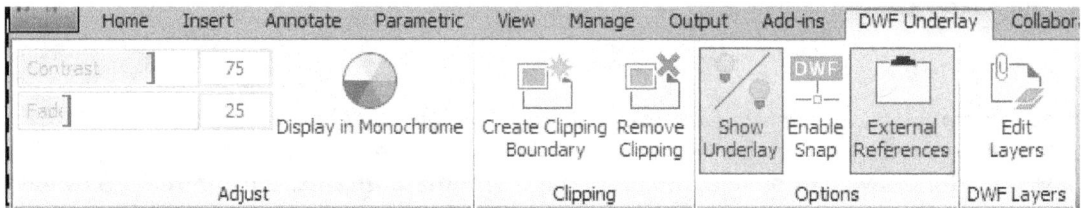

Figure 11-22

- Modification options for drawing reference files include editing the reference, clipping, and access to the *External References* palette, as shown in Figure 11-23.

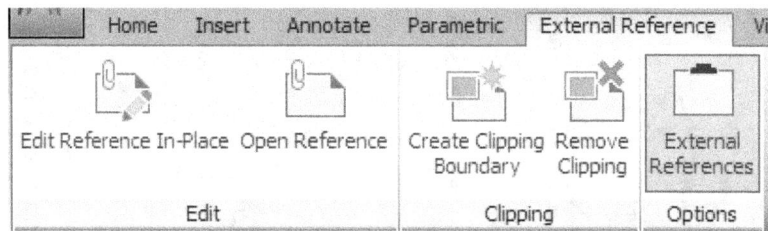

Figure 11-23

- Image panels include *Adjust* and *Clipping*, and an additional **Transparency** option, as shown in Figure 11-24.

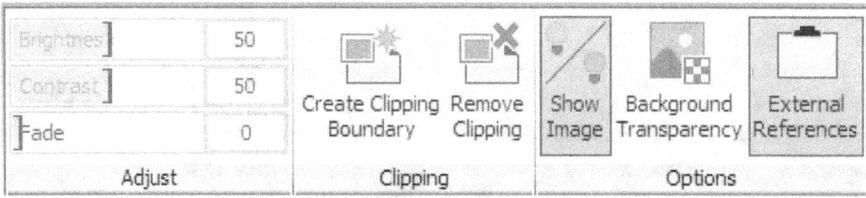

Figure 11-24

- Underlays and image references can only be selected when the frame surrounding them is on. You can change the state of the frames in the *Insert* tab>*Reference* panel, as shown in Figure 11–25.

Figure 11–25

Reference File Properties

DWF, DGN, and Image references have several properties that can be modified, including how and what they display in the drawing.

These options can be modified in the *Properties* palette.

Miscellaneous Options

In the *Misc* area in the *Properties* palette, you can toggle off DWF or DGN underlays or Images without unloading the files. Set *Show image* to **No**, as shown in Figure 11–26.

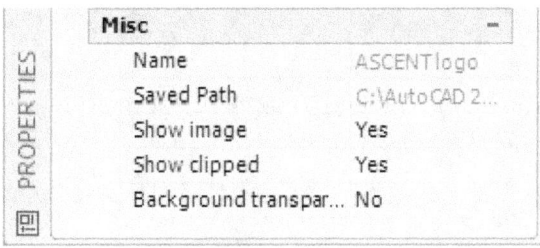

Figure 11–26

- The **Show clipped** option changes the status of displaying whether the object is clipped or not clipped. This is different than displaying the clipping frame.

- Images have the additional **Background Transparency** option. This permits the background of the image to become transparent, so that it matches the general background. However, not all of the file formats enable transparency. You can also access this option in the ribbon and in the shortcut menu under **Image**.

Adjusting Underlays and Images

DWF and DGN underlays and image reference properties can be adjusted.

- With a reference file selected, in the *Properties* palette, in the *Underlay Adjust* or *Image Adjust* areas, you can specify the amount of *Contrast* and *Fade*, as shown in Figure 11–27. DWF and DGN files can be set to **Monochrome** and Image files have an additional **Brightness** adjustment.

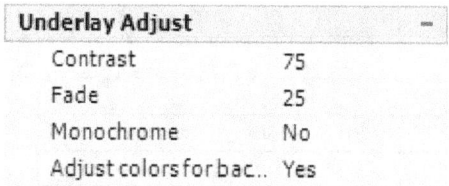

Underlay Adjust	–
Contrast	75
Fade	25
Monochrome	No
Adjust colors for bac..	Yes

Figure 11–27

- DWF underlays have an option to adjust the colors for the background.

- Click (Adjust) in the *Insert* tab>*Reference* panel to adjust the *Fade*, *Contrast*, or *Monochrome* settings for underlay and image files.

- Image references can also be adjusted in the *Image* contextual tab as shown in Figure 11–28. A preview of the changes displays in the drawing window as the modifications are made. The contextual tab is opened by selecting the underlay or image.

Figure 11–28

- The quality of an image can be set to **High** or **Draft** by typing **imagequality** at the Command Line.

💡 **Hint: Creating an Image File**

In the AutoCAD software, there are several ways of creating a raster file, which can then be used as an image:

- You can copy the contents of the current viewport using **saveimg** at the Command Line. The image can be saved in the .BMP, .PCX, .TGA, .TIF, .JPEG, or .PNG file formats.

- You can render the display to a file (usually done with 3D objects). Rendering can create several different raster formats.

DWF Specific Adjustments

DWF reference files have two additional options because they are created from drawing files: toggling layers on and off and snapping to objects in the DWF underlay.

- Layer visibility can be controlled in DWF underlays (as shown in Figure 11–29), if the DWF file was created with the layers toggled on. When you have selected a DWF underlay, in the *DWF underlay* contextual tab, select **Edit Layers**. In the *Underlay Layers* dialog box, select the layers you want to toggle on or off and click **OK**.

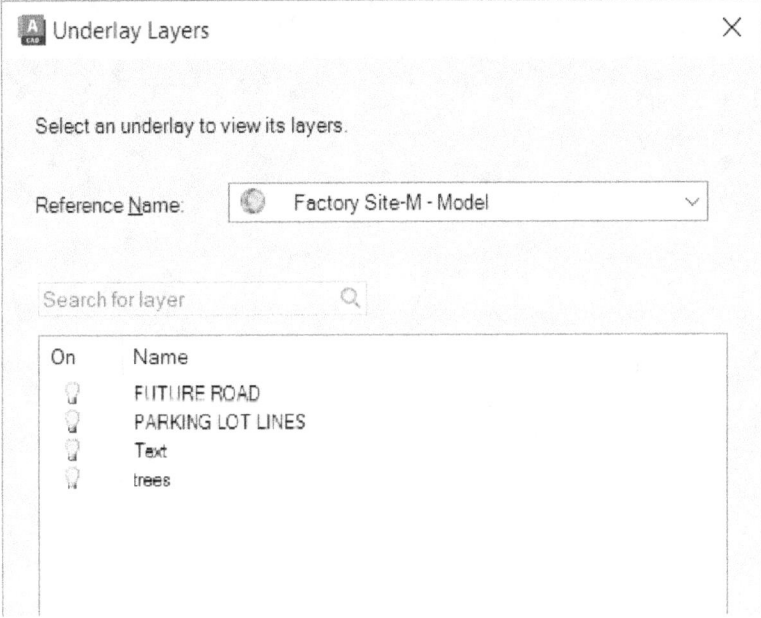

Figure 11–29

- To adjust another reference file's layers, select it in the *Reference Name* drop-down list.

- If a reference file does not contain layers, this is indicated in the *Underlay Layers* dialog box. By default, layers are not saved in the **DWF6ePlot.pc3** file supplied with the software.

- You can snap to objects in a DWF underlay. If you do not want object snaps to work with DWF files, select the DWF underlay, right-click and clear **DWF Object Snap**, as shown in Figure 11–30. You can also clear **Enable Snap** in the *DWF underlay* contextual tab. This impacts all of the DWF underlays in a drawing.

Figure 11–30

11.3 Xref Specific Information

The reference file tools works slightly differently with drawing references (also known as Xrefs). Because drawing reference files (DWG) contain the same components as the host files, you can manipulate them using methods that cannot be applied to raster images, .DWF, and .DGN files. You can set the DWG reference files to be attachments or overlays and can modify Xref layer states in the host drawing without impacting the original file. You can also import (bind) layers and block components of the drawing reference file into your drawing.

Attachments vs. Overlays

You can specify whether a drawing reference file should be an attachment or an overlay when it is originally referenced. Attachments and overlays work in the same way in the host file. You only notice the difference if you reference that host file in another file, as shown in Figure 11-31.

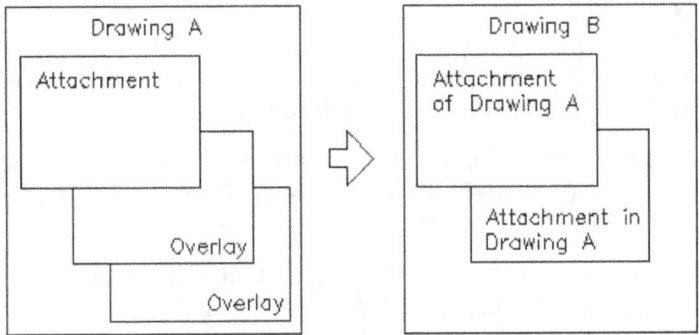

Figure 11-31

Attachment	When a file is referenced as an attachment, it displays with the host file if the host file itself is then referenced in another drawing. Using attachments enables a file to travel along the path with its host. A typical use for this option would be if there were a part referenced inside a subassembly, which is then referenced into a larger assembly.
Overlay	When a file is referenced as an overlay, it does not display in the host file if the host file itself is referenced in another drawing. Using overlays helps to avoid problems of circular references. (Circular references occur when a file references itself, usually indirectly. For example, drawing A references drawing B, which references drawing C, which references drawing A.)

- To change a drawing reference file from an attachment to an overlay, select the reference in the *External References* palette and modify it in the **Details** pane, as shown in Figure 11–32.

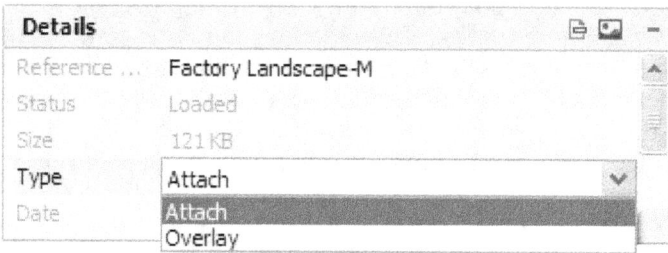

Figure 11–32

- You can also right-click on a filename(s) in the *External References* palette, expand Xref Type, and select **Overlay**.

Xref Layers

When you attach or overlay a drawing reference file, it brings the drawing objects and its named objects, such as layers and blocks, into the host drawing.

- In *Layer Properties Manager*, you can quickly display all of the layers in a specific drawing reference file by selecting the **Xref** filter, as shown in Figure 11–33. The **Xref** filter is automatically created when you attach a drawing reference file.

- A special prefix is added to any named objects from the referenced drawing when the names display in the host drawing, as shown in Figure 11–33. It consists of the name of the referenced drawing and a vertical bar ("|"). For example, a layer named **1F** in a reference file named **Factory Floorplan-M** would display as **Factory Floorplan-M|1F**.

Figure 11–33

- In order to clearly distinguish which layers come from referenced drawings and which layer reside in the active drawing, Xref layers are shown in gray text in *Layer Properties Manager* and the *Layer Control* drop-down list, as shown in Figure 11–34. Additionally, you can change the visibility of Xref layers in the layer panel drop-down.

Figure 11–34

- You can change the Xref layers state or properties (**Freeze/Thaw**, **Color**, etc.) in the current drawing. However, you cannot make an Xref layer current in the host drawing.

- The layer on which the drawing reference file is inserted controls the visibility of the drawing reference file. The drawing reference file is hidden when that layer is frozen. To specify a default layer on which you want the reference files inserted, use the **XREFLAYER** system variable.

- Renaming or deleting an Xref layer in the Xref drawing, automatically renames and deletes the layer when the Xref is reloaded in the host drawing.

- If you change the properties of an Xref layer, the change does not affect the referenced drawing. However, the change is retained in the host drawing by default. The default is controlled by the **VISTRETAIN** system variable. You can also control it in the *Layer Settings* dialog box, in the *Xref Layer Settings* area, by using the **Retain overrides to Xref layers properties** option.

- In the *Layer Settings* dialog box, you can specify the various Xref layer properties that you want to reload, as shown in Figure 11–35. These Xref layer properties are stored in the **VISRETAINMODE** system variable.

Figure 11–35

- In *Layer Properties Manager*, a ⌕ icon is displayed beside Xref layers that contain overrides. Hovering the cursor over this icon displays a tooltip that lists the override information, as shown in Figure 11–36. In the top right corner of *Layer Properties Manager*, the ⌕ icon (shown in Figure 11–36) can be used to toggle the shading background of the layers with overrides.

Figure 11–36

- In *Layer Properties Manager*, an **Xref Overrides** filter is automatically created when some Xref layers have overrides applied to them.

  - Clicking **Xref Overrides** displays only the list of Xref layers with overrides.

  - To reset any or all of the layer properties to their original state, right-click on **Xref Overrides** and select **Reset Xref Layer Properties** to access the options, as shown in Figure 11-37.

Figure 11-37

- You can control the display of layers for objects in an Xref drawing that were not set to "ByLayer" for the layer property updates in the original Xref. The **XREFOVERRIDE** variable enables you to force objects to be set to ByLayer in the host file.

  - Setting the **XREFOVERRIDE** to **1** enables the original file to set the properties and enables Xref objects to be forced to use ByLayer in the host file.

  - Setting the **XREFOVERRIDE** to **0** enables the drawing in which it is referenced to control the properties and only enables Xref objects that are already set to ByLayer to be changed in the host file.

  - This can also be controlled in the *Layer Settings* dialog box>*Xref Layer Settings* area, using the **Treat Xref object properties as ByLayer** option.

Binding Drawing Reference Files

The **Bind** option in a drawing reference file copies all of the referenced drawing's data into the current drawing and then detaches the reference. The referenced drawing becomes an inserted block.

How To: Bind a Drawing Reference File

1. Open the *External References* palette.
2. Right-click on the drawing reference file that you want to bind in the list and select **Bind**.
3. In the *Bind Type* area, select **Bind** or **Insert** (as shown in Figure 11–38) and click **OK**.

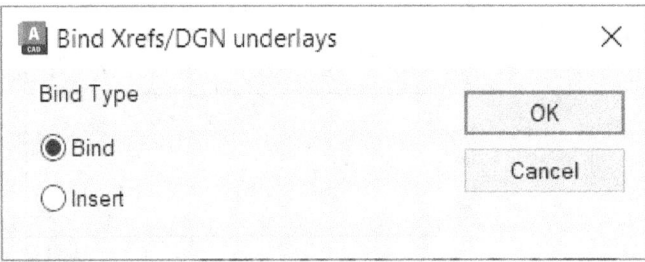

Figure 11–38

When a drawing reference file is bound, it brings all of its layers, blocks, and other named objects into the host drawing. The **Bind Type** controls how these named objects are named in the host drawing.

- When you use the *Bind Type* **Bind**, the object names are prefixed with the name of the reference file (filename0layername). For example, if the layer **Ref¦Floor** (from the drawing **Ref.dwg**) was bound to the current drawing, its name would become **Ref0Floor**. This can result in long names, but keeps the layers that were originally in the drawing reference file separate from the layers that were originally in the host file.

- When a drawing reference file is bound as an **Insert**, the block and layer names are added to the current file without change. For example, the Xref layer **Ref¦Floor** would become **Floor**. If the current file contains a block or layer with the same name, the drawing reference file object is updated to match the definition already in the current drawing.

- Binding a drawing reference file as an **Insert** is equivalent to detaching the reference file and inserting it as a block.

Binding Drawing Reference File Components

Instead of binding the entire drawing reference file, you can bind one or more blocks, layers, linetypes, text styles, and dimension styles. Binding any of these named objects adds their definition to the host drawing so that you can use them in the drawing.

- The **Xbind** command, accessed in the Command Line, enables you to bind specific named objects from a drawing reference file (such as layers or blocks).

- **Xbind** opens the *Xbind* dialog box (shown in Figure 11–39), in which you can select the drawing reference file from which to bind, the type of object (layer, block, etc.), and the specific named object to bind. Click the **+** sign to display the listings under each category. Select the object and click **Add** to add it for binding.

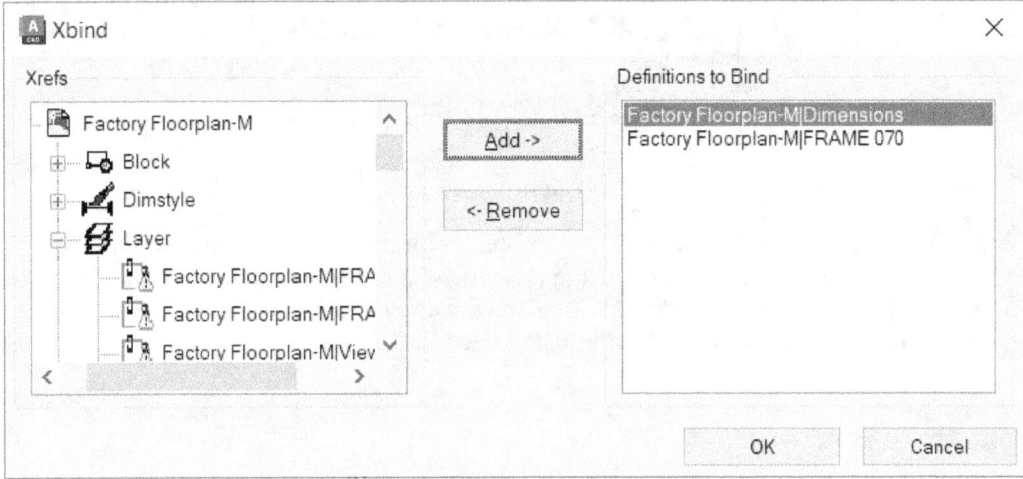

Figure 11–39

- When named objects are bound with **Xbind**, the "¦" in the name is replaced with "0". For example, the block **Office3¦Lamp** becomes **Office3$0$Lamp**. There is no option, such as **Insert**, to add the name without a change. However, you can rename the resulting objects using **Rename**.

- You can use the *DesignCenter* to copy these components into your current drawing without using the long names.

Demand Loading

Demand Loading controls how much of a drawing reference file is loaded. With **Demand Loading** enabled, only the visible parts of the drawing reference file (that are not clipped or on layers that are off or frozen) are loaded. Since it does not have to load the entire drawing reference file, the AutoCAD software responds more quickly.

- **Demand Loading** can be set in the *Options* dialog box, in the *Open and Save* tab, by selecting the **Demand load Xrefs** options, as shown in Figure 11–40.

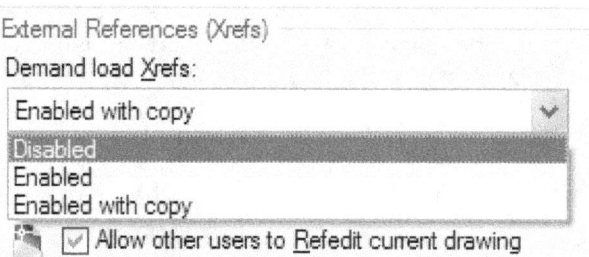

Figure 11–40

- When **Demand Loading** is enabled, others cannot edit the file that is being referenced. To enable others to use the file that is being referenced and take advantage of the improved performance, set *Demand Loading* to **Enabled with copy**. A copy of the file is used in place of the drawing reference file, so that others can use the file.

Practice 11a
Attach External References

Practice Objectives

- Attach and modify external references and overlay drawing references.
- Adjust the layers in a referenced file.
- Bind a reference to a file.

In this practice, you will attach and modify external references using the *External References* palette. You will also attach and overlay drawing references and note how they function in another file. You will then adjust layers in a referenced file and bind a reference to a file, as shown in Figure 11–41.

Figure 11–41

Task 1: Attach external references.

In this task, you will explore the features of the *External References* palette. You will attach a Reference File DWG, Raster Image, and DWF Underlay.

1. Start a new drawing based on **Civil-Meters.dwt**, which is located in your practice files folder and save the drawing as **Factory Site.dwg**.

2. In the *View* tab>*Palettes* panel, click ⬜ (External References Palette) to open the *External References* palette.

3. Near the top of the *External References* palette, click on the arrow with 📄 ▾ (Attach DWG) and select **Attach DWF....**

4. In the *Select Reference File* dialog box, open **Factory Site-M.dwf** from your practice files folder.

5. In the *Attach DWF Underlay* dialog box, for *Insertion point*, clear **Specify on-screen** and verify X,Y,Z values are set as **0,0,0**. Select **Specify on-screen** for the *Scale*, if required. Note that the *Path type* is set to **Relative path**. Click **OK** to continue.

6. At the *Specify scale factor* prompt, right-click and select **Unit**. Verify that **Meter** is selected and press <Enter> to accept the default selection.

7. Press <Enter> to complete the command. The DWF underlay of a site is placed in the drawing window and the DWF file displays as **Loaded** in the *External References* palette.

8. Using the above steps, and using **Attach DWG**, attach **Factory Floorplan-M.dwg** from your practice files folder at **0,0,0** *Insertion point* with the default scale and rotation (*Specify On-screen* cleared for all three). Verify that the *Reference Type* is set to **Attachment**. The floor plan of a building is placed in the center of the site plan.

    *   Note that the 📄 (Manage Xrefs) tool now displays in the *Status Bar*, which can be used to open the *External References* palette at a later time.

9. **Zoom Extents** to display **Factory Site-M.dwf** and **Factory Floorplan-M.dwg**.

10. Similarly, attach **Factory Landscape-M.dwg** from your practice files folder at any location (*Insertion point*: **Specify On-screen**) outside the left side of the site plan (you will move it later).

11. In the *External References* palette, Select **Factory Landscape-M.dwg**. In the *Details* section, click 🖼 (Preview) to display an image of the landscape reference file in the palette.

12. Switch to the **ISO A0** layout. Activate the viewport by double-clicking inside it and **Zoom Extents**.

13. Activate the Paper Space (double-click outside the viewport).

14. In the *External References* palette, using **Attach Image**, attach **ASCENT logo.gif** from your practice files folder at a scale factor of **50**. Place it near the left of the title block, as shown in Figure 11–42. (Select **Specify on-screen** for both *Scale* and *Insertion point*.)

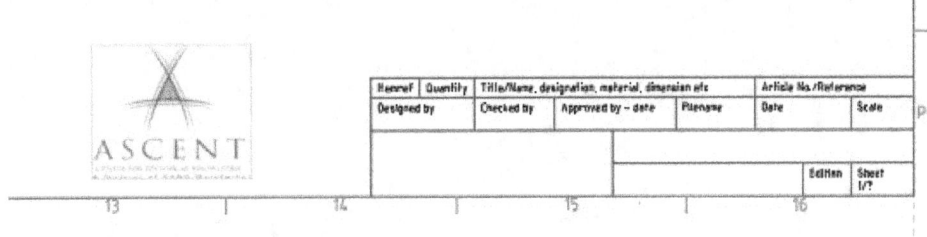

Figure 11–42

15. Save the file.

Task 2: Modify external references.

In this task, you will move a reference file to a new location, clip a DWF file, open a reference file and make a change to that drawing, close and reload it, and detach and unload it. The completed drawing is shown in Figure 11–43.

Figure 11–43

1. Switch to the *Model* tab. In the drawing window, select **Factory Site-M.dwf** (the outer rectangle). Right-click and verify that **DWF Object Snap** is enabled (blue frame), as shown in Figure 11–44. (You can also use **Enable Snap** (highlighted), located in the *DWF Underlay* contextual tab.) Press <Esc> to exit the selection.

Figure 11–44

2. Move **Factory Landscape-M.dwg** (file with trees that was placed along the left side of the drawing) so that the existing road in the DWF file is at the end of the entrance to the parking lot, as shown in Figure 11–45. In the landscape drawing, use the bottom left endpoint of the vertical portion of the road as your base point and snap it to the right endpoint of the top horizontal line of the road in the site DWF, as shown in Figure 11–45.

Figure 11–45

3. In the drawing window, select **Factory Site-M.dwf** (outer rectangle), right-click and select **DWF Clip....** Press <Enter> to accept the **New boundary** option and create a new rectangular boundary close to the landscape elements, building, and road, similar to the area shown previously in Figure 11–43.

4. In the *Insert* tab>*Reference* panel, expand **Frames vary** flyout, and select **Hide frames** to hide the boundary frame.

   • You can also type **dwfframe** and set the *system variable* to **0**.

5. Check the Layer Control, and note that the layers associated with **Factory Floorplan-M.dwg** and **Factory Landscape-M.dwg** are listed but they are grayed out.

6. In the *External References* palette, right-click on **Factory Floorplan-M.dwg** and select **Detach**. The building is removed from the drawing window and the file is removed from the *External References* palette.

7. Save the drawing.

8. Attach **Factory Floorplan-M.dwg** from your practice files folder to your file at an *Insertion point* of **0,0,0** and a *Rotation* of **0**. The building displays in the drawing window and the file is added to the *External References* palette back again.

9. In the E*xternal References* palette, unload **Factory Floorplan-M.dwg** (right-click and select **Unload**). Note that the building is removed from the drawing window but the file is still listed in the palette with a red arrow displayed along with it, as shown in Figure 11–46.

Figure 11–46

10. Reload **Factory Floorplan-M.dwg**. (Right-click and select **Reload**.)

11. In the *External References* palette, select **Factory Floorplan-M.dwg**. Right-click and select **Open**. The **Factory Floorplan-M.dwg** drawing opens in another window and its tab is added to the *File Tabs* bar. It also becomes the currently active drawing.

12. Set the layer **Equipment** to be current and draw a circle with a *radius* of **2** near the approximate center of the floor plan.

13. Save and close **Factory Floorplan-M.dwg**.

14. Activate the **Factory Site.dwg**, and note that the new circle is not displayed there.

15. In the *External References* palette, reload **Factory Floorplan-M.dwg**. Note that the new circle displays.

16. In the *External References* palette, right-click on **Factory Floorplan-M.dwg** and select **Compare>Recent Changes.** Note that the drawing is in the Compare mode, enclosed in a blue border and the *Xref Compare* toolbar displayed along the top of the drawing window, as shown in Figure 11−47. Also note that the circle that you added to **Factory Floorplan-M.dwg** is surrounded by a yellow rectangular revision cloud, as shown in Figure 11−47. Additionally, note that in the *External References* palette, the **Factory Floorplan-M.dwg** displays as **In Compare**, as shown in Figure 11−47.

Figure 11−47

17. Click **X** in the *Compare* toolbar to end the comparison.

18. Save and close the drawing.

Task 3: Attach and overlay drawing references in another file.

In this task, you will attach and overlay drawing references and note how they function in another file. You will then adjust layers in a referenced file and finally bind a reference to a file. The completed drawing is shown in Figure 11−48.

Figure 11−48

1. Open **Factory Floorplan-M.dwg** from your practice files folder.

2. Set layer **0** to be current and attach **Factory Electric-M.dwg** from your practice files folder to the current drawing at **0,0,0** as an attachment. Accept the defaults for the *Scale*, *Rotation*, and other options. Note that there might be some **Unreconciled New Layers**.Close the unreconciled bubble in the *Status Bar*.

3. Attach **Factory Lighting-M.dwg** from your practice files folder to the current drawing at **0,0,0**. Accept the defaults for the other options. Close the unreconciled bubble in the *Status Bar*, if required.

4. In the *External References* palette, right-click on **Factory Lighting-M.dwg**, expand **Xref Type**, and select **Overlay**. Close the palette. The overlay file remains visible in the drawing.

5. Save and close the drawing.

6. Open **Factory Site.dwg** if it is not already open. Note that the attached reference **Factory Electric-M.dwg** displays but the overlaid lighting reference is not displayed.

7. Save and close the drawing.

Task 4: Work with drawing reference file layers.

1. Open **Factory Floorplan-M.dwg** from your practice files folder. Close the unreconciled bubble in the *Status Bar*, if required.

2. Expand the Layer Control and note the layers that begin with **Factory Electric-M** and **Factory Lighting-M** are all gray. All of these layers belong to the drawing reference files.

3. Open *Layer Properties Manager*.

4. In the left pane, note the **Xref** category in the list. It is an Xref filter group that gets added when an Xref is attached.

5. Expand the **Xref** group and select **Factory Electric-M**. All of the layers in the **Factory Electric-M** drawing reference file display in the right pane.

6. In the right pane, right-click and select **Select All**.

7. Select one of the color blocks and change the *color* to **light gray**. The selected layers display in that color in the current drawing.

8. In the left hand pane, note that the **Xref Overrides** filter is added and that the listed layers have a blue background with their icons changed to 🔁. Hover the cursor over the icon to display the Xref override details, as shown in Figure 11−49.

Figure 11−49

9. Open **Factory Electric-M.dwg** from your practice files folder and verify that the layers retain their original colors. Close the file.

10. In the **Factory Floorplan-M.dwg**, note that the layers from the **Factory Electric-M** referenced drawing are still gray.

11. In the left pane, right-click on **Xref Overrides** category. Expand **Reset Xref Layer Properties** and select **All Properties**. Note that all of the layers retain their original color and that the **Xref Overrides** filter category is no longer displayed.

Task 5: Bind drawing reference files.

1. Continue working in **Factory Floorplan-M.dwg**.

2. In the *External References* palette, right-click on **Factory Lighting-M.dwg** (which is an underlay file) and select **Bind...** to bind it to the host file. In the dialog box, ensure that **Bind** is selected and click **OK**.

3. In the *External References* palette, note that the **Factory Lighting-M.dwg** is no longer displayed.

4. In *Layer Properties Manager*, note that all of the *Factory Lighting-M* layers contain **0** and are no longer grayed out, as shown in Figure 11–50. Note that all of the *Factory Electric-M* layers are still grayed out, indicating that they are Xref layers.

Figure 11–50

5. Undo the **Bind** process.

6. **Bind** the same file (**Factory Lighting-M.dwg**) again, but this time as an **Insert** (select **Insert** in the *Bind Xrefs/DGN underlays* dialog box).

7. In the *External References* palette, note that the **Factory Lighting-M.dwg** is no longer displayed.

8. In the *Layer Properties Manager*, note that the **Factory Lighting-M** layers are now integrated into the main layer names.

9. Save and close the drawing.

10. Open **Factory Site.dwg**. In the drawing window, note that the **Factory Lighting-M.dwg** objects are displayed but the file is not listed in the *External References* palette, as it is a part of the **Factory Floorplan-M** drawing file and not an overlay in the referenced file.

11. Save and close the drawing.

End of practice

Chapter Review Questions

1. Which of the following describes how external references are different from blocks? An external reference...

    a. Can contain one or many objects.

    b. Is a link to another file.

    c. Includes layers.

    d. Acts as one object in the drawing.

2. What is the default Path Type that is used when attaching an external reference file to the host drawing?

    a. Relative path

    b. Full path

    c. No path

3. What happens when you open a drawing containing a referenced file that cannot be located by the software? (Select all that apply.)

    a. The *References - Not Found Files* dialog box opens.

    b. A warning symbol displays next to the drawing file in the *External References* palette.

    c. It becomes a block.

    d. It is compressed to take up less memory.

4. Which of the following file formats cannot attach to an AutoCAD drawing as an external reference?

    a. .DWF

    b. .DOC

    c. .DWG

    d. .DGN

5. Drawing A is attached as a drawing reference file to host drawing B and both are then closed. Drawing A is then modified. Drawing B is opened and displays an image of drawing A. What happens to the image of drawing A when drawing B is opened?

   a. It displays a warning message.

   b. It does not change.

   c. It updates to display the changes.

   d. It displays as a blank image.

6. When describing Xref layers, which of the following statements are wrong?

   a. You can change the Xref layers state or properties (**Freeze/Thaw**, **Color**, etc.) in the current drawing.

   b. You can make an Xref layer current in the host drawing.

   c. You can specify a default layer for inserting the reference file on.

   d. Renaming or deleting an Xref layer in the Xref drawing automatically updates the layer when reloaded in the host drawing.

7. Which command or option enables you to bind one or more blocks, layers, linetypes, text styles, or dimension styles?

   a. Reload

   b. Demand Load

   c. Bind

   d. Xbind

Command Summary

Button	Command	Location
	Adjust	• **Ribbon:** *Insert* tab>*Reference* panel • **Command Prompt:** adjust
	Attach Xref	• **Ribbon:** *Insert* tab>*Reference* panel • **Command Prompt:** attach
	Clip Xref	• **Ribbon:** *Insert* tab>*Reference* panel • **Command Prompt:** clip
	External References	• **Ribbon:** *View* tab>*Palettes* panel or *Insert* tab>*Reference* panel arrow • **Command Prompt:** externalreferences

Projects: Drawing

Practice projects are provided for you to gain additional hands-on experience in the topics and commands previously covered. These projects are intended to be self-guided and do not include step-by-step information.

Learning Objectives

- *All:* Create title blocks that contain borders using rectangles and lines.
- *Mechanical:* Create a drill press base using features such as fillet, offset, trim, hatching, and viewports.
- *Architecture:* Create a room layout using features such as hatching, viewports, text, and dimensions. Additionally, setup the drawing for plotting in a layout.
- *P&ID:* Create a piping schematic using drawing and editing commands. Then add a legend in the layout to make the schematic ready for plotting.
- *Civil:* Create a warehouse site using drawing commands and other features such as viewports, text, hatching, and dimensions.

12.1 D-Sized Title Block (36x24)

In this project, you will create a title block. You will add a border using rectangles and lines, and add a logo and permanent text in the title block. This title block (shown in Figure 12-1) works with the DWF6 ePlot plotter with an **ARCH expand D** paper size when inserted at 0,0.

Figure 12-1

1. Start a new drawing based on **Mech-Inches.dwt**, which is located in your practice files folder and save it as **Titleblock3624.dwg**.

2. Set the current layer to **Border**.

3. Draw a **34 x 22** rectangle, starting with the lower left corner at the point **1.0,0.5** (the border starts at this point so that it fits correctly when inserted into the layout at 0,0). Zoom out to display the entire drawing.

4. Draw the lines for the title block, as shown in Figure 12–2. Place it in the lower right corner of the border.

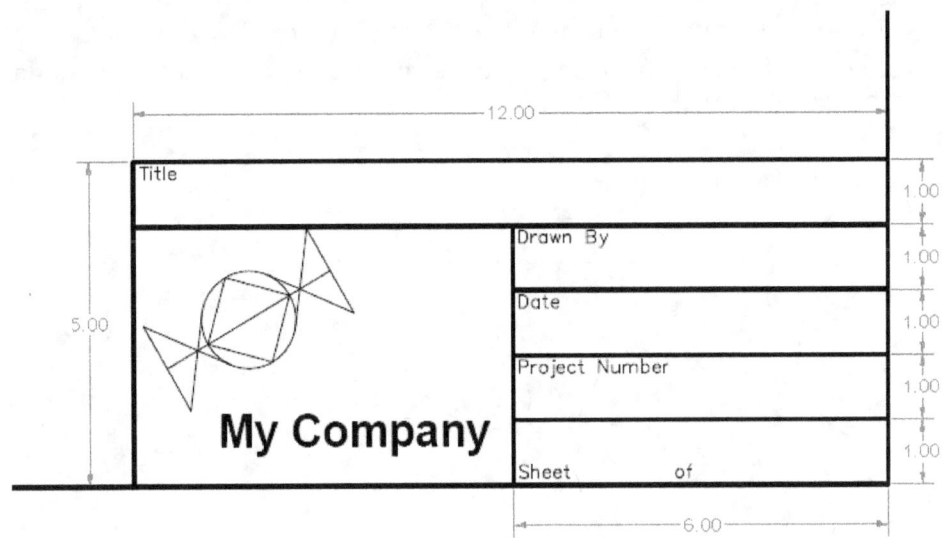

Figure 12–2

5. Change the current layer to **Text**. Draw circles, lines, and rectangles to create a logo in the largest box of the title block.

6. Move, rotate, and/or scale the logo so that it fits inside the box, but with enough room to add text later.

7. Add the text shown in Figure 12–2. All of the small text is **0.2 units** and uses the **Standard** text style. The text style for the logo is **Title** and you can use any height that fits in the space.

8. Save the drawing.

12.2 Mechanical Project: Drill Press Base

In this project, you will create a mechanical drawing of a drill press base and prepare it for plotting. You will draw the top view, insert a pre-drawn side view, and make the drawing ready for plotting in a layout, as shown in Figure 12–3.

Figure 12–3

Task 1: Draw the base.

1. Start a new drawing based on **Mech-Inches.dwt**, which is located in your practice files folder, and save it as **Drill Press Base.dwg**.

2. Draw the objects shown in Figure 12–4 on the layer **Object**. Use **Offset** to help locate the lines correctly. Use **Fillet** or **Trim** to clean up any extra overlapping lines.

Figure 12-4

3. Add the opening shown in Figure 12-5.

Figure 12-5

4. Save the drawing.

Task 2: Create a block.

1. Draw one lug in empty space to the side of the part, as shown in Figure 12–6.

Figure 12–6

2. Make a block called **Lug** from the circle, arc, and lines. Select the center of the circle as the base point, as shown in Figure 12–7.

Figure 12–7

3. Insert the four lugs, as shown in Figure 12–7. When you rotate, you can obtain the angles using grips and by snapping to the centerlines used to place the block.

4. Trim the lines that cross over the lugs.

5. Insert **Section-I.dwg** from your practice files folder. Position it above or below the top view of the base. Do not be concerned with its exact position. You can arrange the layout later in Paper Space.

6. Save the drawing.

Task 3: Set up the drawing for plotting in a layout.

1. In **Drill Press Base.dwg**, create a new layout and rename it **Sheet 1**. Apply a Page Setup to the layout using the plot device **DWF6 ePlot** and the paper size **ARCH expand D (36.00 x 24.00 Inches)**.

2. Set the current layer to **Border** and insert the file **Tblk3624.dwg** (located in your practice files folder) at **0,0**.

3. Erase the existing viewport in the layout.

4. Set the current layer to **Viewports**.

5. Create three new viewports, as shown in Figure 12–8. Scale the *Top View* and *Section View* to **1:1**. Scale the *Lug Detail* to **2:1**.

Figure 12–8

6. If the viewport is not big enough, you can return to Paper Space and stretch the viewport using grips.

7. Make the **Section** viewport active.

8. Set the current layer to **Hatching** and hatch the areas of the section view with the **ANSI31** pattern, as shown in Figure 12–9.

Figure 12–9

9. Save the drawing.

Task 4: Add text to the layout.

1. Set the current layer to **Text** and toggle off the layer **Viewports**. Add labels to each view using the **Hand** text style with a *height* of **0.25**. Change the *title part* of the label to the **Arial** font and the *size* to **0.5**, as shown in Figure 12–10.

Figure 12–10

2. Using multiline text with the **Hand** text style, add the text shown in Figure 12−11 to your drawing. The *text height* is **0.25**. Change the text **Notes:** to the **Arial** font and make it **0.5** units tall.

```
Notes:
1. All fillets and rounds 0.125 R
2. Material: Tempered Steel.
3. To be used with Drill Press 3462.
```

Figure 12−11

3. Position the text from Figure 12−11 so that it is below the **Lug Detail** view, as shown in Figure 12−12.

Figure 12−12

4. Fill out the title block with the **Standard** text style and a *height* of **0.2**.

5. Save and close the drawing.

12.3 Architectural Project: Office Tower

In this project, you will create an architectural drawing of one floor in an office tower. You will draw the floor plan for the building core, mark the areas for various tenants, and lay the drawing out for plotting, as shown in Figure 12–13.

Figure 12–13

Task 1: Draw the interior and exterior walls and elevators.

1. Start a new drawing based on **AEC-Imperial.dwt**, which is located in your practice files folder and save it as **Tower.dwg**.

2. Draw a rectangular building outline of **150'-0" x 125'-0"**, starting with the absolute coordinate **10'-0",10'-0"** in the lower left corner, as shown in Figure 12–14.

3. Fillet the upper left corner with a *radius* of **50'-0"**, as shown in Figure 12–14.

4. Chamfer the lower right corner with *distances* of **40'-0"**, as shown in Figure 12–14.

5. Use **Offset** to create the walls. The exterior walls are **12"** thick, as shown in Figure 12−14.

Figure 12−14

6. Draw the interior walls, as shown in Figure 12−15. Start at the absolute coordinate point of **51'-0",63'-6"** at the intersection of the **4'-6"** and **23'-0"** lines. The interior walls are **6"** thick.

Figure 12−15

7. Use **Trim**, **Extend**, and **Fillet** (with a radius of **0**) as required to clean up the intersections of the walls at the core of the building, as shown in Figure 12–16.

8. Draw a **5'-6" x 8'-0"** elevator in the bottom left elevator shaft space (the 6' wide space). There should be **3"** of clearance between the elevator and the walls (you might want to create an **Elevator** layer).

9. Use **Mirror** to create the other three elevators. They are centered in the middle of the 12'-0" x 17'-0" space, as shown in Figure 12–16.

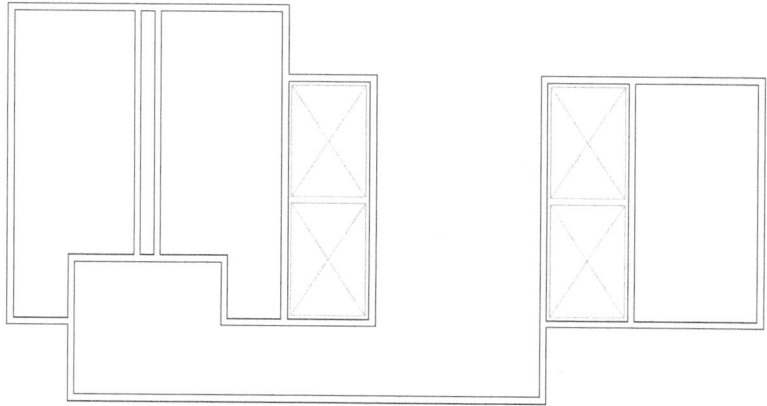

Figure 12–16

10. Save the drawing.

Task 2: Create doors and insert the bathroom block.

1. Cut the door openings, as shown in Figure 12–17. The elevator openings are **6'-0"**. All of the other doors are **3'-0"** wide and either centered on the wall or offset **6"** from the closest wall.

Figure 12–17

2. Set the current layer to **Doors**. Draw the doors shown in Figure 12–18 and create blocks. The door panels are **2"** thick. Do not include the dimensions in the blocks.

Door   *Elevator Door*

Figure 12–18

3. Insert the door blocks, as shown in Figure 12–19. Insert **Restrooms-A-12.dwg** into the restroom areas as well.

Figure 12–19

4. Save the drawing.

Task 3: Set up the drawing for plotting in a layout.

1. Switch to the **D-Sized** layout.

2. Set the current layer to **Viewports** and create three viewports, as shown in Figure 12-20.

Figure 12-20

3. In one viewport, display the entire drawing scaled at **1/16"=1'-0"**.

4. In another viewport, display only the layout of the bathrooms scaled at **1/2"=1'-0"**. Freeze the layer **Hatching** in this viewport only.

5. In the third viewport, display the core of the building scaled at **1/4"=1'-0"**. Freeze the layers **Hatching** and **Restroom**. You might have to change the sizes of the viewports to fit all of the information once you have applied the scale. You can do this in Paper Space with grips.

Task 4: Create a tenant layout.

1. Set the current layer to **Hatching**.

2. In the overall viewport, divide the building into several areas, with lines radiating from the core, as shown in Figure 12–21. These are subdivisions for various tenants.

ACME COMPUTERS
ROAD PLANNERS
EMPTY
BUGS BE GONE
WILEY'S MACHINES
EMPTY

Figure 12–21

3. Set the current layer to **Text**. Add text in each space with the tenant's name.

4. Set the current layer to **Hatching** again. Hatch each tenant's space with a different hatch pattern. Use annotative scales for the hatches.

5. Save the drawing.

Task 5: Add text and dimensions to the layout.

1. In Paper Space, set the current layer to **Text** and freeze the layer **Viewports**. Use the **Title** text style and add a title for each view, as shown in Figure 12–22. The text size should be **1/4"** for the *title* and **1/8"** for the *scale*.

TENANT'S LAYOUT
SCALE: 1/16"=1'-0"

Figure 12–22

2. Set the current layer to **Dimensions**.

3. Dimension the core, as shown in Figure 12–23. Use the annotative **Architectural** dimension style supplied with the template.

   • To check the dimensions, refer to Figure 12–15.

Figure 12–23

4. Save and close the drawing.

12.4 P&ID Project: Oil Lubrication System

In this project, you will create a schematic piping diagram for the oil lubrication system shown in Figure 12–24.

Figure 12–24

Task 1: Draw the schematic layout.

1. Start a new drawing based on **Mech-Inches.dwt**, which is located in your practice files folder, and save it as **Lubesys.dwg**.

2. Create the blocks shown in Figure 12–25. Study the diagram shown in Figure 12–24 to determine an appropriate size and insertion point for each block.

   Note: The grid is meant for approximation purposes so that you know the approximate size of the blocks. You are not required to draw the blocks with exact dimensions.

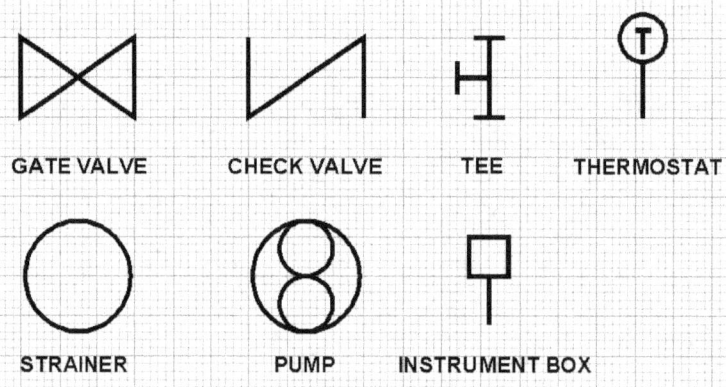

Figure 12–25

   - For the mesh in the Strainer, use the **ANSI37** hatch pattern with the *Scale* set to **1.0**. For the arrow in the Check Valve, use a polyline with the **Width** option.

3. Insert the blocks and draw the other elements to create the diagram.

Tips:

- Exact dimensions are not important because this is a schematic drawing. It might help to start by drawing and positioning some of the large parts (tanks and sumps) and then filling in the connecting pieces.

- Use **Move**, **Rotate**, and **Stretch** as required to arrange the parts correctly. Remember to use Snap or Object Snaps to connect the parts at precise points. Use **Copy** to save time and effort.

- The text should be **0.1** units high.

Task 2: Set up the drawing for plotting.

1. Switch to the **C-Sized** layout.

2. Make the viewport active. Set the *scale* to **1:1** and adjust the view in the viewport by panning until the diagram fits the viewport.

3. Switch back to Paper Space and freeze the layer **Viewports** to hide the viewport border.

4. In Paper Space, add a Legend on the right side of the sheet, and include the symbols used in the diagram and their descriptions, as shown in Figure 12–26.

Figure 12–26

5. Save and close the drawing.

12.5 Civil Project: Warehouse Site

In this project, you will create a drawing of a warehouse site. You will draw the property line, and locate the building, parking, driveway, and existing wetlands area. You will then create drawing views in a layout for plotting. Finally, you will dimension, hatch, and add text, as shown in Figure 12–27.

Figure 12–27

Task 1: Draw the property line, building location, and pavement.

1. Start a new drawing based on **Civil-Feet.dwt**, which is located in your practice files folder, and save it as **Warehouse.dwg**. The drawing is in decimal feet.

2. Draw the property line, building location, existing pavement, and new pavement, as shown in Figure 12–28.

    *   **Note:** Ignore the dimension **N18d0'0"E** of the property line. It is a text object that you will add in Task 3. Draw the right-hand slanting portion of the property line by joining the endpoints of upper and lower horizontal portions of the property lines.

- Use approximate dimensions, if required, to complete the drawing.

Figure 12–28

3. Add a wetlands area and hatch it with the **Swamp** hatch pattern. You need to use a *hatch scale* of **30**.

4. Add the parking area and concrete valley swale to the driveway, as shown in Figure 12–29. Hatch the areas shown in Figure 12–29 on the layer **Pavement Hatching**, using the **AR-Conc** *pattern*, with a *scale* of **1.0**.

Figure 12–29

5. Add the loading dock pad and dumpster pad, as shown in Figure 12–30. Hatch these areas using the **AR-Conc** *pattern* and a *scale* of **1.0**.

Figure 12–30

Task 2: Lay out the drawing for plotting.

1. Switch to the **D-Sized** layout.
2. Set the current layer to **Viewports** and create four viewports, as shown in Figure 12–31.

Figure 12–31

3. Switch to Model Space so that you can adjust the view in each viewport. For the larger view, set the *scale* to **1:40**. For the smaller views, set the *scale* to **1:10** and display the parking area in one, the loading dock in the second, and the dumpster pad in the third. You might need to change the sizes of the viewports to fit all of the information once you have scaled them. You can do this in Paper Space using grips.

4. In the *Linetype Manager* dialog box, in the *Details* area, set the *Global scale factor* to **1.0** and verify that the **Use Paper Space units for scaling** option is selected. This displays the linetypes correctly in Paper Space.

5. Freeze the layer **Pavement Hatching** in the site plan view only.

Task 3: Add dimensions and text.

Note: Refer to Figure 12–28 for a clearer view of the placement of the dimensions.

1. Set the current layer to **Dimensions** and add the required dimensions to each viewport, as shown in Figure 12–32. Use the annotative **Civil** dimension style. Use text to input the property line dimension information, as shown previously in Figure 12–28.

Figure 12–32

2. In the **Text** layer, add titles to label each view and the other text as required. The *text height* for titles is **0.25** with the **Hand** text style. All of the other text (refer to Figure 12–28) is **0.18** with the **Standard** text style. The titles of the viewports are as follows:

- **Viewport 1:** Site Plan, Scale: 1:40
- **Viewport 2:** Parking Plan, Scale: 1:10
- **Viewport 3:** Loading Dock Plan, Scale: 1:10
- **Viewport 4:** Dumpster Pad Plan, Scale: 1:10

3. Freeze the layer **Viewports**.

4. Save and close the drawing.

Skills Assessment

To test your knowledge on the course material, answer the questions that follow. Select the best answer for each question.

1. Which of the following statements is correct when you display multiple drawings at the same time as floating windows? (Select all that apply)

    a. You can pull each drawing tab and display it as a separate drawing window.

    b. You cannot resize each drawing window separately.

    c. Each floating window has its own separate Command Line and Dynamic Input.

    d. Each floating window has its own separate ribbon, *Quick Access Toolbar*, and *Status Bar*.

2. When defining a block, you specify a base point. Which of the following is true of the base point?

    a. It should always be at the center of the block.

    b. It should always be at the bottom of the block.

    c. It should always be an end point.

    d. It is the handle by which the block is held when being inserted.

3. What technique could you use to draw a circle with its center point 3 units over and 8 units up from the center of an existing circle?

    a. Temporary Tracking Point

    b. Measure

    c. Locate Point

    d. Array

4. Settings you can build into a template file include:
   a. Layers
   b. Units
   c. Text and Dimension Styles
   d. All of the above

5. How can you add blocks to a Tools palette?
   a. Use **Insert Block**.
   b. Use **Make Block**.
   c. Use **Wblock**.
   d. Drag and drop blocks from drawing window onto the palette.

6. Which key enables you to make multiple grips hot?
   a. <Shift>
   b. <Alt>
   c. <Esc>
   d. <Ctrl>

7. Which phrase describes relative coordinates?
   a. They are relative to the current screen display.
   b. They are relative to the object snap.
   c. They are measured from the last point picked.
   d. They are measured from the origin (0,0).

8. What layer properties can you override in viewports?
   a. Color
   b. Freeze
   c. Linetype
   d. All of the above

9. Which of the following statements is true?

    a. If you change the properties of an Xref layer, the change affects the referenced drawing.

    b. If you rename an Xref layer in the Xref drawing, the layer is automatically renamed when the Xref is reloaded in the host drawing.

    c. Any Xref layer can be made current in the host drawing.

    d. It is impossible to distinguish which layers come from referenced drawings, and which layers reside in the active drawing.

10. Which command converts a local block or selected objects into a separate drawing file?

    a. Explode

    b. Wblock

    c. Group

    d. Purge

Optional Topics

You will explore how to use the calculator to perform standard calculations. You will also learn to navigate the drawing using additional zoom commands, use advanced text and dimensioning tools, as well as create boundaries and lengthen objects.

Learning Objectives

- Perform calculations and send the output to the Command Line.
- Create and modify single line text.
- Change the size of multiline text objects and change the justification point (alignment) of selected text objects.
- Make temporary changes to a dimension style and compare various dimension styles.
- Set and compare dimension styles in a part or assembly.
- Create a closed, complex polyline from existing objects.
- Create a single object that contains an outline and holes.
- Combine regions by adding, subtracting, or intersecting them.
- Change the length of an object or the included angle of an arc.

B.1 Using QuickCalc

QuickCalc is a calculator that is included with the AutoCAD® software (as shown in Figure B–1) and can be used for standard calculations. It sends the output to the Command Line.

Quickcalc is similar to other palettes in that it can be left floating, docked, or hidden while you are working in other commands.

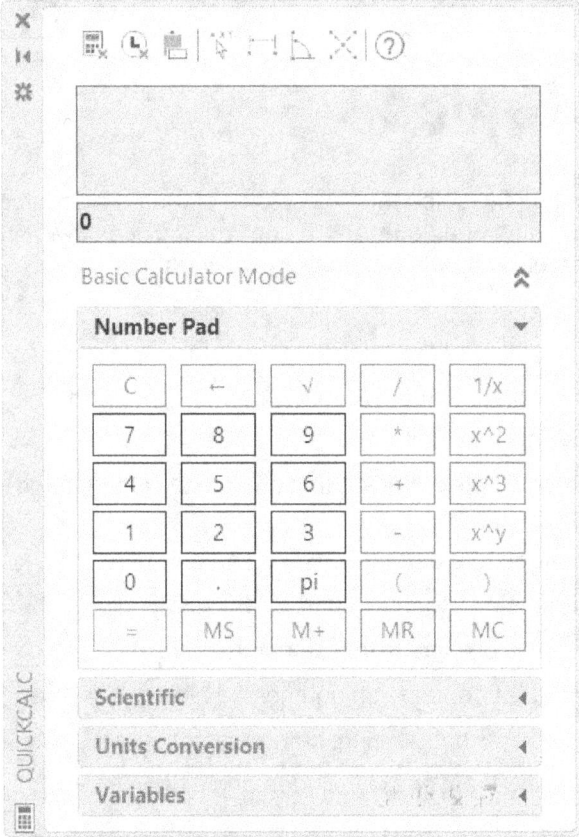

Figure B–1

- To paste a value from the *QuickCalc* Input box to the Command Line, click 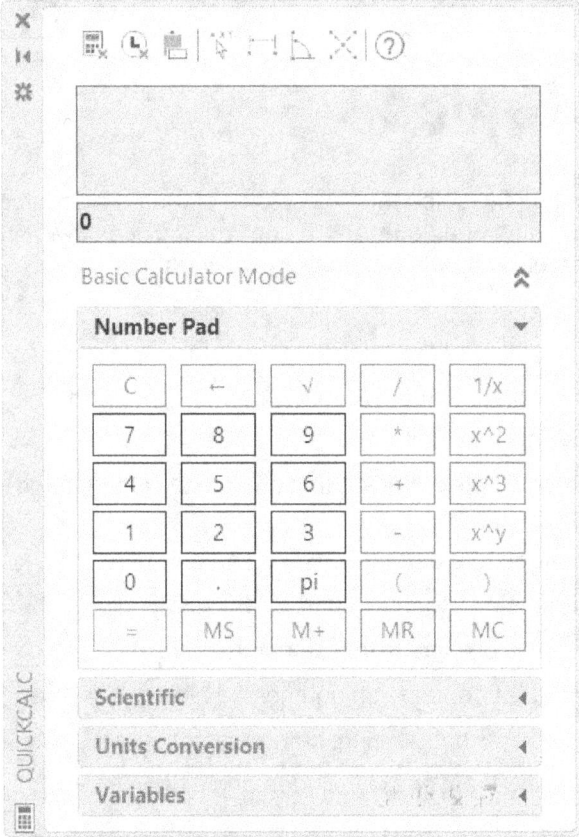 (Paste value to command line) located in the toolbar near the top of the palette.

- In the *Units Conversion* area, you can obtain equivalent values for different units of measurement as shown in Figure B–2. Unit conversions are available for length, area, volume, and angular values as shown on the right in Figure B–2. Based on the unit type selected, you can select a list of units to convert from and a list of units to convert to.

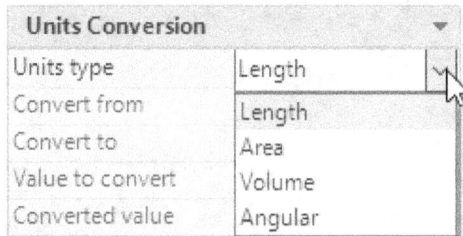

Figure B–2

How To: Convert Units of Measurement with QuickCalc

1. In the *View* tab>*Palettes* panel or the *Home* tab>*Utilities* panel, click 🔲 (Quick Calculator).
2. In the *Units Conversion* area, expand the *Units type* drop-down list and select a unit category.
3. Expand the *Convert from* drop-down list and select the type of unit from which you want to convert.
4. Expand the *Convert to* drop-down list and select the type of unit to which you want to convert.
5. In the *Value to convert* field, enter the value you want to convert. Press <Enter>.
6. The converted value displays in the *Converted value* field.

B.2 Additional Zoom Commands

While these **Zoom** command options are not used frequently, you can access them in the Navigation Bar, as shown in Figure B-3.

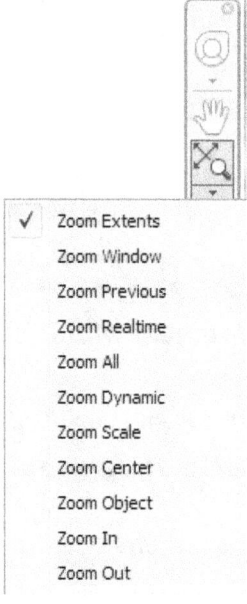

Figure B-3

	Dynamic	Enables you to define an area to display using an overall view of the drawing. The screen zooms out to display the full drawing, and a *view box* opens to represents the viewport. Click to resize the view box. Move the box to the location that you want to display and press <Enter> to zoom to that area.
	Scale	Changes the scale (magnification) of the display. The scale can be entered as a function of the limits of the drawing and press <Enter>. You can also enter the scale as a function of the size of the active display where you type the scale followed by **X**, and press <Enter>.
	Center	Enables you to pick a point to be the new center of the display and to change the scale.
	Object	Zooms to fit the object(s) that you select on the screen.
	In	Makes the drawing twice as large as the current display (half of the area displays), while keeping the same center.
	Out	Makes the drawing half as large as the current display (twice as much area displays), while keeping the same center.

B.3 Additional Text Tools

Several text tools add to the versatility of the AutoCAD software. You can create single line text where multiline text is not required. There are also special tools for scaling and justifying text.

Creating Single Line Text

Single-line text adds each line of text as a separate object, as shown in Figure B–4. This type of text is quick and easy to use. However, multiline text offers more options in formatting and is better for paragraph editing.

Figure B–4

How To: Create Single Line Text

1. In the *Home* tab>*Annotation* panel or the *Annotate* tab>*Text* panel, click A (Single Line).
2. Select a start point.
3. Specify the paper height or press <Enter> to accept the default height.
4. Specify the rotation angle or press <Enter> to accept the default angle.
5. Start typing.
6. When you press <Enter> at the end of the line, you are prompted for another line.
7. Press <Enter> at an empty line to finish the command.

- While still in the command, you can select another point to place another line of text. It is a separate text object in the drawing.

- To make single-line text annotative, set an annotative text style to be current before creating the text, or change the existing text in the Properties palette.

- The **Single Line Text** command enables multiple lines of text to be entered in one sequence. However, each line is a separate text object.

Editing Single Line Text

Double-click on any line of text to edit it. It highlights on the screen and you can make changes as shown in Figure B–5. The *Text Editor* contextual tab and the ruler do not display with a single line text.

This is a line of single-line text.
This is a second separate line.
This is a third separate line.

Figure B–5

- You can change the style, height, justification, and a few other text properties in the Properties palette.

Justify Text

(Justify Text) in the *Annotate* tab>*Text* panel, changes the justification point (alignment) of selected text objects without changing the location of the text, as shown in Figure B–6. If you use other methods to change the justification, such as **Edit Text** or the Properties palette, the text shifts generally.

New College Art Building
Project No: 0125
513 Main Street
Alexandria, Virginia
Left Justified

New College Art Building
Project No: 0125
513 Main Street
Alexandria, Virginia
Center Justified

Figure B–6

The options that can be used with the **Justify Text** command are as follows.

Left	Aligns text to be left-justified against an end point on the left side of the text string.
Align	Aligns text between any two selected points and determines the text height automatically (similar to **Fit**).
Fit	Places text between any two selected points at a user-specified height.
Center	Places text in the drawing, centered above the selected point.
Middle	Places text in the drawing, centered at the top of the selected point. Middle text is convenient for marking callouts and tags.
Right	Aligns text to be right-justified against an end point on the right side of the text string.

- Other alignments are for top, middle, bottom, left, center, or right (TL for Top Left, TC for Top Center, etc.).

- Once a justification has been set, it remains the default each time Single Line Text is used and until it is modified.

- You can also use ᴬ (Text Align) in the *Annotate* tab>*Text* panel to align Single Line text. The command also works with multiline text. First select the text objects that you want to align and then select the text to which you want them to be aligned.

Scale Text

With the regular **Scale** command, scaling several text objects at once changes the location of the text. Aₙ (Scale Text) in the *Annotate* tab>expanded *Text* panel, changes the size of multiple text objects without changing their location as shown in Figure B–7.

| FCV 1561 |
| 6.101S GATE VALVE |
| 6.130S GLOBE VALVE |
| 150# M.I. TEE |

Before Scaling

| FCV 1561 |
| 6.101S GATE VALVE |
| 6.130S GLOBE VALVE |
| 150# M.I. TEE |

After Scaling

Figure B–7

- You can scale the text around existing base points or specify a different justification base point for scaling (Top Left, Middle Center, etc.).

- The scaling can be specified as a text height, as a scale factor, or to match another text object.

Model Space Text and Paper Space Text

It is recommended that you use Annotation Scaling for most of the text in your drawings. However, text can be placed in either Model Space or Paper Space. In Paper Space, as with an annotative text style, you make the text the required printed height. For example, 1/8" text is exactly that height when you print the layout.

For text placed in Model Space without annotation scaling, some calculation is involved for the height, because this text is scaled along with the model when it is printed. For example, room labels in a floor plan would normally be placed directly on the model. If you want the labels to be 1/8" on the paper, and you are printing at a scale of 1/8"=1', the labels need to be 1' high in Model Space. The table displays some of the common values.

Scale	Paper Text Size	Model Text Size
1/8"=1'-0"	3/32"	9"
	1/8"	12"
	1/4"	24"
1/4"=1'-0"	3/32"	4 1/2"
	1/8"	6"
	1/4"	12"
1/2"=1'-0"	3/32"	2 1/4"
	1/8"	3"
	1/4"	6"

Convert Text to Mtext

In the *Express Tools* tab>*Text* panel, use the **Convert to Mtext** tool (shown in Figure B−8) to combine multiple individual text objects to create one multi-line text object.

Figure B−8

- When you start this command, you can select the individual single line text objects and then press <Enter>. In the Command Line, it displays the number of Text line objects that were converted to a single multiline object, as shown in Figure B–9.

```
3 Text objects removed, 1 MText object added.
>_ ▾ Type a command
```

Figure B–9

- Before selecting the individual text lines, you can select the *Settings* option (<Down Arrow>) which opens the *Text to MText Settings* dialog box, as shown in Figure B–10. You can use the default **Sort top-down** setting, which sorts the collinear multiple text lines as they are on the same line with a space between them.

Figure B–10

- If you clear the **Combine into a single mtext object** option, the selected multiple single line text objects are converted to individual multi-line text objects, without combining them into one object.

- The **Force uniform line spacing** option keeps the existing line spacing between the individual text lines.

B.4 Additional Dimensioning Tools

When you work in Dimension Style Manager, advanced tools can be used to override and display the differences between dimension styles as shown in Figure B–11.

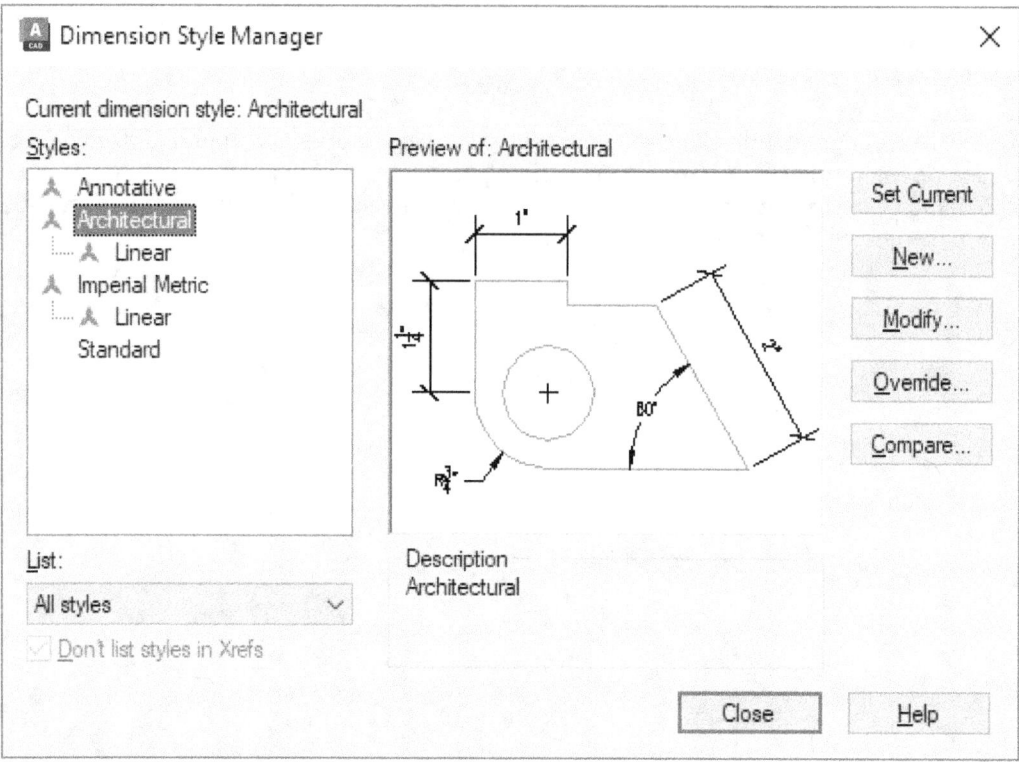

Figure B–11

Dimension Style Manager

Adding Style Overrides

With the **Override** option, you can make temporary changes to a style and add several dimensions with those changes. For example, you might need to add a few dimensions with a different precision or tolerance value from others in the drawing.

How To: Apply a Style Override

1. In the *Dimension Style Manager*, make the style you want to override current.

2. Click **Override...**.

3. In the *Override Current Style* dialog box, make the required override changes to the style. Click **OK**.

4. Overrides display in the styles list below the style. The *Description* area displays the overrides that you have applied.

5. Click **Close**. In the drawing, add the required dimensions with the overrides.

   Note: To stop using the overrides, set the original style (or any other style) to be current. The override changes are discarded.

Comparing Dimension Styles

In the *Dimension Style Manager*, click **Compare...** to open a table listing the differences between two styles, as shown in Figure B–12. You can pick any two styles or sub-styles that have been defined in the current drawing in the *Compare* and *With* lists. The AutoCAD software lists all of the dimension variables that differ and the settings of the variable in each style.

Figure B–12

Inspection Dimensions

The **Inspect (dimension)** command creates special types of dimensions for quality control in mechanical drafting and manufacturing. They are used in Inspection Drawings to indicate dimensions that must be checked for the part or assembly, as shown in Figure B–13. They are useful for companies who out-source parts and must ensure that specific dimensions are met so that the parts fit into an assembly correctly.

Figure B–13

- You can add Inspection dimensions to any dimension object. Inspection dimensions consist of text and a frame and contain three information fields:

- **Inspection Label:** Located on the left side and used to identify the dimension.

- **Dimension Value:** Located in the middle and containing the original dimension text, tolerances, and prefix and suffix text.

- **Inspection Rate:** Located on the right side, indicates inspection frequency, and is shown as a percentage.

- **Remove Inspection:** Removes an inspection dimension from the selected dimension.

How To: Add an Inspection Dimension

1. In the *Annotate* tab>*Dimensions* panel, click ⊢✓⊣ (Inspect). The *Inspection Dimension* dialog box opens as shown in Figure B−14.

Figure B−14

2. Click ▦ (Select dimensions) and select the dimensions to be used as inspection dimensions.
3. Press <Enter> to return to the dialog box.
4. Set the *Shape* to **Round**, **Angular**, or **None**.
5. Select **Label** and type an identifier for the inspection dimension.
6. Type a percentage for the **Inspection rate** option or accept the default of 100%.
7. Click **OK** to close the *Inspection Dimension* dialog box and add the inspection dimensions.

B.5 Creating Boundaries and Regions

Creating Boundaries

Sometimes you need to create a complex polyline from several existing objects using the **Boundary** command, as shown in Figure B–15.

Figure B–15

• The **Boundary** command can also create regions.

How To: Create Boundaries

1. In the *Home* tab>*Draw* panel, in the *Hatch* flyout, click ⊞ (Boundary).
2. In the *Boundary Creation* dialog box, select the required options.
3. Click ▦ (Pick Points) or click **OK**.
4. Select a point inside a closed area, as shown in Figure B–16. You can select points in multiple closed areas.

   • The AutoCAD software creates a closed polyline or region that is defined by the edges of the first objects it detects.

Figure B–16

5. Press <Enter> to create the boundary.

Boundary Options

When you create boundaries, you can specify what is included in the boundary area with the options shown in Figure B–17. You can either create a polyline object or a region of the boundary area.

*   The new polyline is placed directly on top of the existing boundary lines. It is recommended that you create the boundary on a separate layer from the other objects.

Figure B–17

Island detection	Select this option if you want the **Boundary** command to find any interior objects (*islands*) and create polylines around them, in addition to finding the exterior boundary.
Object type	You can create a polyline or a region. If a boundary set includes ellipses, elliptical arcs, or splines, the **Boundary** command automatically creates a region.
Boundary set	The default option, **Current viewport**, calculates the boundary based on all of the objects that are visible in the current viewport.
	To select the objects that should be considered when calculating the boundary, click (New - Select new boundary set). This enables you to exclude objects from the boundary calculation and it can make the boundary calculation faster in a complex drawing.

Working with Regions

A polyline is a continuous object. It can be closed, but cannot contain holes. Regions are used to create single objects that contain an outline and holes, as shown in Figure B-18.

Figure B-18

- A *region* is a 2D solid object or infinitely thin surface. The edges cannot be separated from the shape. Therefore, if you move an edge, the entire surface moves. Typical uses for regions include a plate with holes or a wall with windows.

- You can create objects with holes that are part of the object.

- Regions can be used in many cases to quickly create complex geometry using the **Union**, **Subtract**, and **Intersect** commands.

- The area of a region, even one with holes, can easily be found using the **Area** command with the **Object** option.

How To: Create a Region

1. Draw the closed shape for the region using lines, polylines, etc. The lines must connect precisely end point to end point.

2. In the *Home* tab>expanded *Draw* panel, click ⬚ (Region).

3. Select the objects. You can select several closed shapes and convert them all into regions at the same time. In the Command Line, the AutoCAD software reports the number of regions it has created.

    *   Regions can be created out of existing closed shapes made of lines, arcs, polylines, circles, etc.
    *   If the closed shape consists of separate segments, the segments must connect end point to end point to make a region.

4. The original objects are consumed when you use them to create a region.

*   You can **Explode** a region to convert it into lines, arcs, splines, or circles, depending on the shapes involved.

Combining Regions

Regions are useful construction tools because of the ways in which they can be combined. For example, you can create a hole or cutout in a region by subtracting one region from another. You can also add regions and find the intersection of regions as shown in Figure B–19. The addition (union), subtraction, and intersection actions are called *Boolean Operations.*

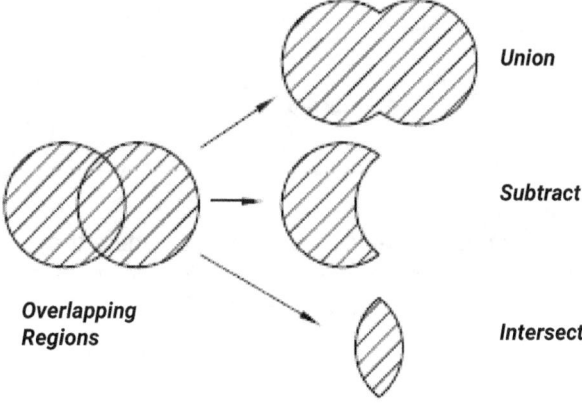

Figure B–19

*   You can union, subtract, or intersect two or more regions at a time.

*   The regions on which the Boolean Operations are performed do not need to intersect. However, the intersection of two objects that do not overlap erases the regions.

- Regions are considered solid objects and the tools for editing them are located in the *Home* tab>*Solid Editing* panel (as shown in Figure B–20) when the *3D Modeling* workspace is active.

   Note: You are required to be in the 3D Modeling workspace for the 3D ribbon to display.

Figure B–20

- You can type the name of the command if you do not want to switch workspaces.

Union

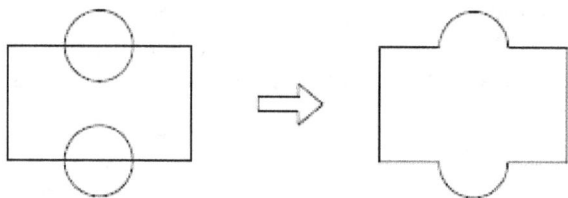 (Union) combines two or more regions into a single region as shown in Figure B–21.

Figure B–21

Subtract

 (Subtract) removes the area of one region from another where they overlap as shown in Figure B–22. You can also use **Subtract** to create regions containing holes. By subtracting the holes, you can also find out the area of the closed shape.

Figure B–22

- Select the region(s) to *subtract from* first. Then select the regions that you want to subtract.

Intersect

 (Intersect) finds the common area of two or more regions as shown in Figure B–23. Only the area that is shared by the selected regions remains in the new region.

Figure B–23

B.6 Modifying Length

You can use the **Lengthen** command to change the length of an object or the included angle of an arc as shown in Figure B–24. However, you cannot change the length of a closed object.

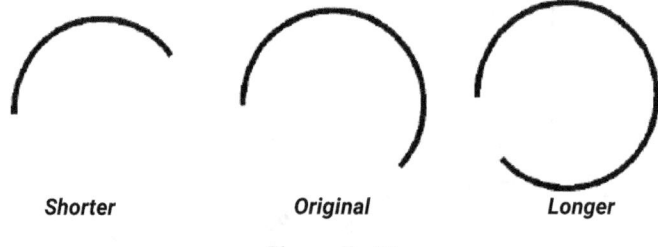

| Shorter | Original | Longer |

Figure B–24

How To: Lengthen an Object

1. In the *Home* tab>expanded *Modify* panel, click   (Lengthen).
2. Select the object. Its current length displays in the Command Line.
3. Select an option to modify the object's length:
   - **Delta:** Specify the increments by which the object's length is to be modified. To extend the object, enter a positive value. To shorten it, enter a negative value. The length is always measured from the closest end point to the selection point. Use the same method to change the angle of an arc.
   - **Percent:** Modify the object by a percentage of its length.
   - **Total:** Modify the object's length by a specific amount from a fixed end point. Specify the total required angle to modify the included angle of an arc.
   - **Dynamic:** Toggle on Dynamic Dragging mode. Pick an object's end point and drag it to the required length. The other end point does not change.
4. Hover over the object to preview the changes depending on the selected option and the specified values. Select the object to change it.
5. Press <Enter> to end the command.

Chapter Review Questions

1. You can use the **QuickCalc** command to obtain equivalent values for different units of measurement.

   a. True

   b. False

2. The **Dynamic Zoom** command:

   a. Makes the drawing twice as large as the current display.

   b. Makes the drawing half as large as the current display.

   c. Enables you to define an area to display using an overall view of the drawing.

   d. Zooms to fit the object(s) that you select on the screen.

3. Which one of the following is true of single-line text?

   a. You can only type in one line at a time and then have to start the command again.

   b. There are no options for alignments of single-line text.

   c. You can type in multiple lines, but each line is separate from the last.

   d. You can format the text using the *Text Editor* contextual tab.

4. In which of the following industries are Inspection Dimensions most useful?

   a. Architectural building inspection

   b. Electrical control inspection

   c. Plumbing flow control

   d. Manufacturing quality control

5. When you want to inquire about the area of a closed shape that contains holes, you can create a region and use which of the following Boolean commands?

   a. Union

   b. Remove

   c. Intersect

   d. Subtract

6. What does the **Delta** option of the **Lengthen** command do?

    a. Modifies the object's length by specified increments.

    b. Modifies the object by a percentage of its length.

    c. Modifies the object's length by a specific amount from a fixed end point.

    d. Modifies the object's length by dragging its end point to the required length.

Command Summary

Button	Command	Location
	Boundary	• **Ribbon:** *Home* tab>*Draw* panel
	Inspect	• **Ribbon:** *Annotate* tab>*Dimension* panel
	Intersect	• **Ribbon:** *Home* tab>*Solid Editing* panel (*in the 3D Modeling workspace*)
	Justify Text	• **Ribbon:** *Annotate* tab>*Text* panel
	Lengthen	• **Ribbon:** *Home* tab>expanded *Modify* panel
	QuickCalc	• **Ribbon:** *View* tab>*Palettes* panel
	Region	• **Ribbon:** *Home* tab>expanded *Draw* panel
	Scale Text	• **Ribbon:** *Annotate* tab>expanded *Text* panel
	Single Line Text	• **Ribbon:** *Home* tab>*Annotation* panel or *Annotate* tab>*Text* panel
	Subtract	• **Ribbon:** *Home* tab>*Solid Editing* panel (*in the 3D Modeling workspace*)
	Union	• **Ribbon:** *Home* tab>*Solid Editing* panel (*in the 3D Modeling workspace*)
	Zoom Center	• **Navigation Bar** • **Ribbon:** *Home* tab>*Utilities* panel
	Zoom Dynamic	• **Navigation Bar** • **Ribbon:** *Home* tab>*Utilities* panel
	Zoom In	• **Navigation Bar** • **Ribbon:** *Home* tab>*Utilities* panel
	Zoom Object	• **Navigation Bar** • **Ribbon:** *Home* tab>*Utilities* panel
	Zoom Out	• **Navigation Bar** • **Ribbon:** *Home* tab>*Utilities* panel
	Zoom Scale	• **Navigation Bar** • **Ribbon:** *Home* tab>*Utilities* panel

Autodesk AI Features in AutoCAD

You learn how Autodesk AI is used to enhance your AutoCAD workflow by leveraging instant, AI-powered support for an improved user experience. You will also learn to convert selected geometry into blocks with Smart Blocks, automate common tasks using the AI-driven Macro Advisor, and seamlessly integrate feedback from imported PDFs into DWG files with Markup Assist.

Learning Objectives

- Enhance the user experience by providing immediate AI-driven tailored support directly within AutoCAD.
- Convert multiple instances of selected geometry into blocks using the **Smart blocks** solutions.
- Provide context-specific recommendations that help automate frequent, multi-step tasks using the AI driven Macro Advisor.
- Incorporate feedback into your DWG files from imported PDFs using the Markup Assist in AutoCAD.

C.1 Autodesk Assistant

Autodesk Assistant is an AI tool that is built into the AutoCAD software to enhance user experience. This conversational tool, with its AI-powered interface, offers self-service features that provide personalized support for users directly within the software. Serving as a real-time expert assistant, Autodesk Assistant delivers instant, context-specific answers, helpful resources, and command suggestions. You can type your question into the chat box to quickly get answers to common queries. If you have a commercial AutoCAD account, you can also chat with a product support agent for more detailed assistance, request a callback for direct communication, or create a support case for more complex issues.

How To: Use Autodesk Assistant

1. In the Infocenter, click (Autodesk Assistant) to open the *Autodesk Assistant* palette.

2. Enter your question in the chat box, as shown on the left in Figure C–1. It provides you with AI generated answers, as shown on the right in Figure C–1.

 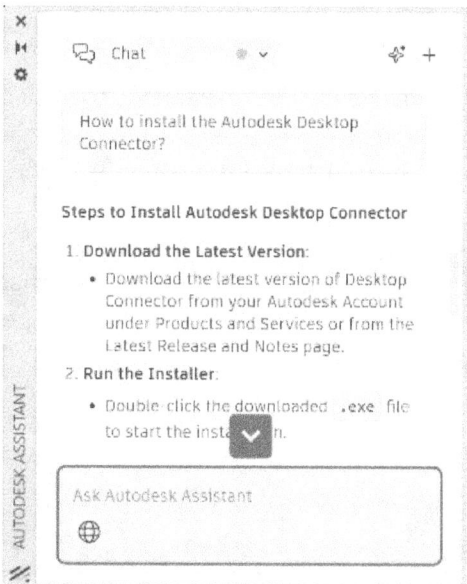

Figure C–1

*Note: Your Autodesk Assistant palette may appear differently from what is shown here, as this feature was in **Tech Preview** mode at the time of publishing this guide. Tech preview means that the software is still under development and could be refined to make improvements.*

*Note: The **Contact a support agent** feature is only available for those users that have commercial account of AutoCAD.*

C.2 Smart Blocks

The Smart blocks solutions in AutoCAD offers two AI driven tools that automatically identifies and converts multiple instances of selected geometry into block. They are **Search and Convert** and **Detect and Convert.** Both these tools are available through the *Insert* tab>*Block* panel in the Ribbon as shown in Figure C−2.

Figure C−2

Search and Convert

AutoCAD offers the **Search and Convert** tool, which provides an efficient method to convert multiple instances of the selected geometry into blocks. This feature enables you to streamline repetitive work and maintain consistency across your projects.

With the **Search and Convert** tool, you can select the required geometry in your drawing, and AutoCAD automatically identifies and highlights every occurrence of the selected geometry within that drawing. When converting the geometry into a block, you can select an existing block from the current drawing or from recently used blocks list. You can also use similar blocks suggested by Autodesk AI from your block library. Additionally, this tool can find text variations and convert them into block attributes, making it especially useful for organizing repetitive text elements such as hotel room numbers or room names.

How To: Use Search and Convert

1. Hover your cursor over different geometry and note that they are all separate objects, as shown in Figure C−3.

Figure C−3

2. In the *Insert* tab>*Block* panel, click (Search and Convert).

3. At the *Select object to find matching instances* prompt, select a chair's geometry. (Use a crossing/window to select all the geometry that makes up the chair, as shown in Figure C−4.)

Figure C−4

4. Press <Enter>. The drawing opens in a *Search* window and note that all similar objects are highlighted and zoomed in, with a bounding box surrounding the initially selected geometry, as shown in Figure C–5.

Figure C–5

5. Select the bounding box around the selected chair and select **Convert**.

6. In the *Convert to block* dialog box, click **New block**. Enter the name for the block. You can change the basepoint of the block and also move the block to layer **0**, if required. In Figure C−6, the name of the block is entered as **Chairs** and the layer is set to **PDF_Chairs**. Verify that **Include existing blocks** is selected.

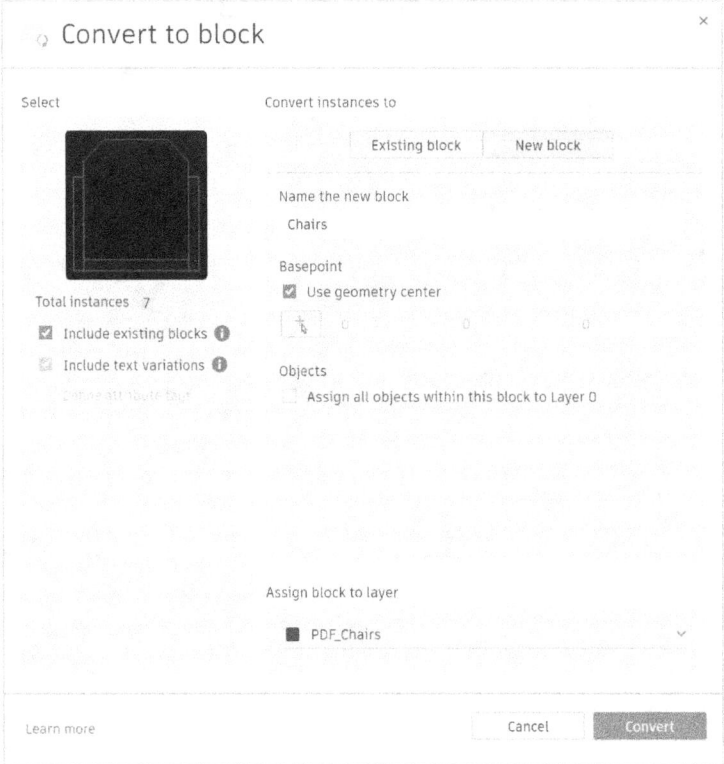

Figure C−6

7. In the *Convert to block* dialog box, click **Convert**. Note that all the chairs (including the originally selected chair) are converted to blocks, as shown in Figure C−7.

Figure C−7

Detect and Convert

The **Detect and Convert** tool analyzes drawing geometry to detect objects that are suitable for conversion into blocks. The process begins with the object detection tool identifying sets of geometry in a drawing. Once these sets are identified, you can convert them into blocks. The blocks can then be organized and edited faster, making the process more streamlined and efficient.

Object detection is especially useful when you need to import a PDF file into AutoCAD. When a PDF is imported, the original geometry that were used to create the objects are displayed as separate elements (circles, arcs, lines, and text). Manually editing these individual elements can be a tedious and time-consuming process, which can lead to errors and inefficiencies. By using object detection, you can quickly identify complete objects (like doors and windows) and convert them from separate geometric elements into unified blocks. This significantly improves workflow efficiency and accuracy.

How To: Use Detect and Convert

1. Hover your cursor over different geometry and note that they are all separate objects, as shown in the Figure C-8.

Figure C-8

2. In the *Insert* tab>Block panel, click 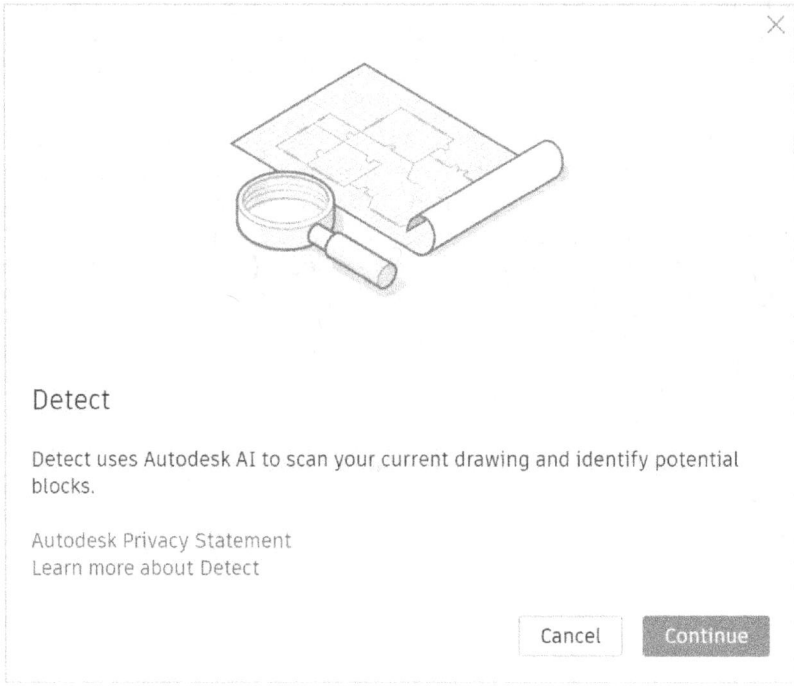 (Detect and Convert) to open the *Detect* dialog box, as shown in the Figure C-9. Click **Continue**.

Detect

Detect uses Autodesk AI to scan your current drawing and identify potential blocks.

Autodesk Privacy Statement
Learn more about Detect

Cancel   Continue

Figure C-9

3. In the *Detect* palette that opens, the software scans the document and detects the various sets of geometry that can be converted to blocks, as shown in Figure C-10.

Figure C-10

4. Select any one of the sets. Note that the drawing is opened in a *Detect* window and the set is highlighted and the objects are zoomed into with a bounding box around the primary geometry of the set. In Figure C–11, **Set 2** is selected and the geometry set consisting of **7** chairs are highlighted.

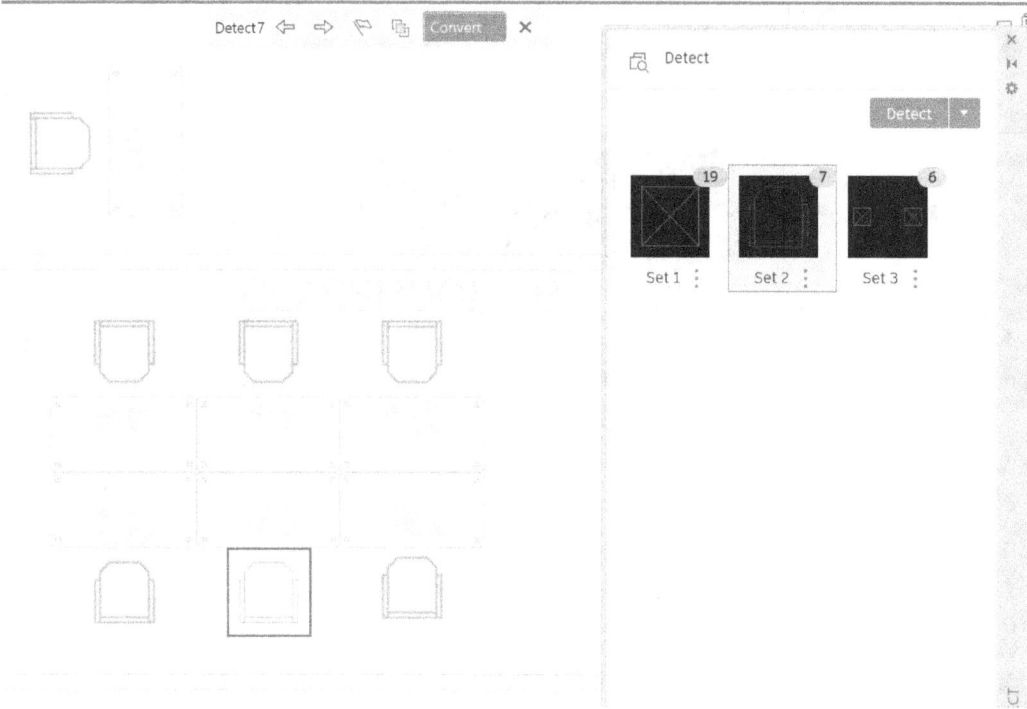

Figure C–11

5. Select the boundary around the primary set and select **Convert,** as shown in Figure C–12.

Figure C–12

6. In the *Convert to block* dialog box, click **New block**. Enter the name for the block. You can change the basepoint of the block and also move the block to layer **0**, if required. In Figure C–13, the name of the block is entered as **Chairs** and the layer is set to **PDF_Chairs**.

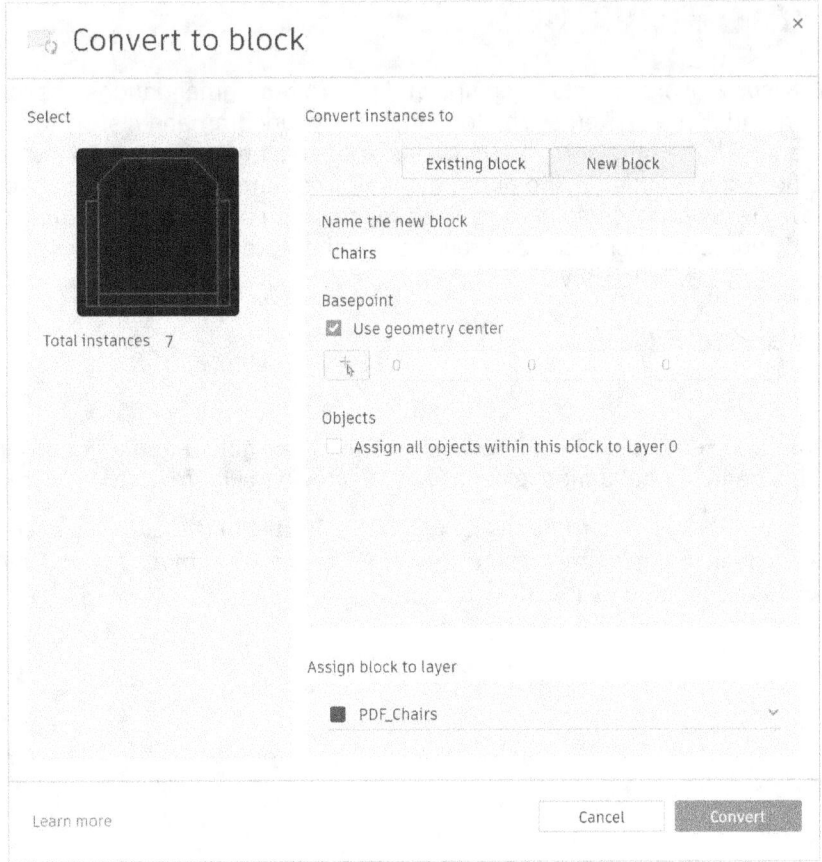

Figure C–13

7. In the *Convert to block* dialog box, click **Convert**. Note that the set has been removed from the *Detect* dialog box and all the chairs are converted to blocks, as shown in Figure C–14.

Figure C–14

C.3 Macro Advisor

The **Macro Advisor** tool provides tailored tips and macro recommendations based on your AutoCAD command usage patterns. The tool analyzes your command history to understand how you interact with the AutoCAD software. Based on this analysis, the tool provides context-specific recommendations to automate your frequently used command sequences. You can review these ready-to-use personalized macros and save them for later use. These macros simplify complex operations and reduce repetitive tasks to help you maintain CAD standards and workflow efficiency.

How To: Use Macro Advisor

1. Use a command sequence a few times. In the *Status Bar*, note that the ⬚ (Macro Advisor) along with a balloon notification is displayed as shown in Figure C−15.

    - For example, the **Copy** command along with the **Rotate** command was used to copy and rotate the desk multiple times in the drawing. The *New Command Macro* for **Copy Rotate Previous** is suggested by the software.

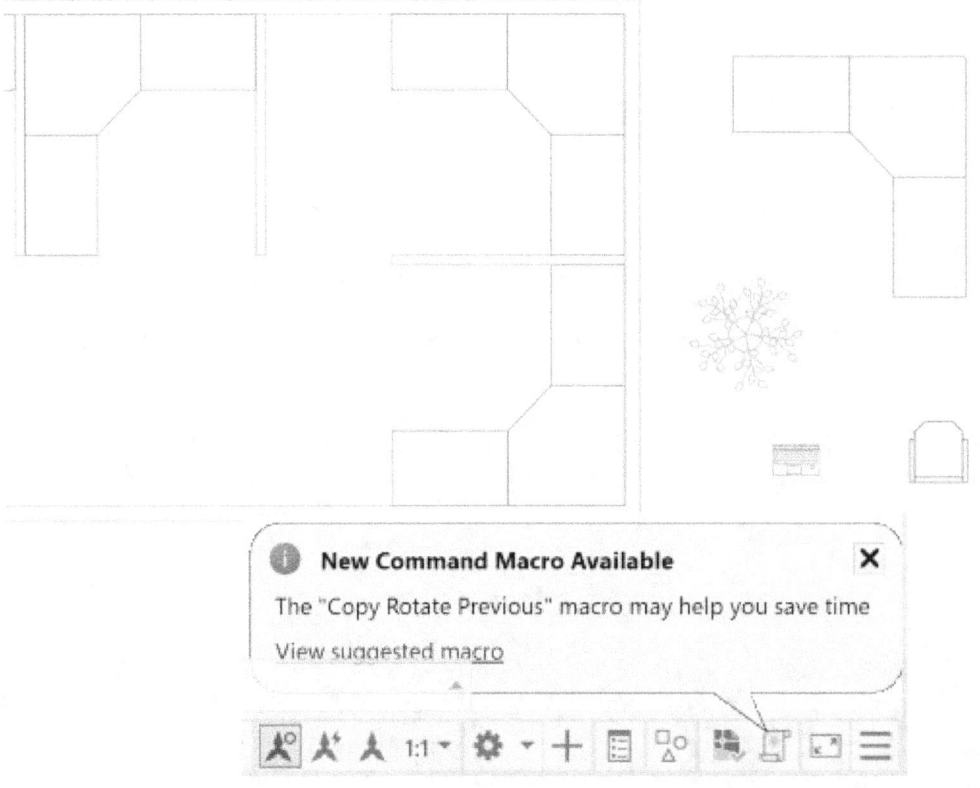

Figure C−15

2. In the balloon notification, click on **View suggested macro**. It opens the *Command Macros* palette in the *Insights* tab where it displays the macro name and its description along with the macro string as shown in Figure C−16.

Figure C−16

3. In the *Insights* tab, you can **Try** the recommended macro and if you find it useful, you can click **Save** to save it in the *Saved* tab (as shown in Figure C−17) for later use.

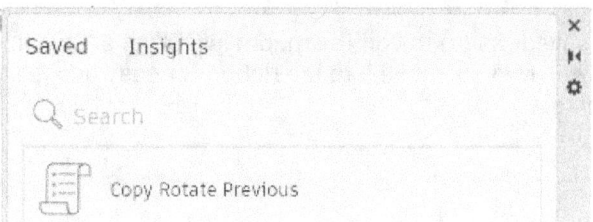

Figure C−17

4. Use the saved macro to copy and rotate the chair in a single command as shown in Figure C–18.

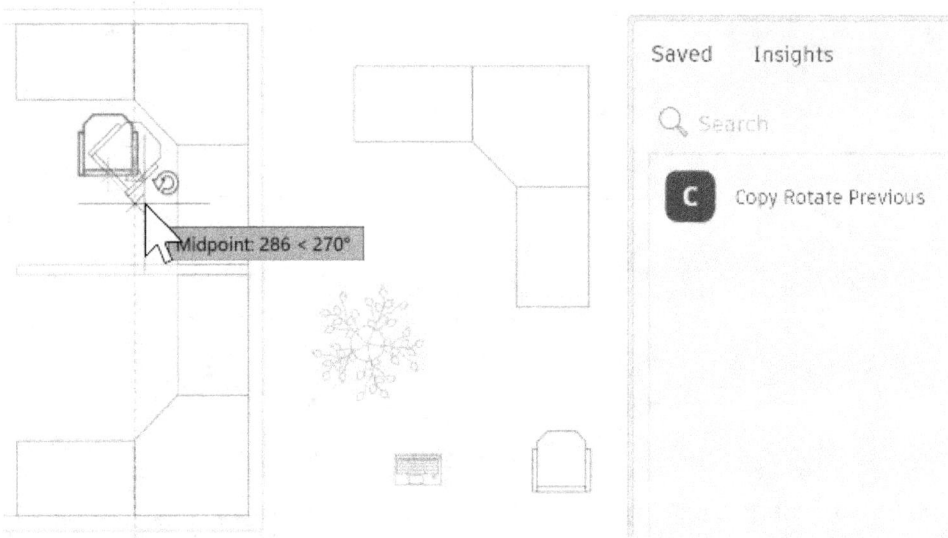

Figure C–18

5. Right-click on the saved macro to edit the macro in CUI, as shown in Figure C–19. If the macro is working well for you, move it to the ribbon for easy access. You can also rename and delete the macro.

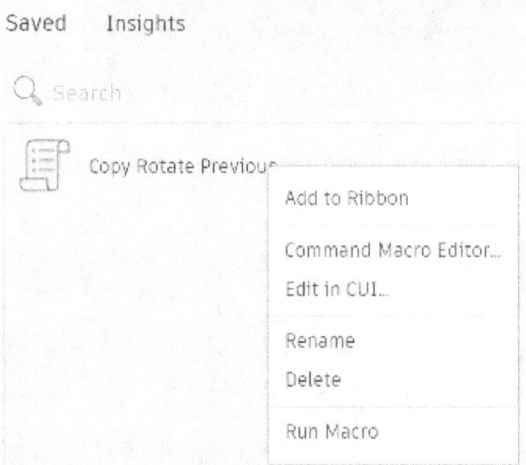

Figure C–19

Note: The ***Insights*** *tab in the Command Macros palette will display insights only if you have a commercial AutoCAD license.*

C.4 Markup Import and Markup Assist

Markup Import and **Markup Assist** are features designed to streamline the process of incorporating feedback into your DWG files. Using machine learning, these tools can identify handwritten or digital feedback from imported PDFs and automatically convert them into actionable text, revision clouds, or other objects within your drawing. This significantly accelerates the revision process.

To get started, use **Markup Import** to overlay markups in the *Trace* workspace. Then, use **Markup Assist** to quickly incorporate those markups into the drawing, ensuring that revisions are efficiently integrated into your workflow.

How To: Use Markup Import and Markup Assist

1. Open the drawing file where you want to incorporate the feedback.

2. In the *Collaborate* tab>*Traces* panel, click 　 (Markup Import).

3. In the *Select a markup file to import* field, select a jpg, png, or pdf (as required) of the current drawing that contains either hand-drawn or digitally drawn markups. Note that the markup pdf file is placed on top of the drawing file in the *Trace* workspace, as shown in Figure C–20.

Figure C–20

4. If required, move, align, rotate, or scale the markup file such that it is properly overlaid on the drawing. Click **aCcept** in the menu once the trace is aligned with the drawing file.

5. In the *Trace* toolbar, click **Drawing** for the **Markup Assist** to be used. In the *Markup Assist* mode, the markups are detected and are indicated by the blue dotted boundary, as shown in Figure C–21.

    *   Verify that the   (Markup Assist) is toggled on for the markups to show.

Figure C–21

6. Click on the markup boundary to display its options list and select **Rectangular Revcloud**, as shown in Figure C–22.

Figure C–22

7. In the *Trace* toolbar, click ⚙ (Settings) to change the visibility of the markups and the revcloud by using the Markup Transparency as shown in Figure C–23.

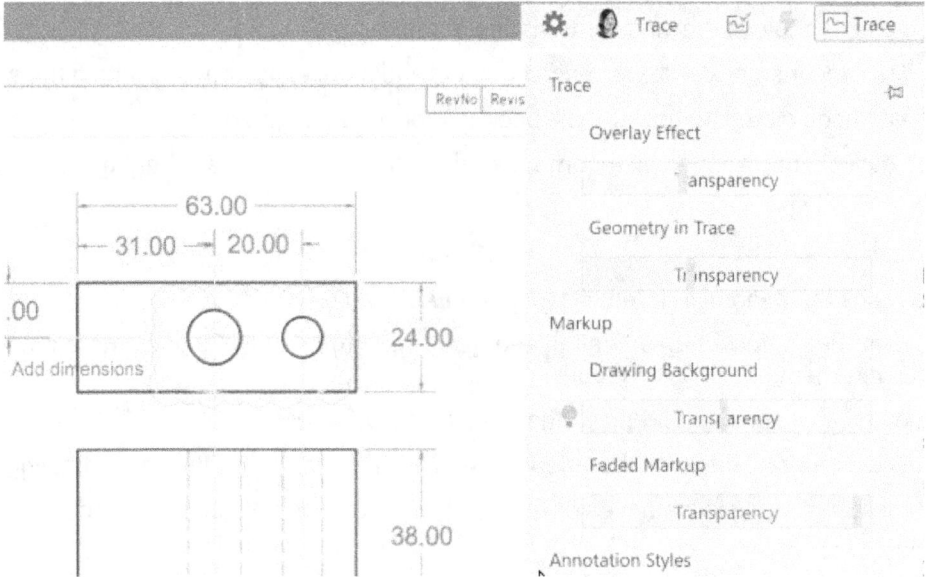

Figure C–23

8. In the *Settings* palette, toggle off the ⚙ drawing transparency to display the accepted markups only as shown in Figure C–24.

Figure C–24

Chapter Review Questions

1. What is the primary function of **Autodesk Assistant** in AutoCAD?

   a. To create and edit drawings automatically without user input.

   b. To provide instant, context-specific support and self-service options within the software.

   c. To manage cloud storage and file backups for AutoCAD projects.

   d. To deliver context-specific recommendations that help automate frequent, multi-step tasks.

2. What does the **Search and Convert** tool do in AutoCAD?

   a. It identifies handwritten or digital feedback from imported PDFs and automatically convert them into revision clouds.

   b. It enables users to export drawings directly to PDF format.

   c. It allows for real-time collaboration between multiple users on the same drawing.

   d. It identifies multiple instances of the same geometry and enables you to convert them into blocks.

3. Which of the following is true for **Macro Advisor** in AutoCAD? (Select all that apply.)

   a. **Macro Advisor** quickly finds answers to your common queries and enables you to engage in a chat session.

   b. **Macro Advisor** provides tailored tips and macro recommendations based on your command usage patterns.

   c. Using this command, you can only use the recommended macro once in the current drawing but the macro cannot be saved for later use.

   d. The *Insights* tab in the *Command Macros* palette will display insights only if you have a commercial AutoCAD license.

4. **The Markup Import** and **Markup Assist** tools can identify handwritten or digital feedback from imported PDFs and automatically convert them into actionable text, and revision clouds.

   a. True

   b. False

Command Summary

Button	Command	Location
	Autodesk Assistant	• **Infocenter**
	Detect and Convert	• **Ribbon:** *Insert* tab>*Block* panel
	Macro Advisor	• **Status Bar**
	Markup Import	• **Ribbon:** *Collaborate* tab>*Traces* panel
	Search and Convert	• **Ribbon:** *Insert* tab>*Block* panel

Index

www.ingramcontent.com/pod-product-compliance
Lightning Source LLC
Chambersburg PA
CBHW082011230526
45468CB00022B/1838

* 9 7 8 1 9 6 7 6 2 5 5 9 8 *